VOLUME 9

EMERGING POWERS

THE ILLUSTRATED
HISTORY OF THE WORLD

VOLUME 9

EMERGING POWERS

J. M. ROBERTS

New York
Oxford University Press

The Illustrated History of the World

This edition first published in 1999 in the United States of America by
Oxford University Press, Inc.,
198 Madison Avenue, New York, N.Y. 10016
Oxford is a registered trademark of Oxford University Press

EMERGING POWERS
Copyright © Editorial Debate SA 1998
Text Copyright © J. M. Roberts 1976, 1980, 1983, 1987, 1988, 1992, 1998
Artwork and Diagrams Copyright © Editorial Debate SA 1998
(for copyright of photographs and maps, see acknowledgments on page 192, which are
to be regarded as an extension of this copyright)

Art Direction by Duncan Baird Publishers
Produced by Duncan Baird Publishers, London, England,
and Editorial Debate, Madrid, Spain

Series ISBN 0-19-521529-X
Volume ISBN 0-19-521527-3

DBP staff:
Senior editor: Joanne Levêque
Assistant editors: Georgina Harris, Kirsty Seymour-Ure
Senior designer: Steven Painter
Assistant designer: Anita Schnable
Picture research: Julia Ruxton
Sales fulfilment: Ian Smalley
Map artwork: Russell Bell
Decorative borders: Lorraine Harrison

Editorial Debate staff:
Editors and picture researchers:
Isabel Belmonte Martínez, Feliciano Novoa Portela,
Ruth Betegón Díez, Dolores Redondo
Editorial coordination: Ana Lucía Vila

Typeset in Sabon 11/15 pt
Color reproduction by Trescan, Madrid, Spain
Printed in Singapore by Imago Limited

NOTE
The abbreviations CE and BCE are used throughout this book:
CE Common Era (the equivalent of AD)
BCE Before Common Era (the equivalent of BC)

10 9 8 7 6 5 4 3 2

CONTENTS

EMERGING POWERS

IN 1900 EUROPEANS COULD LOOK BACK on two, perhaps three, centuries of astonishing growth. Most of them would have said that it was growth for the better – that is, progress. Their history since the Middle Ages looked very much like a continuing advance to evidently worthwhile goals questioned by few. Whether the criteria were intellectual and scientific, or material and economic (even if they were moral and aesthetic, some said, so persuasive was the gospel of progress), a look at their own past assured them that they were set on a progressive course – which meant that the world was set on a progressive course, for their civilization was spread worldwide. What was more, limitless advance seemed to lie ahead. Europeans showed in 1900 much the same confidence in the continuing success of their culture as the Chinese élite had shown in theirs a century earlier. The past, they were sure, proved them right.

Even so, a few did not feel so confident. They felt that the evidence could equally well imply a pessimistic conclusion. Though there were far fewer pessimists than optimists, they numbered in their ranks men of acknowledged standing and powerful minds. Some of them argued that the civilization in which they lived had yet to reveal its full self-destructive potential and sensed that the time when it would do so might not be far away. Some of them saw a civilization more and more obviously drifting away from its moorings in religion and moral absolutes, carried along by the tides of materialism and barbarity – probably to complete disaster.

As it turned out, neither optimists nor pessimists were wholly right, perhaps because their eyes were glued too firmly to what they thought were the characteristics of European civilization. They looked to its own inherent powers, tendencies, or weaknesses for guidance about the future; not many of them paid much attention to the way Europe was changing the world in which her own ascendancy had been built and was thus to alter once again the balance between the major centres of civilization. Few looked further than Europe and Europe beyond the seas except the unbalanced cranks who fussed about the "Yellow Peril", though Napoleon had a century earlier warned that China was a sleeping giant best left undisturbed.

It is tempting to say in retrospect that the pessimists have had the best of the argument; it may even be true. But hindsight is sometimes a disadvantage to the historian; in this instance it makes it difficult to see how the optimists could once have felt so sure of themselves. Yet we should try to do so. For one thing, there were men of vision and insight among them; for another, optimism was for so long an obstacle to the solution of certain problems in the twentieth century that it deserves to be understood as a historical force in its own right. And much of what the pessimists said was wrong too. Appalling though the disasters of the twentieth century were, they fell on societies more resilient than those shattered by lesser troubles in earlier times, and they were not always those feared a hundred years ago. In 1900, optimists and pessimists alike had to work with data which could be read in more than one way. It is not reprehensible, merely tragic, that they found it so hard to judge exactly what lay ahead. With better information available to us, we have not been so successful in shorter-term prediction that we are in a position to condemn them.

The sense of optimism about the future that many Europeans had felt in the late 19th century was swept away by the outbreak of the First World War in 1914. This image of Verdun, France, four years later shows a scene of the devastation suffered by so many French cities and towns. Material disaster and unprecedented slaughter in 1914–1918 bequeathed poisonous legacies to the inter-war years.

1 A NEW ASIA IN THE MAKING

Industrial expansion meant that Japanese cities grew increasingly crowded during the 1920s, as this traffic jam in Tokyo's slum district of Honjo shows.

EUROPE'S TROUBLES COULD NOT be confined to one continent. They were bound soon to cramp her ability to dominate affairs elsewhere and the earliest signs of this came in Asia. European colonial power in Asia was, in the perspective of world history, only very briefly unchallengeable and unchallenged. By 1914 one European power,

Great Britain, had made an ally of Japan in order to safeguard her interests in the Far East, rather than rely on her own resources. Another, Russia, had been beaten by Japan in war and had turned back towards Europe after twenty years of pressure towards the Yellow Sea. Even the bullying of China which seemed likely to prove fatal at the time of the Boxer rebellion was relaxed; she lost no more territory to European imperialists after that. As tensions in Europe mounted and the difficulty of frustrating Japanese ambitions indefinitely became clear, European statesmen realized that the time for acquiring new ports or dreaming of partitions of the Sick Man of the Far East was over. It would suit everyone better to turn to what was always, in effect, British policy, that of an Open Door through which all countries might seek their own commercial advantage. That advantage, too, showed signs of being much less spectacular than had been thought in the sanguine days of the 1890s and here was another reason to tread more softly in the Far East.

THE TWILIGHT OF COLONIALISM

The peak of the European onslaught on Asia and its greatest successes were past by 1914. The revolutionizing of Asia by colonialism, cultural interplay, and economic power had already produced defensive reflexes which had to be taken seriously. They had gone furthest in Japan and it was their indirect operation as catalysts of modernization, channelled through this local and Asian force, which set the pace of the next phase of the

Hundred Years' War of East and West. Japanese dynamism dominates Asian history in the first forty years of this century; China's revolution had no similar impact until after 1945 when, together with new change-making forces from outside, that country again surpassed Japan in importance as a shaper of Asian affairs and closed the Western age in Asia.

JAPAN

JAPAN'S DYNAMISM showed itself both in economic growth and territorial aggressiveness. For a long time the first was more obvious. It was part and parcel of an overall process of what was seen as "westernizing" which could in the 1920s still sustain a mood of liberal hopefulness about Japan and helped to mask Japanese imperialism. In 1925 universal suffrage was introduced and in spite of much European evidence that this had no necessary connexion with liberalism or moderation, it seemed to confirm once again a pattern of steady constitutional progress begun in the nineteenth century.

POST-WAR INDUSTRIAL EXPANSION

Confidence in Japan's constitutional progress, shared both by foreigners and by Japanese, was for a time helped by her industrial growth, notably in the mood of expansive

optimism awoken by the Great War, which gave her great opportunities: markets (especially in Asia) in which she had been faced by heavy Western competition were abandoned to her when their former exploiters found they could not meet the demands of the war in their own countries; the Allied governments ordered great quantities of munitions from Japanese factories; a world shipping shortage gave her new shipyards the work they needed. The Japanese gross national product went up by forty per cent during the war years. Though interrupted in 1920 expansion was resumed later in the decade and in 1929 the Japanese had an industrial base which (though it still engaged less than one in five of the population) had in twenty years seen its steel production rise almost tenfold, its textile production tripled, and its

During an election campaign in Japan in 1914 a speaker, who is wearing Western-style clothes, addresses an audience, most of whom are dressed in traditional Japanese attire.

Tidstavle (1911-37)				
	1919 Versaillestraktaten		1937 Det japanske angreb på Kina	
1900			1940	
	1911-12 Den Kinesiske Revolution	1926-27 Guomindang-ekspeditionen mod nord	1934-35 Den Lange March	

coal output doubled. Her manufacturing sector was beginning to influence other Asian countries, too; she imported iron ore from China and Malaya, coal from Manchuria. Still small though her manufacturing industry was by comparison with that of the Western powers, and though it coexisted with an enduring small-scale and artisan sector, Japan's new industrial strength was beginning to shape both domestic politics and foreign relations in the 1920s. In particular, it affected her relations with mainland Asia.

The 1911 Chinese Revolution ended the Ch'ing Dynasty. Pu-Yi (1906–1967), who ruled as the last emperor of China from 1908 to 1912, is pictured right with his father, Prince Chun Tsai-Feng and his younger brother. Pu-Yi was forced to abdicate in February 1912 but later ruled, under the name of K'ang Te, as Japan's puppet emperor of Manchukuo from 1934 to 1945.

CHINA AFTER THE 1911 REVOLUTION

A CONTRAST TO THE PRE-EMINENT and dynamic role of Japan was provided there by the continuing eclipse of China, potentially the greatest of Asian and world powers. The 1911 revolution had been of enormous importance, but did not by itself end this eclipse. In principle, it marked an epoch far more fundamentally than the French or Russian revolutions: it was the end of more than two thousand years of history during which the Confucian state had held China together and Confucian ideals had dominated Chinese culture and society. Inseparably intertwined, Confucianism and the legal order fell together. The 1911 revolution proclaimed the shattering of the standards by which traditional China lived. On the other hand, the revolution was limited, in two ways especially. In the first place, it was destructive rather than constructive. The monarchy had held together a vast country, virtually a continent, of widely different regions. Its collapse meant that the centrifugal regionalism which so often expressed itself in Chinese history could again have full rein. Many of the revolutionaries were animated by a bitter envy and distrust of Peking (Beijing). Secret societies, the gentry and military commanders were all ready and willing to step forward and take a grip of affairs in their own regions. These tendencies were somewhat masked while Yuan Shih-k'ai remained at the head of affairs (until 1916), but then burst out. The revolutionaries were split between a group round Sun Yat-sen called the Chinese National People's Party, or Kuomintang (KMT), and those who upheld the central government based on the parliamentary structure at Peking. Sun's support was drawn mainly from Canton businessmen and certain soldiers in the south. Against this background

warlords thrived. They were soldiers who happened to have control of substantial forces and arms at a time when the central government was continuously weak. Between 1912 and 1928 there were some 1,300 of them, often controlling important areas. Some of them carried out reforms. Some were simply bandits. Some had considerable status as plausible pretenders to government power. It was a little like the end of the Roman Empire, though less drawn out. Nothing took the place of the old scholar-bureaucrats and the soldiers stepped forward to fill the void. Yuan Shih-k'ai himself can be regarded as the outstanding example of the type.

"NEW YOUTH" REFORMERS

The second limitation of the revolution of 1911 was that it provided no basis of agreement for further progress. Sun Yat-sen had said that the solution of the national question

The republic presided over by Yuan Shih-k'ai (1859–1916) – shown here in full military regalia – was in fact a dictatorship. Political power was in the hands of the military leaders and this was to continue. Between 1916 and 1919 a series of armed struggles between regional governors and warlords plagued the country and made life even harsher for the poverty-stricken Chinese people.

The Kuomintang (KMT)

The Kuomintang, the Chinese Nationalist Party, was the centre of the Chinese nationalist revolution of 1911. Comprising members of the upper- and middle-class bourgeoisie, workers and peasants, the Kuomintang was strongest in the industrial coastal areas, which left the rural areas as fertile ground for Communist agitation.

Between 1927 and 1937 China was governed by the Kuomintang, which unified the country, consolidating a nationalist government and becoming an authoritarian, military power, linked to Western neo-colonial interests. The government was able to balance the budget and it abolished special privileges for foreigners. However, when Japan attacked China in 1937 the Kuomintang proved incapable of resolving the situation. In 1949 the Chinese Communist Party triumphed over the Kuomintang, which they saw as a liberal-bourgeois body.

Members of the Kuomintang are pictured in 1927, shortly after the conference that unified "left" and "right" factions.

would have to precede that of the social. But even about the shape of a nationalist future there was much disagreement, and the removal of the dynasty took away a common enemy that had delayed its emergence. Although eventually creative, the intellectual confusion marked among the revolutionaries in the first decade of the Chinese Revolution was deeply divisive and symptomatic of the huge task awaiting China's would-be renovators.

From 1916 a group of cultural reformers began to gather particularly at the university of Peking. The year before, one of them, Ch'en Tu-hsiu, had founded a journal called *New Youth* which was the focus of the debate they ignited. Ch'en preached to Chinese youth, in whose hands he believed the revolution's destiny to lie, a total rejection of the old Chinese cultural tradition. Like other intellectuals who talked of Huxley and Dewey and introduced to their bemused compatriots the works of Ibsen, Ch'en still thought the key lay in the West; in its Darwinian sense of struggle, its individualism and utilitarianism, it still seemed to offer a way ahead. But important though such leadership was and enthusiastic though its disciples might be, an emphasis on a Western re-education for China was a handicap. Not only were many educated and patriotic Chinese sincerely attached to the traditional culture, but Western ideas were only sure of a ready welcome among the most untypical elements of Chinese society, the seaboard city-dwelling merchants and their student offspring, often educated abroad. The mass of Chinese could hardly be touched by such ideas and appeals, and the demand of other reformers for a vernacular literature was one evidence of this fact.

POVERTY AMONG THE PEASANTS

In so far as they were touched by nationalist feeling the Chinese were likely to turn against the West and against the Western-inspired capitalism which, for many of them, meant one more kind of exploitation and was the most obvious constituent of the civilization some modernizers urged them to adopt. But for the most part China's peasant masses seemed after 1911 relapsed in passivity, apparently unmoved by events and unaware of the agitation of angry and westernized young men. It is not easy to generalize about their economic state: China was too big and too varied. But it seems clear that while the population steadily increased, nothing was done to meet the peasants' hunger for land; instead, the number of the endebted and

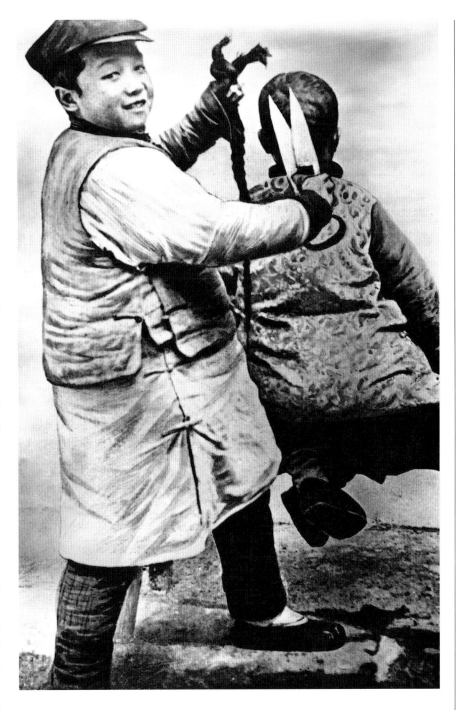

landless grew, their wretched lives frequently made even more intolerable by war, whether directly, or through its concomitants, famine and disease. The Chinese Revolution would only be assured success when it could activate these people, and the cultural emphasis of the reformers sometimes masked an unwillingness to envisage the practical political steps necessary for this.

The revolution of 1911 created a class of intellectuals and reformers, whose campaign against the traditional symbols of the old imperial régime included cutting off Manchu-style pigtails.

JAPAN'S DEMANDS ON CHINA

China's weakness remained Japan's opportunity. A world war was the occasion to push forward again her nineteenth-century policies. The advantages offered by the Europeans' quarrels with one another could be exploited. Japan's allies could hardly object to her seizure of the German ports in China; even if they did, they could do nothing about it while they needed Japanese ships and manufactures. There was always the hope, too, that the Japanese might send their own army to Europe to fight, though nothing like this happened. Instead, the Japanese finessed by arousing fears that they might make a separate peace with the Germans and pressed ahead in China.

Early in 1915 the Japanese government presented to the Chinese government a list of twenty-one demands, following them up with an ultimatum. In their entirety they amounted to a proposal for a Japanese protectorate over China. The United Kingdom and United States did what diplomacy could do to have them reduced but, in the end, the Japanese got much of what they asked for. It included further confirmation of their special commercial and leasehold rights in Manchuria. Chinese patriots were enraged, but there was nothing they could do at a moment when their internal politics were in disorder. They were so confused that Sun Yat-sen was himself at this moment seeking Japanese support.

THE PEACE SETTLEMENT

The next Japanese intervention in China came in 1916, when Japanese pressure was brought to bear on the British to dissuade them from approving Yuan Shih-k'ai's attempt to restore stability by making himself emperor. In the following year came another treaty, this time extending the recognition of Japan's special interests as far as Inner Mongolia. In August 1917 the Chinese government went to war with Germany, partly in the hope of winning goodwill and support which would ensure her an independent voice at the peace, but only a few months later the United States formally recognized the special interests of Japan in China in return for endorsement of the principle of the "open door" and a promise to maintain Chinese integrity and independence. All that the Chinese had got from the Allies was the ending of German and Austrian extra-territoriality and the concession that payment of Boxer indemnities to the Allies should be delayed. The Japanese, moreover, secured more concessions from China in secret agreements in 1917 and 1918.

Yet, when the peace came, it deeply disappointed both the great Asian powers of the future. Japan was now indisputably a world power; she had in 1918 the third largest navy in the world. It was true, too, that she won solid gains at the peace: she retained the former German rights in Shantung (promised to her by the British and French in 1917), and was granted a mandate over many of the former German Pacific islands and a permanent seat on the Council of the League of Nations. But the gain in "face" implied in such recognition was offset in Japanese eyes by a failure to have a declaration in favour of racial equality written in to the Covenant of the League. The Chinese had much more to feel aggrieved about, for in spite of widespread sympathy over the Twenty-One Demands (notably in the United States) they were unable to obtain a reversal of the Shantung decision. Disappointed of American diplomatic support and crippled by the divisions within their own delegation between the representatives of the Peking government and those of the Kuomintang at Canton, the Chinese refused to sign the treaty.

THE MAY 4TH MOVEMENT

A N ALMOST IMMEDIATE consequence was a movement in China to which some commentators have given an importance as great as that of the 1911 revolution itself. This was the "May 4th Movement" of 1919. It stemmed from a student demonstration in Peking against the peace, which had been planned for 7 May, the anniversary of China's acceptance of the 1915 demands, but was brought forward to anticipate action by the authorities. It escalated, though at first only into a small riot and the resignation of the head of the university. This then led to a nationwide student movement (one of the first political reflexions of the widely spread establishment in China of new colleges and universities after 1911). This in turn spread to embrace others than students and to manifest itself in strikes and a boycott of Japanese goods. A movement which had begun with intellectuals and their pupils spread to include other city-dwellers, notably industrial workers and the new Chinese capitalists who had benefited from the war. It was the most important evidence yet seen of the mounting rejection of Europe by Asia.

CHINESE INDUSTRIALIZATION

For the first time, an industrial China entered the scene. China, like Japan, had enjoyed an economic boom during the war. Though a decline in European imports to China had been partly offset by increased Japanese and American sales, Chinese entrepreneurs in the ports had found it profitable to invest in production for the home market. The first important industrial areas outside Manchuria began to appear. They belonged to progressive capitalists who sympathized with revolutionary ideas all the more when the return of peace brought renewed Western competition and evidence that China had not earned her liberation from tutelage to the foreigner. The workers, too, felt this resentment: their jobs were threatened. Many of them were first-generation town-dwellers, drawn into the new industrial areas from the countryside by the promise of employment. An uprooting from the tenacious soil of peasant tradition was even more important in China than in Europe a century before. Family and village ties were especially strong in China. The migrant to the town broke with patriarchal authority and the reciprocal obligations of the independent producing unit, the household: this was a further great weakening of

S un Yat-sen, pictured here in 1925, was the founder of the Kuomintang. He was a particularly westernized Chinese leader. Unlike this rare image, most photographs of Sun Yat-sen show him in European-style dress.

the age-old structure which had survived the revolution and still tied China to the past. New material was thus made available for new ideological deployments.

THE SEEDS OF FURTHER REVOLUTION

The May 4th Movement first showed what could be made of new ideological forces by creating the first broadly based Chinese revolutionary coalition. Progressive Western liberalism had not been enough; implicit in the movement's success was the disappointment of the hopes of many of the cultural reformers. Capitalist Western democracy had been shown up by the Chinese government's helplessness in the face of Japan. Now, that government had another humiliation from its own subjects: the boycott and demonstration forced it to release the arrested students and

dismiss its pro-Japanese ministers. But this was not the only important consequence of the May 4th Movement. For all their limited political influence, reformers had for the first time, thanks to the students, broken through into the world of social action. This aroused enormous optimism and greater popular political awareness than ever before. This is the case for saying that contemporary Chinese history begins positively in 1919 rather than 1911.

Yet ultimately the explosion had come because of an Asian force, Japanese ambition. That force, not in itself a new one in China's affairs, was by 1919 operating on a China whose cultural tradition was dissolving fast. The ending of the examination system, the return of the westernized exiles and the great literary and cultural debate of the war years had all pushed things too far for any return to the old stable state. The warlords could provide no new authority to identify and

In this scene from Shanghai in April 1919 coolies carry luggage to the wharf where foreigners are waiting to depart, anxious about the growing political unrest.

sustain orthodoxy. And now even the great rival of the Confucian past, Western liberalism, was under attack because of its association with the exploiting foreigner. Western liberalism had never had mass appeal; now its charm for intellectuals was threatened just as another rival ideological force from the West had appeared on the scene. The Bolshevik revolution gave Marxism a homeland to which its adherents abroad could look for inspiration, guidance, leadership and, sometimes, material support, a great new factor now introduced into an already-dissolving historical epoch, and bound to accelerate its end.

MARXISM IN CHINA

BOTH THE FEBRUARY 1917 REVOLUTION and the Bolshevik victory had been warmly welcomed by one of the contributors to *New Youth*, Li Ta-chao, who was from 1918 a librarian at Peking University. Soon he saw in Marxism the motive force of world revolution and the means to vitalize the Chinese peasantry. At that moment of disillusion with the West, Russia was very popular among Chinese students. It seemed that the successors of the tsar had driven out the old imperialist Adam, for one of the first acts of the Soviet government had been a formal renunciation of all extra-territorial rights and jurisdictions enjoyed by the tsarist state. In the eyes of the nationalists, Russia, therefore, had clean hands. Moreover, her revolution – a revolution in a great peasant society – claimed to be built upon a doctrine whose applicability to China seemed especially plausible in the wake of the industrialization provoked by the war. In 1918 there had begun to meet at Peking University a Marxist study society. One of its members was an assistant in the university library, Mao Tse-

tung, and others were prominent in the May 4th Movement. By 1920 there was an outlet for Marxist ideas in one of the student magazines which expressed the aspirations of that movement and the first attempts had been successfully made to deploy Marxist and Leninist principles by organizing strikes in support of it.

Yet Marxism opened divisions between the reformers. Ch'en Tu-hsiu himself turned to it as a solution for China's problems in 1920. He threw his energies into helping to organize the emerging Chinese Left around Marxism. The liberals were beginning to be left behind. The Comintern observed its opportunities and had sent its first man to China in 1919 to help Ch'en and Li Ta-chao. The effects were not entirely happy; there were quarrels. Nevertheless, in circumstances still obscure – we know precisely neither names nor dates – a Chinese communist party was formed in Shanghai in 1921 by delegates from different parts of China (Mao Tse-tung among them).

The Chinese Communist Party was founded in June 1921. Among its founding members was Mao Tse-tung (1893–1976), seen here in a photograph taken in 1967. The CCP's beginnings were extremely modest: it had very few card-carrying members, no national organization, no funds and no experience, and many of the details of the founding of the party remain obscure.

CHINESE COMMUNISM

With the foundation of the Chinese Communist Party began the last stage of the Chinese Revolution and the latest twist of that curious dialectic which has run through the relations of Europe with Asia. Once more an alien Western idea, Marxism, born and shaped in a society totally unlike the traditional societies of the East, embodying a background of assumptions whose origins were rooted in Judaeo-Christian culture, was taken up by an Asian people and put to their use. It was to be deployed not merely against the traditional sources of inertia in China, in the name of the Western goals of modernization, efficiency and universal human dignity and equality, but against the source from which it, too, came – the European world.

Communism benefited enormously in China from the fact that capitalism could easily be represented as the unifying, connecting principle behind foreign exploitation and aggression. In the 1920s, China's divisions were thought to make her of little account in international affairs, though nine powers with Asiatic interests were got to guarantee her territorial integrity and Japan agreed to hand back former German territories in China which she had taken in the Great War. This was part of a complicated set of agreements made at Washington whose core was the international limitation on naval strength (there was great uneasiness about the cost of armaments); these in the end left Japan relatively stronger. The four major powers guaranteed one another's possessions, too, and thus provided a decent burial for the Anglo-Japanese alliance, whose ending had long been sought by the Americans. But the guarantee to China, everyone knew, was worth no more than the preparedness of the

In this view of late 19th-century Shanghai the European-style buildings housing foreign commercial companies and embassies can be seen.

Americans to fight to support it; the British had been obliged by the treaties *not* to build a naval base at Hong Kong. Meanwhile, foreigners continued to administer the customs and tax revenues on which the Peking government of an "independent" China depended and foreign agents and businessmen dealt directly with the warlords when it suited them. Though American policy had further weakened the European position in Asia, this was not apparent in China.

THE KMT MOVES TOWARDS MARXISM

The apparently continuing grip of the foreign devils on China's life was one reason why Marxism's appeal to intellectuals went far beyond the boundaries of the formal structure of the Chinese Communist Party. Sun Yat-sen stressed his doctrinal disagreement with it but adopted views which helped to carry the KMT away from conventional liberalism and in the direction of Marxism. In his view of the world, Russia, Germany and Asia had a common interest as exploited powers against their oppressors and enemies, the four imperialist powers (Germany was well regarded after she had undertaken in 1921 to place her relations with China on a completely equal footing). He coined a new expression, "hypo-colony", for the state of affairs in which China was exploited without formal subordination as a dependency. His conclusion was collectivist: "On no account must we give more liberty to the individual," he wrote; "let us secure liberty instead for the nation." This was to give new endorsement to the absence of individual liberty which had always been present in the classical Chinese outlook and tradition. The claims of family, clan and state had always been paramount and Sun Yat-sen envisaged a period of one-party rule in order to make

possible mass indoctrination to reconfirm an attitude which had been in danger of corruption by Western ideas.

COOPERATION BETWEEN THE CCP AND THE KMT

There was apparently, then, no grave obstacle to the cooperation of the Chinese Communist Party (CCP) and the KMT. The behaviour of the Western powers and of the warlords provided common enemies and the Russian government helped to bring them together. Cooperation with the anti-imperialist power with which China had her longest land

When this photograph was taken of Chiang K'ai-shek (1887–1975) – seen here in the foreground of the picture on the left – Chiang was still merely a high-ranking soldier of the new régime.

frontier seemed at least prudent and potentially very advantageous. The policy of the Comintern, for its part, favoured cooperation with the KMT to safeguard Russian interests in Mongolia and as a step towards holding off Japan. Russia had been left out of the Washington conferences, though no power had greater territorial interests in the Far East. For her, cooperation with the likely winners in China was an obvious course even if Marxist doctrine had not also fitted such a policy. From 1924 onwards the CCP was working with the KMT under Russian patronage, in spite of some doubts among Chinese Communists. As individuals, though not as a party, they could belong to the KMT. Sun Yat-sen's able young soldier, Chiang K'ai-shek, was sent to Moscow for training, and a military academy was founded in China to provide ideological as well as military instruction.

KMT SUCCESSES

In 1925 Sun Yat-sen died; he had made Communist cooperation with his followers easier, and the united front still endured. Sun Yat-sen's will (which Chinese schoolchildren learnt by heart) had said that the revolution was not yet complete and while the Communists made important advances in winning peasant support for the revolution in certain provinces, the new revolutionary army led by idealistic young officers made headway against the warlords. By 1927 something of a semblance of unity had been restored to the country under the leadership of the KMT. Anti-imperialist feeling supported a successful boycott of British goods, which led the British government, alarmed by the evidence of growing Russian influence in China, to surrender its concessions at Hankow and Kiukiang. It had already promised to return

Wei-hai-wei to China (1922), and the United States had renounced its share of the Boxer indemnity. Such successes added to signs that China was on the move at last.

RURAL REVOLUTION

One important aspect of the Chinese Revolution long went unremarked. Theoretical Marxism stressed the indispensable revolutionary role of the industrial proletariat. The Chinese Communists were proud of the progress they had made in politicizing the new urban workers, but the mass of Chinese were peasants. Still trapped in the Malthusian vice of rising numbers and land shortage, their centuries of suffering were, if anything, intensified by the breakdown of central authority in the warlord years. Some Chinese Communists saw in the peasants a revolutionary potential which, if not easy to reconcile with contemporary Marxist orthodoxy (as retailed by the Moscow theorists), none the less embodied Chinese reality. One of them was Mao Tse-tung. He and those who agreed with him turned their attention away from the cities to the countryside in the early 1920s and began an unprecedented effort to win over the rural masses to Communism. Paradoxically, Mao seems to have continued to cooperate with the Kuomintang longer than other Chinese Communists just because it was more sympathetic to the organization of the peasants than was his own party.

A great success followed. It was especially marked in Hunan, but altogether some ten million or so peasants and their families were by 1927 organized by the Communists. "In a few months," wrote Mao, "the peasants have accomplished what Dr Sun Yat-sen wanted, but failed, to accomplish in the forty years he devoted to the national revolution."

Organization made possible the removal of many of the ills which beset the peasants. Landlords were not dispossessed, but their rents were often reduced. Usurious rates of interest were brought down to reasonable levels. Rural revolution had eluded all previous progressive movements in China and was identified by Mao as the failure of the 1911 revolution; the Communist success in reaching this goal was based on the discovery that it could be brought about by using the revolutionary potential of the peasants themselves. This had enormous significance for the future, for it implied new possibilities of historical development through Asia. Mao grasped this and revalued urban revolution accordingly. "If we allot ten points to the democratic revolution," he wrote, "then the achievements of the urban dwellers and the military units rate only three points, while the remaining seven points should go to the peasants in their rural revolution." In an image twice-repeated in a report on the Hunan movement he compared the peasants to an elemental force; "the attack is just like a tempest or hurricane; those who submit to it survive, those who resist perish." Even the image is significant; here was something rooted deeply in Chinese tradition and the long struggle against landlords and bandits. If the Communists tried hard to set aside tradition by eradicating superstition and breaking family authority, they nevertheless drew upon it, too.

THE KMT "RIGHT" TURNS ON THE COMMUNISTS

Communism's rural lodgement was the key to its survival in the crisis which overtook its relations with the KMT after Sun Yat-sen's

Chiang K'ai-shek

As a young man, Chiang K'ai-shek studied at military academies in Peking and Tokyo. After failing in business in Shanghai, he joined Sun Yat-sen, whom he had met during his two-year stay in Japan, and became one of the most outstanding officers in the Kuomintang. On Sun's death in 1925, he took over the presidency of the party and initiated the reunification of China by launching an expedition against the warlords who had controlled the north. Chiang, representing capitalist interests, broke off the alliance with the Chinese Communist Party and the Kuomintang's own left wing and began brutally to persecute the Communists. He was defeated in the civil war (1945–1949) and took refuge with his followers in Formosa (present-day Taiwan), where he installed a Nationalist government. As the elected president of the republic – a post he held from 1950 until his death – Chiang led the efforts to create a modern industrialized state in Taiwan.

Chiang K'ai-shek (1887–1975) is pictured here in 1949.

A British naval unit marches up Nanking Road in Shanghai's international settlement in 1927. Sailors sometimes formed some of the forces stationed in Shanghai to protect the European and US business interests in the city during the period of unrest; this parade was intended as a display of force.

death. Sun's removal permitted a rift to open in the KMT between a "left" and a "right" wing. The young Chiang, who had been seen as a progressive, now emerged as the military representative of the "right", which reflected mainly the interests of capitalists and, indirectly, landlords. Differences within the KMT over strategy were resolved when Chiang, confident of his control of his troops, committed them to destroying the left factions and the Communist Party's organization in the cities. This was accomplished with much bloodshed in Shanghai and Nanking in 1927, under the eyes of contingents of European and American soldiers who had been sent to China to protect the concessions. The CCP was proscribed, but this was not quite the end of its cooperation with the KMT, which continued in a few areas for some months, largely because of Russian unwillingness to break with Chiang. Russian direction had already made easier the destruction of the city Communists; the Comintern in China, as

elsewhere, myopically pursued what were believed to be Russian interests refracted through the mirror of dogmatic Marxism. These interests were for Stalin in the first place domestic; in external affairs, he wanted someone in China who could stand up to the British, the greatest imperialist power, and the KMT seemed the best bet for that. Theory fitted these choices; the bourgeois revolution had to precede the proletarian, according to Marxist orthodoxy. Only after the triumph of the KMT was clear did the Russians withdraw their advisers from the CCP, which gave up open politics to become a subversive, underground organization.

Chinese nationalism had in fact done well out of Russian help even if the CCP had not. Nevertheless, the KMT was left with grave problems and a civil war on its hands at a time when the revolution needed to satisfy mass demands if it was to survive. The split within the revolution was a setback, making it impossible to dispose finally of the warlord problem and, more serious, weakening the anti-foreign front. Pressure from Japan had continued in the 1920s after the temporary relaxation and handing back of Kiao-chou. Its domestic background was changing in an important way.

JAPANESE ECONOMIC DEPRESSION

When the wartime economic boom finally ended in 1920, hard times and growing social strains followed, even before the onset of the world economic depression. By 1931, half Japan's factories were idle; the collapse of European colonial markets and the entrenchment of what remained of them behind new tariff barriers had a shattering effect as Japanese exports of manufactures went down by two-thirds. The importance of Japan's outlets on the Asian mainland was now crucial. Anything that seemed to threaten them provoked intense irritation. The position of the Japanese peasant deteriorated, too, millions being ruined or selling their daughters into prostitution in order to survive. Grave political consequences were soon manifest, though less in the intensification of class conflict than in the provocation of nationalist extremism. The forces which were to pour into this had for a long time been absorbed in the struggle against the "unequal treaties". With those out of the way, a new outlet was needed, and the harsh operation of industrial capitalism in times of depression provided anti-Western feeling with fresh fuel.

JAPAN'S CUE TO ACT

The circumstances seemed propitious for further Japanese aggression in Asia. The Western colonial powers were clearly on the defensive, if not in full retreat. The Dutch faced rebellions in Java and Sumatra in the 1920s, the French a Vietnamese revolt in 1930; in both places there was the sinister novelty of Communist help to nationalist rebels. The British were not in quite such difficulties in India. Yet though some in Britain were not yet reconciled to the idea that India must move towards self-government, it was the proclaimed aim of British policy. In China the British had already shown in the 1920s that they wanted only a quiet accommodation with a nationalist movement they found hard to assess, and not too grave a loss of face. Their Far Eastern policies looked even feebler after economic collapse, which also knocked the stuffing out of American opposition to Japan. Finally, Russian power, too, seemed in the eclipse after its attempt to influence events in China. Chinese nationalism, on the contrary, had won notable successes, showed no sign of retreat and was considered to be beginning to threaten the long-established Japanese presence in Manchuria. All these factors were present in the calculations made by Japanese statesmen as the depression deepened.

Chaos reigned in post-revolutionary China, not only on a political and social level, but also when natural disasters, such as the flooding of the Yangtze River in 1931, took place. In Hankow, pictured here, the entire population of the region was forced to carry its household goods to safety on improvised rafts.

Japanese imperialism

Japanese imperialist tendencies were already emerging in the period between the two World Wars. Since her victory in the war with Russia in 1905, Japan had become a great industrial nation, dependent on a large amount of foreign trade. Ideological values influenced by traditional religious feelings, militarism and extreme right-wing nationalism combined with the failure of multi-party government in domestic politics to create a favourable environment in which the new Japanese imperial spirit could flourish.

In eastern Asia, Japan took on a dominant role, although it had abandoned, for a time, its designs on China. This was mainly thanks to the moderation of the minister for foreign affairs, Kijuro Shidehara, who, during his terms in office (from 1924 to 1927 and again from 1929 to 1931), urged economic rather than military expansion. But by the late 1920s, the Japanese were concerned with keeping their rights over Port Arthur, Darien and the south of Manchuria, and therefore, in 1927, Tokyo sent troops to Tsingtao, the Shantung port that it had renounced in 1922, and the Japanese invasion of northern China started in 1931.

By that time, the international peace system was deteriorating all over the world. The Japanese armed forces had always been a powerful group with political interests. Disillusionment with multi-party politics had been growing, particularly among the young officers who focused their activities on secret societies and the Kwantung expeditionary force in Manchuria. At the beginning of the 1930s, an authoritarian régime was established and an aggressive foreign policy adopted. Particularly in the region of Manchuria, the liberal-bourgeois parties gave way to the rising nationalist force of the military High Command and of the patriotic secret societies.

Japan took control of Manchuria in 1931, renaming it Manchukuo and running it as a puppet state. This photograph captures a moment in the Japanese occupation.

THE MANCHURIAN CRISIS

Manchuria was the crucial theatre. The Japanese presence there went back to 1905. Heavy investment had followed. At first the Chinese acquiesced, but in the 1920s began to question it, with support from the Russians who foresaw danger from the Japanese pushing their influence towards Inner Mongolia. In 1929 the Chinese in fact came into conflict with the Russians over control of the railway which ran across Manchuria and was the most direct route to Vladivostok, but this can only have impressed the Japanese with the new vigour of Chinese power; the nationalist KMT was reasserting itself in the territories of the old empire. There had been armed conflict in 1928 when the Japanese had tried to prevent KMT soldiers from operating against warlords in north China whom they found it convenient to patronize. Finally, the Japanese government was by no means unambiguously in control on the spot. Effective power in Manchuria rested with the commanders of the Japanese forces there, and when in 1931 they organized an incident near Mukden which they used as an excuse for taking over the whole province, those in Tokyo who wished to restrain them could not do so.

There followed the setting up of a new puppet state, Manchukuo (to be ruled by the last Manchu emperor), an outcry against Japanese aggression at the League of Nations, assassinations in Tokyo, the establishment there of a government much more under military influence, and the expansion of the quarrel with China. In 1932 the Japanese replied to a Chinese boycott of their goods by landing forces at Shanghai; in the following year they came south across the Great Wall to impose a peace which left Japan dominating a part of historic China itself and trying unsuccessfully to organize a secessionist north China. There matters stood until 1937.

THE COMMUNISTS ORGANIZE THE PEASANTS

The KMT government proved unable, after all, to resist imperialist aggression. Yet from its new capital, Nanking, it appeared to control successfully all save a few border areas. It continued to whittle away at the treaties of inferiority and was helped by the fact that as the Western powers saw in it a means of opposing Communism in Asia, they began to show themselves somewhat more accommodating. These achievements, considerable though they were, none the less masked important weaknesses which compromised the KMT's domestic success. The crux was that though the political revolution might have continued, the social revolution had come to a stop. Intellectuals withdrew their moral support from a régime which had not provided reforms of which a need to do something about land was the

From Manchukuo, whose puppet emperor Pu-Yi (known as K'ang Te) appears in the photograph, the Japanese continued to attack Chinese territory. They advanced along the coast to the outskirts of Peking. Their troops also overran the five northern provinces, which until 1937 supplied Japanese industry with iron and coal.

China 1918–1949

The area controlled by the Kuomintang up to 1937 was mainly along the country's east coast. The CCP was strong in specific areas all over China. An important step came when, in search of a safe sanctuary, Mao Tse-tung moved the Kiangsi

Soviet from the central southern region to the far north. Participants in this "Long March" covered more than 6,000 miles (9,650 km) on foot in order to penetrate the mountainous region of Shansi, which was better suited to guerrilla activities.

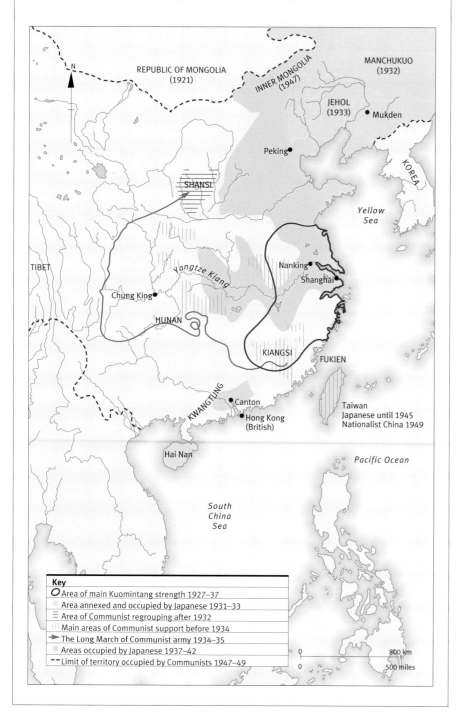

Key
- ⃝ Area of main Kuomintang strength 1927–37
- Area annexed and occupied by Japanese 1931–33
- ≡ Area of Communist regrouping after 1932
- ‖‖ Main areas of Communist support before 1934
- ▶ The Long March of Communist army 1934–35
- Areas occupied by Japanese 1937–42
- ‑‑ Limit of territory occupied by Communists 1947–49

most pressing. The peasants had never given the KMT their allegiance as some of them had given it to the Communists. Unfortunately for the régime, Chiang fell back more and more at this juncture upon direct government through his officers and showed himself more and more conservative at a time when the traditional culture had decayed beyond repair. The régime was tainted with corruption in the public finances, often at the highest level. The foundations of the new China were therefore insecure. And there was once more a rival waiting in the wings.

THE LONG MARCH

The central leadership of the CCP for some time continued to hope for urban insurrection; in the provinces, none the less, individual Communist leaders continued to work along the lines indicated by Mao in Hunan. They dispossessed absentee landlords and organized local soviets, a shrewd appreciation of the value of the traditional peasant hostility to central government. By 1930 they had done better than this, by organizing an army in Kiangsi, where a Chinese Soviet Republic ruled fifty million people, or claimed to. In 1932 the CCP leadership abandoned Shanghai to join Mao in this sanctuary. KMT efforts were directed towards destroying this army, but always without success. This meant fighting on a second front at a time when Japanese pressure was strongest. The last great KMT effort had a partial success, it is true, for it drove the Communists out of their sanctuary, thus forcing on them the "Long March" to Shansi which began in 1934, the epic of the Chinese Revolution and an inspiration ever since. Once there, the seven thousand survivors found local Communist support, but were still hardly safe; only the demands of resistance

Japanese troops enter Peking's Forbidden City in 1937. By the end of the following year, Japan ruled over the most important areas of economic activity and controlled territory inhabited by 42 per cent of the Chinese population.

to the Japanese prevented the KMT from doing more to harass them.

JAPAN ATTACKS CHINA

Consciousness of the external danger explains why there were tentative essays in cooperation between CCP and KMT again in the later 1930s. They owed something, too, to another change in the policies of the Comintern; it was an era of "Popular Fronts" elsewhere which allied Communists with other parties. The KMT was also obliged to mute its anti-Western line and this won it a certain amount of easy sympathy in England and, above all, the United States. But neither the cooperation of Communists nor the sympathies of Western liberals could prevent the Nationalist régime from being forced on the defensive when the Japanese launched their attack in 1937.

The "China incident", as the Japanese continued to call it, was to take eight years' fighting and inflict grave social and physical damage on China. It has been seen as the opening of the Second World War. At the end of 1937 the Chinese government removed itself for safety's sake to Chungking in the far west while the Japanese occupied all the important northern and coastal areas. League condemnation of Japan and Russian deliveries of aircraft seemed equally unable to stem the onslaught. The only bonus in the first black years was an unprecedented degree of patriotic unity in China; Communists and Nationalists alike saw that the national revolution was at stake. This was the view of the Japanese, too; significantly, in the area they occupied, they encouraged the re-establishment of Confucianism. Meanwhile, the Western powers felt deplorably unable to intervene. Their protests, even on behalf of their own citizens, were brushed aside by the Japanese who by 1939 made it clear that they were prepared to blockade the foreign settlements if recognition of the Japanese new order in Asia was not forthcoming. For British and French weakness there was an obvious explanation: they had troubles enough elsewhere. American ineffectiveness had deeper roots; it went back to a long-established fact that however the United States might talk about mainland Asia, Americans would not fight for it, perhaps wisely. When the Japanese bombed and sank an American gunboat near Nanking the State Department huffed and puffed but eventually swallowed Japanese "explanations". It was all very different from what had happened to the USS *Maine* in Havana harbour forty years before, though the Americans did send supplies to Chiang K'ai-shek.

CHINA HUMILIATED

By 1941, China was all but cut off from the outside world, though on the eve of rescue. At the end of that year her struggle would at last be merged with a world war. By then, though, much damage had been done to her. In the long duel between the potential Asian rivals, Japan had been so far clearly the winner. On the debit side of Japan's account had to be placed the economic cost of the struggle to her and the increasing difficulty experienced by her occupying forces in China. On the other hand, her international position had never seemed stronger; she showed it by humiliating Western residents in China and by forcing the British in 1940 to close the Burma Road by which supplies reached China, and the French to admit an occupying army to Indo-China. Here was a temptation

A child cries alone in the aftermath of a Japanese bombardment of Shanghai. The Japanese bombed the city extensively during the Sino-Japanese War of 1937–1945, with the intention of destroying the foreign concessions that were based there.

A Japanese officer, standing on Nanking's historic wall in 1938 and holding the Rising Sun flag, symbolizes the Japanese conquest of China. The war, however, had severe repercussions in Japan; what was called the "China incident" required general military mobilization and centralized economic planning.

to further adventure, and it was not likely to be resisted while the prestige of the military and their power in government remained as high as it had been since the mid-1930s.

DECOLONIALIZATION BEGINS

There was also a negative side to Japanese military success. Aggression made it more and more imperative for Japan to seize the economic resources of Southeast Asia and Indonesia. Yet it also slowly prepared the Americans psychologically for armed defence of their interest. It was clear by 1941 that the United States would have to decide before

long whether it was to be an Asian power at all and what that might mean. In the background, though, lay something even more important. For all her aggression against China, it was with the window-dressing slogan of "Asia for the Asians" that Japan advanced on the crumbling Western position in Asia. Just as her defeat of Russia in 1905 marked an epoch in the psychological relations of Europe and Asia, so did the independence and power which Japan showed in 1938–41. When followed by conquest of the European empires, as it was to be, it would signal the beginning of the era of decolonialization; this was to be fittingly inaugurated by the one Asian power at that time successful in its "westernization".

2 THE OTTOMAN HERITAGE AND THE WESTERN ISLAMIC LANDS

DURING THE NINETEENTH CENTURY the Ottoman Empire all but disappeared in Europe and Africa. In each continent, the basic causes were the same: the disintegrating effect of nationalism and the predatory activities of European powers. The Serbian revolt of 1804 and Mehemet Ali's establishment of himself as the governor of Egypt in 1805 together opened the final, though drawn out, era of Turkish decline. In Europe the next step was the Greek revolt; from that time the story of the Ottoman Empire in Europe can be told in the dates of the establishment of new nations, until in 1914 Turkey was left with only eastern Thrace. In Islamic Africa the decline of Ottoman power had by then gone even further, and much of North Africa had already been virtually independent of the sultan's rule early in the nineteenth century.

EGYPT UNDER MEHEMET ALI

One result of the decline of Ottoman power in the region was that nationalism in Islamic Africa tended to be directed more against Europeans than against the Ottomans. It was

Fighting in the name of a disappearing empire: young Turkish recruits are photographed in 1914 in Istanbul. Following its defeat in the First World War, the Ottoman Empire lost all its non-Turkish territories.

also a culturally revolutionary force. The story again begins with Mehemet Ali. Though he himself never went further west than his birthplace, Kavalla, he admired European civilization and thought Egypt could learn from it. He imported technical instructors, employed foreign consuls in the direction of health and sanitation measures, printed translations of European books and papers on technical subjects, and sent boys to study in France and England. Yet he was working against the grain. His practical achievements disappointed him, though he opened Egypt to European (especially French) influence as never before. Much of it flowed through educational and technical institutions and reflected an old French interest in the trade and affairs of the Ottoman Empire. French was soon the second language of educated Egyptians and a large French community grew up in Alexandria, one of the great cosmopolitan cities of the Mediterranean.

PAN-ARABISM

Few modernizing statesmen in the non-European world have been able to confine their borrowings from the West to technical knowledge. Soon, young Egyptians began to pick up political ideas, too; there were plenty of them available in French. A compost was forming which would in the end help to transform Europe's relations with Egypt. Egyptians would draw the same lesson as Indians, Japanese and Chinese: the European

disease had to be caught in order to generate the necessary antibodies against it. So, modernization and nationalism became inextricably intertwined. Here lay the origin of an enduring weakness in Middle Eastern nationalism. It was long to be the creed of advanced élites cut off from a society whose masses lived in an Islamic culture still largely uncorroded by Western ideas. Paradoxically, the nationalists were usually the most Europeanized members of Egyptian, Syrian and Lebanese societies, and this was true until well into the twentieth century. Yet their ideas were to come to have wider resonance. It was among Christian Arabs of Syria that there seems first to have appeared the idea of pan-Arabian or Arab nationalism (as opposed to Egyptian, Syrian or some other kind), an assertion that all Arabs, wherever they were, constituted a nation. This was an idea distinct from that of the brotherhood of Islam which not only embraced millions of non-Arabs, but also excluded many non-Muslim Arabs. The potential complications of this for any attempt actually to realize an Arab nation in practice were, like other weaknesses of pan-Arabist ideas, not to appear until well into the twentieth century.

ISMAIL LEADS EGYPT INTO DEBT

Another landmark in the history of the former Ottoman lands was the opening of the Suez Canal in 1869. This did more (though indirectly) than any other single fact to doom

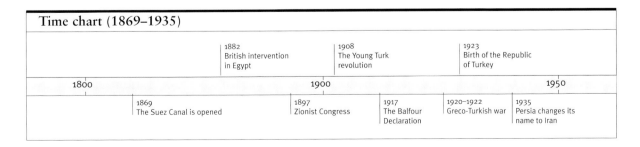

Time chart (1869–1935)

1800		1900				1950	
	1882 British intervention in Egypt		1908 The Young Turk revolution		1923 Birth of the Republic of Turkey		
	1869 The Suez Canal is opened		1897 Zionist Congress	1917 The Balfour Declaration	1920–1922 Greco-Turkish war	1935 Persia changes its name to Iran	

Egypt to intervention and therefore increasing irritation by the foreigner. Yet the canal was not the immediate cause of the start of nineteenth-century interference by Europeans in Egypt's government. That came about because of the actions of Ismail (the first ruler of Egypt to obtain from the sultan the title of khedive, in recognition of his substantial de facto independence). Educated in France, Ismail liked Frenchmen and up-to-date ideas, and travelled much in Europe. He was very extravagant. When he became ruler, in 1863, the price of cotton, Egypt's main export, was high because of the American Civil War and Ismail's financial prospects therefore looked good. Unhappily, his financial management was less than orthodox. The results were to be seen in the rise in the Egyptian national debt; £7,000,000 at Ismail's accession, it stood at nearly £100,000,000 only thirteen years later. The interest charges amounted to £5,000,000 a year, in an age when such sums mattered. In 1876 the Egyptian government was bankrupt and ceased to pay its debts, so foreign managers were put in. Two controllers, one British, one French, were

Dated 1882 – the year of the British army's intervention to put down an Egyptian revolution – this illustration depicts English soldiers in Alexandria searching Arabs for hidden weapons.

appointed to make sure that Egypt was governed by Ismail's son with the priority of keeping up revenue and paying off the debt. They were soon blamed by nationalists for the huge burdens of taxation laid upon the Egyptian poor in order to provide the revenue to pay debt interest as well as for economies, such as the reduction of government salaries. The European officials who worked in the name of the khedive were, in the nationalists' eyes, simply the agents of foreign imperialism. There was growing resentment of the privileged legal position of the many foreigners in Egypt and their special courts.

BRITISH INTERVENTION IN EGYPT

Grievances against European officials led to nationalist conspiracy and eventually to revolution. As well as the westernizing xenophobes a few now began to urge the reform of Islam, the unity of the Muslim world and a pan-Islamic movement adapted to modern life. Some took a more local view, antagonized by the preponderance of Turks in the khedive's entourage. But such divisions mattered less than British intervention in frustrating a revolution in 1882. This was not intervention for financial reasons. It took place because British policy, even under a Liberal prime minister who favoured nationalism in other parts of the Ottoman Empire, could not accept the danger that the security of the canal route to India might be jeopardized by an unfriendly government at Cairo. It was unthinkable at the time, but British soldiers were to remain in the Canal Zone until 1955, tied down by strategical dogma.

After 1882 the British became the prime targets of nationalist hatred in Egypt. They said they wanted to withdraw as soon as a dependable government was available, but could not do so for none acceptable to them was conceivable. Instead, British administrators took on more and more of the government of Egypt. This was not wholly deplorable; they reduced the debt, and mounted irrigation schemes which made it possible to feed a growing population (it doubled to about twelve million between 1880 and 1914). They antagonized Egyptians, though, by keeping them out of government service in the interests of economy, by imposing high taxes and by being foreign. After 1900 there was growing unrest and violence. The British and the puppet Egyptian government proceeded firmly against agitation, and also sought ways out through reform. At first administrative, this led in 1913 to a new constitution providing for more representative elections to a more powerful legislative assembly. Unfortunately, the assembly met only for a few months before it was suspended at the outbreak of war. The Egyptian government was pushed into war with Turkey, a khedive suspected of anti-British plotting was replaced, and at the end of the year the British proclaimed a protectorate. The khedive now took the title of sultan.

THE YOUNG TURK MOVEMENT

BY THE TIME WAR BROKE OUT, the Ottoman government had lost Tripolitania to the Italians, who had invaded it in 1911 partly because of another manifestation of reforming nationalism, this time in Turkey itself. In 1907 a successful rebellion had been started there by the "Young Turk" movement, which had a complicated history, but a simple purpose. As one Young Turk put it: "we follow the path traced by Europe ... even in our

In 1875 the British prime minister Benjamin Disraeli (1804–1881) bought shares in the Suez Canal from the khedive of Egypt. Having acquired control of this major strategic waterway, Great Britain had more reason than ever to intervene in Egyptian political affairs.

refusal to accept foreign intervention." The first part of this meant that they wished to end the despotic rule of Abdul Hamid and restore a liberal constitution granted in 1876 and subsequently withdrawn. But they wanted this less for its own sake than because they thought it would revive and reform the empire, making possible modernization and an end to the process of decay. Both this programme and the Young Turks' methods of conspiracy owed much to Europe; they used, for example, masonic lodges as cover and organized secret societies such as those which had flourished among European liberals in the days of the Holy Alliance. But they much resented the increasing interference in Ottoman internal affairs by Europeans, notably in the management of finance, for, as in Egypt, the securing of interest on money

This engraving, which dates from 1879, shows the traditional irrigation system at work on the banks of the Nile in Upper Egypt.

lent for internal development had been followed by loss of independence. European bullying had also resulted (they felt) in the Ottoman government's long and humiliating retreat from the Danube valley and the Balkans.

THE COUP AND THE REFORMS

After a series of mutinies and revolts, the sultan gave way over the constitution in 1908. Liberals abroad smiled on constitutional Turkey; it seemed that misrule was at last to end. But an attempted counter-revolution led to a Young Turk coup which deposed Abdul Hamid and installed a virtual dictatorship. From 1909 to 1914 the revolutionaries ruled with increasingly dictatorial means from behind the façade of constitutional monarchy. Ominously, one of them announced that "there are no longer Bulgars, Greeks, Romanians, Jews, Muslims ... we glory in being Ottoman". This was something

The Young Turks

The Young Turks were the first group to succeed in modernizing the Ottoman political system. Led by a minister and a high-ranking army officer, and taking advantage of the turbulent times both nationally and internationally, the Young Turks managed to convince the sultan, Abdul Hamid II, to rework a constitution first granted and then suspended in 1876. This instituted a parliament and ministers who would answer to it (although the first elected parliament only lasted for a year).

Turkey's younger generation had been increasingly exposed to European ideas. Young people gradually became sceptical about the legitimacy of the traditional Ottoman institutions, which led them to consider the possibility of deposing the greatest exponent of that power, the sultan himself. In 1908 a group of Young Turks (army officers garrisoned in Macedonia) began an uprising which spread rapidly and was joined by the troops sent to quash it.

Although the 1876 constitution was restored and the sultan deposed, the Young Turks' government was unable to prevent army interference in politics, especially when the Balkan Wars broke out in 1912. Factional infighting led to the forcible ejection of a more conservative wing of the movement in January 1913 and the emergence of a Young Turk dictatorship.

The Young Turks hesitated between neutrality and alliance with Germany as the Great War approached. Here, their minister of war, Enver Pasha (formerly Enver Bey), is seen in conversation with the British ambassador's military attaché.

quite new: the announcement of the end of the old multinational régime.

With hindsight, the Young Turks seem more comprehensible than they did at the time. They faced problems like those of many modernizers in non-European countries and their violent methods have been emulated by many since from necessity or imagined necessity. They threw themselves into reform of every branch of government (importing many European advisers). To seek (for instance) to improve the education of girls was a significant gesture in an Islamic country. But they took power in the middle of a shattering succession of diplomatic humiliations which weakened their appeal and led them to rely on force. After the Habsburg annexation of Bosnia, the ruler of Bulgaria won an acknowledgement of Bulgarian independence, and the Cretans announced their union with Greece. A brief pause then was followed by the Italian attack on Tripoli, and the Balkan Wars.

REFORMISTS RESORT TO TYRANNY

Under such strain, it was soon apparent that the post-reform harmony among the peoples to which liberals had looked forward was a chimera. Religion, language, social custom and nationality still fragmented even what was left of the empire. The Young Turks were driven back more and more upon the assertion of one nationalism among many, that of the Ottomans. This, of course, led to resentment among other peoples. The result was once more massacre, tyranny and assassination, the time-honoured instruments of rule at Constantinople; from 1913 they were deployed by a triumvirate of Young Turks who ruled as a collective dictatorship until the outbreak of the Great War.

In January 1913 a group of Young Turk officers, led by Colonel Enver Bey, crossed the Sublime Gateway in Constantinople, as depicted in this contemporary illustration, and announced the overthrow of the Turkish cabinet installed by another army faction the year before.

Though they had disappointed many of their admirers, these men had the future on their side. They represented the ideas which would one day remake the Ottoman heritage: nationalism and modernization. They had even – willy-nilly – done something towards this by losing most of the little that was left of the Ottoman Empire in Europe, thus releasing themselves from a burden. But their heritage was still too encumbering in 1914. Before them lay no better alternative as a vehicle for reform than nationalism. How little pan-Islamic ideas would mean was to be shown by what happened after 1914 in the largest remaining block of Ottoman territory, the largely Muslim provinces of Asia.

ASIA'S MUSLIM PROVINCES

IN 1914 THE MUSLIM PROVINCES of Asia covered a large and strategically very important area. From the Caucasus the frontiers with Persia ran down to the Gulf near

Theodor Herzl (1816–1904) established political Zionism and the movement to found a Jewish homeland. In 1896, in his pamphlet *The Jewish State*, he proposed that a world council of nations should be created to settle the Jewish political question.

Basra, at the mouth of the Tigris. On the southern shore of the Gulf Turkish rule ran round Kuwait (with an independent sheik and under British protection) and then back to the coast as far south as Qatar. From here the coasts of Arabia right round to the entrance of the Red Sea were in one way or another under British influence, but the whole interior and Red Sea coast were Ottoman. Under British pressure the Sinai desert had been surrendered to Egypt a few years before, but the ancient lands of Palestine, Syria and Mesopotamia were still all Turkish. This was the heartland of historical Islam, and the sultan was still caliph, its spiritual leader.

This heritage was to crumble as the strategy and politics of world war played upon it. Even within the historic Islamic heartland, there had been signs before 1914 that the new nationalist forces were at work. In part, they stemmed from old-established European cultural influences, which operated in Syria and the Lebanon much more strongly than in Egypt. French influence had been joined in those countries by American missionary efforts and the foundation of schools and colleges to which there came Arab boys, both Muslim and Christian, from all over the Arab world. The Levant was culturally advanced and literate. On the eve of the world war over a hundred Arabic newspapers were published in the Ottoman Empire outside Egypt.

GROWING DISSENT

An important crystallization had followed the triumph of the Young Turks and their Ottomanizing tendencies. Secret societies and open groups of dissidents were formed among Arab exiles, notably in Paris and Cairo. In the background was another uncertain factor: the rulers of the Arabian peninsula, whose allegiance to the sultan was shaky. The most important of them was Hussein, sherif of Mecca, in whom by 1914 the Turkish government had no confidence. A year earlier there had also been the ominous sign of a meeting of Arabs in Persia to consider the independence of Iraq. Against this, the Turks could only hope that the divisiveness of the different interests represented among the Arabs would preserve the status quo.

ZIONISM

Finally, although it did not present an immediate danger, the latest converts to the religion of nationalism were the Jews. Their history had taken a new turn when, in 1897, there appeared a Zionist Congress whose aim was the securing of a national home. Thus, in the long history of Jewry, assimilation, still barely achieved in many European countries after the liberating age of the French Revolution, was now replaced as an ideal by that of territorial nationalism. The desirable location had not at once been clear; Argentina, Uganda were suggested at different times, but by the end of the country Zionist opinion had come to rest finally on Palestine. Jewish immigration there had begun, though still on a small scale. The unrolling of the war was to change its significance.

WORLD WAR I

CURIOUS PARALLELS EXISTED between the Ottoman and Habsburg empires in 1914. Both sought war, seeing it, in part, as a solution to their problems. Yet both were bound to suffer from it, because too many

The Young Turk government's leanings towards Germany were obvious as it began the rearmament and training of the Turkish army. Although the Ottoman Empire had been exhausted by the Balkan Wars, Enver Pasha insisted that Turkey enter the Great War as Germany's ally. This announcement led to anti-war demonstrations in the streets of Constantinople, such as this one in October 1914.

people inside and outside their borders saw in war an opportunity to score at their expense. In the end, both empires were to be destroyed by it. Even at the outset, Russia, the historic enemy, seemed likely to benefit since Turkey's entry to the war at last evaporated the long resistance of the British and French to the establishment of tsarist power at Constantinople. For their part, the French had their own fish to fry in the Middle Eastern pan. Though their irritation over a British presence in Egypt had subsided somewhat with the making of the entente and a free hand for France in Morocco, there was a tradition of a special French role in the Levant. The evocations of St Louis and the crusaders with which some enthusiasts made play did not have to be taken seriously, but, undeniably, French governments had for a hundred years exercised a special protection

of Catholicism in the Ottoman Empire, especially in Syria, to which Napoleon III had sent a French army in the 1860s. There was also the cultural predominance evinced by the wide use of the French language among the educated in the Levant, and much French capital was invested there. These were not forces which could be overlooked.

Nevertheless, in 1914 Turkey's main military antagonists outside Europe were likely to be Russia in the Caucasus, and Great Britain at Suez. The defence of the canal was the foundation of British strategic thinking in the area, but it soon became clear that no great danger threatened it. Then occurred events announcing the appearance of new factors which would in the end turn the Middle and Near East upside-down. At the end of 1914 an Indian-British army landed at Basra to safeguard oil supplies from Persia. This was the beginning of the interplay of oil and politics in the historical destiny of this area, though it was not to show itself fully until well after the Ottoman Empire had ceased to exist. On the other hand, an approach which the British governor of Egypt made to Hussein in October 1914 bore fruit very quickly. This was the first attempt to use the weapon of Arab nationalism.

AN ARABIAN ALLIANCE

The attraction of striking a blow against Germany's ally became all the greater as fighting went on bloodily but indecisively in Europe. An attempt in 1915 to force the Dardanelles by combined naval and land operations, in the hope of taking Constantinople, bogged down. By then Europe's civil war had already set in train forces one day to be turned against her. But there was a limit to what could be offered to Arab allies. Terms were not agreed with Hussein until the beginning of 1916. He had demanded independence for all the Arab lands south of a line running along the 37th degree of latitude – this was about eighty miles north of a line from Aleppo to Mosul and included, in effect, the whole of the Ottoman Empire outside Turkey and Kurdistan. It was much more than the British could take at the gallop. The French had to be consulted, too, because of their special interest in Syria. When an agreement was made between the British and French on spheres of influence in a partitioned Ottoman Empire it left many questions still unsettled

British troops are pictured at a makeshift position during the disastrous Dardanelles campaign of 1915, in which the Allies invaded the Gallipoli peninsula. But they failed to achieve their aim of occupying the northern side of the Dardanelles channel and then Istanbul (Constantinople). British Commonwealth casualties alone totalled more than 214,000, and the defeat led Winston Churchill to resign as first lord of the Admiralty.

for the future, including the status of Iraq, but an Arab nationalist political programme had became a reality.

THE ARAB REVOLT

The future of such undertakings was soon in doubt. The Arab revolt began in June 1916 with an attack on the Turkish garrison of Medina. The rising was never to be more than a distraction from the main theatres of war, but it prospered and became a legend. Soon the British felt they must take the Arabs more seriously; Hussein was recognized as king of the Hejaz. Their own troops pressed forwards in 1917 into Palestine, taking Jerusalem. In 1918 they were to enter Damascus together with the Arabs. Before this, though, two

Edmund Allenby (1861–1936), the British commander-in-chief of the Egypt expeditionary force against the Turks, launched an offensive to take Jerusalem in 1917. On entering the city, he was warmly welcomed by the Jewish community.

The Balfour Declaration

"I have much pleasure in conveying to you, on behalf of His Majesty's Government, the following declaration of sympathy with Jewish Zionist aspirations which has been submitted to, and approved by, the Cabinet.

"His Majesty's Government view with favour the establishment in Palestine of a national home for the Jewish people, and will use their best endeavours to facilitate the achievement of this object, it being clearly understood that nothing shall be done which may prejudice the civil and religious rights of existing non-Jewish communities in Palestine, or the rights and political status enjoyed by Jews in any other country.

"I should be grateful if you would bring this declaration to the knowledge of the Zionist Federation."

A letter from Arthur James Balfour, the British foreign secretary, to Lord Rothschild, dated 2 November, 1917.

other events had further complicated the situation. One was the American entry into the war; in a statement of war aims President Wilson said he favoured "an absolute unmolested opportunity of development" for the non-Turks of the Ottoman Empire. The other was the Bolshevik publication of their predecessors' secret diplomacy; this revealed Anglo-French proposals for spheres of influence in the Middle East. One part of this agreement had been that Palestine should be administered internationally. Another irritant was added when it was announced that British policy favoured the establishment of a national home in Palestine for the Jewish people. The "Balfour Declaration" can be accounted the greatest success of Zionism down to this time. It was not strictly incompatible with what had been said to the Arabs, and President Wilson had joined in the good work by introducing to it qualifications to protect Palestinians who were not Jews, but it

Lawrence of Arabia

In 1916, when the British tried to advance into Sinai to protect their access to the Suez Canal, Hussein, the sherif of Hejaz, began an uprising against the Turks. Keen to support him, the British sent two Arab specialists into Hejaz: Ronald Storrs and Thomas Edward Lawrence. The latter, a captain attached to the British army, was to become a fierce defender of the cause of Faisal, Hussein's son.

Lawrence persuaded Faisal to abandon the siege of Medina and centre his activities on severing Turkish communications along the railway line to Damascus. Together, they conquered Aqaba and entered Palestine; his heroic adventures won the British captain the nickname "Lawrence of Arabia". At the end of the war Lawrence acted as adviser to the Arab delegation at the Paris Peace Conference, but failed to achieve Faisal's great hope of creating a pan-Arab state that would cover the whole of the Middle East. Lawrence was killed in a motorcycle accident in 1935.

T. E. Lawrence (1888–1935) is pictured in Arabia.

is almost inconceivable that it could ever have operated unchallenged, especially when further British and French expressions of goodwill towards Arab aspirations followed in 1918. On the morrow of Turkish defeat, the outlook was thoroughly confused.

MIDDLE EASTERN MANDATES

Following the Turkish defeat Hussein was recognized as king of the Arab peoples by Great Britain, but this did little for him. It was mainly the British and French, with the help of the League of Nations, who were to lay out the main lines of the map of the modern Arab world, not Arab nationalism. During a confused decade the British and French became embroiled with the Arabs whom they had themselves conjured on to the stage of world politics, while the Arab leaders quarrelled among themselves. Islamic unity

once more disappeared but, mercifully, so did the Russian threat (even if only briefly), so only two great powers were involved in the Middle East. They distrusted one another, but could agree, roughly on the basis that if the British had their way in Iraq, the French could have theirs in Syria. This was legitimized subsequently by the League of Nations awarding three main mandates to them for Arab lands. Palestine, Transjordan and Iraq went to the British and Syria to the French, who governed high-handedly from the start, having to install themselves by force after a national congress had asked for independence or a British or American mandate. They evicted the king the Arabs had chosen, Hussein's son. Subsequently they had to face a full-scale insurrection. The French were still holding their own by force in the 1930s, though there were by then signs that they would concede some power to the nationalists. Unfortunately, the Syrian situation soon also showed the disintegrating power of nationalism when the Kurdish people of north Syria revolted against the prospect of submergence in an Arab state, so introducing to Western diplomats another Middle Eastern problem with a long life before it.

INDEPENDENCE FOR THE PENINSULA STATES

The Arabian peninsula was meanwhile racked by a struggle between Hussein and yet another king with whom the British had negotiated a treaty (his followers, to make things more difficult still, were members of a particularly puritanical Islamic sect who added religious to dynastic and tribal conflict). Hussein was displaced, and in 1932 the new kingdom of Saudi Arabia emerged in the place of the Hejaz. From this flowed other problems, for sons of Hussein were by this time kings of Iraq and Transjordan. After heavy fighting had shown the difficulties ahead, the British had moved as fast as they dared towards the ending of the mandate over Iraq, seeking only to secure British strategic interests by preserving a military and air force presence. In 1932, accordingly, Iraq entered the League as an independent and fully sovereign state. Earlier, Transjordan had been recognized as independent by the British in 1928, again with some retention of military and financial powers.

THE PALESTINIAN PROBLEM

Palestine was much more difficult. From 1921, when there were anti-Jewish riots by Arabs alarmed over Jewish immigration and Jewish acquisition of Arab land, that unhappy country was never to be long at peace. More was at stake than merely religious or national feeling. Jewish immigration meant the irruption of a new westernizing and modernizing force, its operation changing economic relationships and imposing new demands on a traditional society. The British mandatory power was caught between the outcry of the Arabs if it did not restrict Jewish immigration, and the outcry of the Jews if it did. But Arab governments now had to be taken into account, and they occupied lands which were economically and strategically important to British security. World opinion was becoming involved, too. The question became more inflamed than ever when in 1933 there came to power in Germany a régime which persecuted Jews and began to take away the legal and social gains they had been making since the French Revolution. By 1937 there were pitched battles between Jews and Arabs in Palestine. Soon a British army was trying to hold down an Arab insurrection.

BRITISH ECONOMIC INTERESTS

The collapse of the paramount power in the Arab lands had often in the past been followed by a period of disorder. What was unclear this time was whether disorder would be followed – as earlier periods of anarchy had eventually been – by the establishment of a new imperial hegemony. The British did not want that role; after a brief spell of imperial intoxication in the aftermath of victory, they desired only to secure their own fundamental interests in the area, the protection of the Suez Canal and the swelling flow of oil from Iraq and Iran. Between 1918 and 1934 a great pipeline had been built from northern Iraq across Transjordan and Palestine to Haifa, thus giving yet another new twist to the future of these territories. The consumption of oil in Europe was not yet so large that there was any general dependence on it, nor had the great discoveries been made which would again change the political position in the 1950s. But a new factor was making itself felt; the Royal Navy had turned over to oil for its ships.

INDEPENDENT EGYPT

The British believed Suez to be best secured by keeping forces in Egypt, but this caused increasing trouble. The war had intensified Egyptian feeling. Armies of occupation are never popular; when the war sent up prices the foreigner was blamed. Egyptian nationalist leaders attempted in 1919 to put their case to the Paris Peace Conference but were prevented from doing so; there followed a rising against the British which was quickly put down. But the British were in retreat. The protectorate was ended in 1922 in the hope of getting ahead of nationalist feeling. Yet the new kingdom of Egypt had an electoral system which returned nationalist majority after nationalist majority, thus making it impossible for an Egyptian government to come to terms on safeguards for British interests which any British government would find acceptable. The result was a prolonged constitutional crisis and intermittent disorder until in 1936 the British finally agreed to be content with a right to garrison the Canal Zone for a limited number of years. An end was also announced to the jurisdictional privileges of foreigners.

PAN-ARAB FEELING GROWS

These concessions were among other signs of the beginning of a British retreat from empire which can be detected elsewhere after 1918; it was in part a reflexion of an overstretching of power and resources, as British foreign policy began to be preoccupied by other challenges. Changes in world relationships far from the Middle East thus helped to shape post-Ottoman developments in Islamic lands. Another novel factor was Marxist communism. During the whole of the years between the wars, Russian radio broadcasting to the Arab countries supported the first Arab communists. But for all the worry they caused, communism showed no sign of being able to displace the strongest revolutionary influence of the area, still that of Arab nationalism, whose focus had come by 1938 to be Palestine. In that year a congress was held in Syria to support the Palestinian Arab cause. Arab resentment of the brutality of the

The Druzes, a group of whom are shown here, revolted against the French in 1926. The rebellion reached Damascus, and continued throughout the summer, but – after several bombings of Damascus – most of the trouble had died out by the following summer.

Jubilant Turkish nationalists celebrate Turkey's success in reclaiming the town of Smyrna (now Izmir) from Greece during the war between Greece and Turkey of 1921–1922.

French in Syria was beginning to be evident, too, as well as an Arab response to the outcry of the Egyptian nationalists against the British. In pan-Arab feeling lay a force which some thought might in the end override the divisions of the Hashemite kingdoms.

EUROPEANS IN TURKEY AFTER THE WAR

Allied agreements during the war also complicated the history of the Ottoman homeland, Turkey (as it was soon to be renamed) itself. The British, French, Greeks and Italians had all agreed on their shares of the booty; the only simplification brought by the war had been the elimination of the Russian claim to Constantinople and the Straits. Faced with Greek and Italian invasion, the sultan signed a humiliating peace. Greece was given large concessions, Armenia was to be an independent state, while what was left of Turkey was divided into British, French and Italian spheres of influence. This was the most blatant imperialism. To drive home the point, European financial control was re-established.

THE END OF THE OTTOMAN EMPIRE

THIS DIVISION of historic Turkey provoked the first successful revision of any part of the peace settlement. It was largely the work of one man, a former Young Turk and an outstanding soldier, Mustafa Kemal, who drove out French and Greeks in turn after frightening away the Italians. With Bolshevik help he crushed the Armenians. The British decided to negotiate and so a second treaty was made with Turkey in 1923. It was a triumph of nationalism over the decisions at Paris, and it was the only part of the peace settlement which was negotiated between equals and not imposed on the defeated. It was also the only one in which Russian negotiators took part and it lasted better than any of the other peace treaties. The capitulations and financial controls disappeared. Turkey gave up her claims to the Arab lands and the islands of the Aegean, Cyprus, Rhodes and the Dodecanese. A big exchange of Greek and Turkish population followed and the hatred of these peoples for one another received fresh reinforcement. So the Ottoman Empire outside Turkey was wound up after six centuries, and a new republic came into existence in 1923 as a national state under a dictator who proved rapidly to be one of the most effective of modernizers. Appropriately, the caliphate followed the empire, being abolished in 1924. This was the end of Ottoman history; of Turkish history, it was a new beginning. The Anatolian Turks were now for the first time in five or six centuries the majority people of their state.

ATATÜRK'S MODERNIZATION OF TURKEY

Kemal, as he tended to call himself (the name meant "Perfection"), was something of a

Peter the Great (though he was not interested in territorial expansion after the successful revision of the dictated peace) and something of a more enlightened despot. The law was secularized (on the model of the Napoleonic code), the Muslim calendar abandoned, and in 1928 the constitution was amended to remove the statement that Turkey was an Islamic state. Polygamy was forbidden. In 1935 the weekly day of rest, formerly Friday, the Islamic holy day, became Sunday and a new word entered the language: *vikend* (the period from 1.00 p.m. Saturday to midnight Sunday). Schools ceased to give religious instruction. The fez was forbidden; although it had come from Europe it was considered Muslim. Kemal was conscious of the radical nature of the modernization he wished to achieve and such symbols mattered to him. They were signs, but signs of something very important, the replacement of traditional Islamic society by a European one. One Islamic ideologist urged his fellow Turks to "belong to the Turkish nation, the Muslim religion and European civilization" and did not appear to see difficulties in achieving that. The alphabet was latinized and this had great importance for education, henceforth obligatory at the primary level. A national past was rewritten in the schoolbooks; it was said that Adam had been a Turk.

Kemal – on whom the National Assembly conferred the name of Atatürk, or "Father of the Turks" – is an immensely significant figure. He is what Mehemet Ali perhaps wanted to be, the first transformer of an Islamic state by modernization. He remains strikingly interesting; until his death in 1938 he seemed determined not to let his revolution congeal. The result was the creation of a state in some ways among the most advanced in the world at that date. In Turkey, a much greater break with the past was involved in giving a new role to women than in Europe, but in 1934

The Turkish sultan Muhammad VI (centre) is shown offering prayers to Allah at the tomb of Muhammad the Conqueror in Istanbul in 1922. When the sultan was forced into exile and the caliphate was abolished, there were uprisings all over Turkey and negative reactions from the Islamic communities.

Mustafa Kemal

Mustafa Kemal twice made history. He won the crucial battle of the Dardanelles campaign and, after the war ended, he brought his Turkish-speaking Muslim compatriots to see themselves as citizens of a republic and members of a new Turkish nation.

Kemal's landing in Samsun in 1919, after the Greek invasion, is generally thought to represent the start of the Turkish revolution. By 1920, he was head of the civil government in Ankara. He was also commander-in-chief of the army, which carried out a successful counter-attack against the Greeks in the Battle of Sakarya in 1921.

As president of the People's Republican Party, Kemal officially proclaimed the Republic of Turkey on 29 October, 1923, and became its first president. He upheld a firm belief in progress and science, but was also aware of the importance of historical, ethnic and cultural forces in society. Although he wielded a vast amount of personal power, Kemal also managed to win wide support in the republic's assembly.

Mustafa Kemal (1880–1938) is pictured as commander-in-chief of the Turkish army in 1922.

Turkish women received the vote and they were encouraged to enter the professions.

PERSIA

THE MOST IMPORTANT Islamic country neither under direct imperial rule by Europeans nor Ottomans before 1914 was Persia. The British and Russians had both interfered in her affairs after agreeing over spheres of influence in 1907, but Russian power had lapsed with the Bolshevik revolution. British forces continued to operate on Persian territory until the end of the war. Resentment against the British was excited when a Persian delegation, too, was not allowed to state its case to the Peace Conference. There was a confused period during which the British struggled to find means of maintaining resistance to the Bolsheviks after withdrawal of their forces. There could be no question of retaining Persia by force, given the over-taxing of British strength. Almost by accident, a British general had already discovered the man who was to do this, though hardly in the way anticipated.

REZA KHAN'S REFORMS

Reza Khan was an officer who carried out a *coup d'état* in 1921 and at once used the Bolshevik fear of the British to get a treaty conceding all Russian rights and property in Persia and the withdrawal of Russian forces. Reza Khan then went on to defeat separatists who had British support. In 1925 he was given dictatorial powers by the national assembly and a few months later was proclaimed "shah of shahs". He was to rule until 1941 (when the Russians and the British together turned him off the throne), somewhat in the style of an Iranian Kemal. The abolition of the veil and religious schools showed secularist aims, though they were not pressed so far as in Turkey. In 1928 the capitulations were abolished, an important symbolic step; meanwhile industrialization and the improvement of communications were pressed forward. A close association with Turkey was cultivated. Finally, the Persian strong man won in 1933 the first notable success in a new art, the diplomacy of oil, when the concession held by the Anglo-Persian Oil Company was cancelled. When the British government took the question to the League of Nations, another and more favourable concession was Reza Shah's greatest victory and the best evidence of the independence of Persia. A new era had opened in the Gulf, fittingly marked in 1935 by an official change of the name of the state: Persia became Iran.

The shah of Iran, Reza Khan (1878–1944), portrayed here, admired Mustafa Kemal and imitated many of the methods that Kemal had used to modernize Turkey.

3 THE SECOND WORLD WAR

THE DEMONSTRATION that the European age was at last over was made in another world war. It began (in 1939) like its predecessor, as a European struggle, and like it became a combination of wars. Like it, too, but to a far greater degree, it made unprecedented demands; this time they were on a scale which left nothing untouched, unmobilized, undisturbed. It was realistically termed "total" war.

ECONOMIC DISINTEGRATION

By 1939, there were already many signs for those with eyes to see that a historical era was ending. Though 1919 had brought a few last extensions of territorial control by colonial powers, the behaviour of the greatest of them, Great Britain, showed that imperialism was on the defensive, if not already in retreat. The vigour of Japan meant that Europe was no longer the only focus of the international power system; a prescient South African statesman said as early as 1921 that "the scene has shifted away from Europe to the Far East and to the Pacific". His prediction now seems more than ever justified and it was made when the likelihood that China might soon again exercise her due weight was far from obvious. Ten years after he spoke, the economic foundations of Western

French refugees flee during the bombing of Dunkirk in northern France in 1940. When Dunkirk was liberated in 1945 only a quarter of its buildings were still standing.

preponderance had been shaken even more plainly than the political; the United States, greatest of industrial powers, had still ten million unemployed. Though none of the European industrial countries was by then in quite such straits, the confidence which took for granted the health of the basic foundations of the economic system had evaporated for ever. Industry might be picking up in some countries – largely because rearmament was stimulating it – but attempts to find recovery by international cooperation came to an end when a World Economic Conference broke down in 1933. After that, each nation had gone its own way; even the United Kingdom at last abandoned free trade. Laissez-faire was dead, even if people still talked about it. Governments were by 1939 deliberately interfering with the economy as they had not done since the heyday of mercantilism.

CHANGING INTELLECTUAL AND MORAL TRENDS

IF THE POLITICAL AND ECONOMIC assumptions of the nineteenth century had gone, so had many others. It is more difficult to speak of intellectual and spiritual trends than of political and economic, but though many people still clung to old shibboleths, for the élite which led thought and opinion the old foundations were no longer firm. Many people still attended religious services – though only a minority, even in Roman Catholic countries – but the masses of the

industrial cities lived in a post-Christian world in which the physical removal of the institutions and symbols of religion would have made little difference to their daily lives. So did intellectuals; they perhaps faced an even greater problem than that of loss of religious belief, because many of the liberal ideas which had helped to displace Christianity from the eighteenth century were by now being displaced in their turn. In the 1920s and 1930s, the liberal certainties of the autonomy of the individual, objective moral criteria, rationality, the authority of parents, and an explicable mechanical universe all seemed to be going under along with the belief in free trade.

The "Roaring Twenties" were a time of economic recovery during which many people felt able to enjoy a new lease of life after the horrors and deprivation of the First World War. Nightclubs such as the Charleston Contest Parody Club, shown here in 1926, became very popular.

Time chart (1919–1945)				
	1931 Japanese invasion of Manchuria	1933 Hitler comes to power Roosevelt's New Deal	1939 The German-Soviet pact is signed Poland is divided The Second World War begins	
1900				1950
1919–1920 Peace Treaties of the Paris Conference The Weimar Republic is established	1929 The Wall Street Crash	1936–1939 The Spanish Civil War Germany takes Czechoslovakia Creation of the Anschluss	1941 The Japanese attack Pearl Harbor	1945 Atomic bombs are dropped on Hiroshima and Nagasaki End of the Second World War The UN is created

Art and changing values

In the early 20th century, recent major scientific discoveries and theories began to undermine the solid scientific and cultural paradigms of the previous century. The new ideas derived from Darwin's theory of evolution had a widespread impact, as did Freud's uncovering of a new field of knowledge, the unconscious mind. The formulation of relativist theories also transformed prevailing attitudes: humanity began to seem ever less significant in relation to other species (we are just one more of them), in relation to ourselves (we are not governed only by rational forces) and in relation to the universe (time and space do not have an absolute value).

The late 19th-century philosophers, in particular Arthur Schopenhauer and Friedrich Nietzsche, had considerable impact both on literature and on music. Artists, influenced by the spirit of the time, moved away from naturalism and immersed themselves in a private world. In literature, Virginia Woolf, James Joyce and Franz Kafka explored the human ego and laid the foundations of 20th-century narrative. In music, dodecaformism, or the twelve-tone technique, which was first used by Arnold Schoenberg in 1923, emerged as an alternative to classical tonal systems. In painting, after Impressionism came Cubism, Dadaism and Surrealism.

Animal Composition *was painted by the Spanish artist Joan Miró (1893–1983), who became a leading figure in the field of abstract art and Surrealist fantasy.*

THE ARTS

Change was most obvious in the arts. For three or four centuries, since the age of humanism, Europeans had believed that the arts expressed aspirations, insights and pleasures accessible in principle to ordinary men, even though they might be raised to an exceptional degree of fineness in execution, or be especially concentrated in form so that not everyone would always enjoy them. At any rate, it was possible for the whole of that time to retain the notion of the cultivated individual who, given time and study, could discriminate with taste among the arts of his or her time because they were expressions of a shared culture with shared standards. This idea was somewhat weakened when the nineteenth century, in the wake of the Romantic movement, came to idealize the artist as genius – Beethoven was one of the first examples – and formulated the notion of the avant-garde. By the first decade of the twentieth century, though, it was already very difficult for even trained eyes and ears to recognize art in much of what was done by contemporary artists. The best symbol of this was the dislocation of the image in painting. Here, the flight from the representational still kept a tenuous link with tradition as late as Cubism, but by then it had long ceased to be apparent to the average "cultivated man" – if he still existed. Artists retired into a less and less accessible chaos of private visions, whose centre was reached in the world of Dada and Surrealism. The years after 1918 are of the greatest interest as something of a culmination of disintegration; in Surrealism even the notion of the objective disappeared, let alone its representation. As one Surrealist put it, the movement meant "thought dictated in the absence of all control exerted by reason, and outside all aesthetic or moral preoccupations". Through chance, symbolism, shock, suggestion and violence the Surrealists sought to go beyond consciousness itself. In so doing, they were only doing what many writers and musicians were trying to do, too.

Such phenomena provide evidence in widely different forms of the decay of liberal culture which was the final outcome of the high civilization of the European age. It is significant that such disintegratory movements were often prompted by a sense that the traditional culture was too limited because of its exclusion of the resources of emotion and experience which lay in the unconscious. Probably few of the artists who would have agreed with this would have read the work of the man who, more than any other, gave the twentieth century a language in which to explore this area and the confidence that it was there that the secrets of life lay.

THE ROLE OF SIGMUND FREUD

Sigmund Freud was the founder of psychoanalysis. He deserves a place in the history of culture beside Newton or Darwin, for he changed the way educated men and women thought of themselves. He introduced several new ideas into ordinary discourse: the special meanings we now give to the words "complex", "unconscious" and "obsession", and the appearance of the familiar terms "Freudian slip" and "libido" are monuments to the power of his teaching. His influence quickly spread into literature, personal relations, education, politics. Like that of many prophets, his message was often distorted. What he was believed to have said was much more important than the specific clinical studies which were his contribution to science. Again like Newton and Darwin, Freud's

The work carried out by Sigmund Freud (1856–1939) in Vienna transformed thinking about the human consciousness around the world. Because Freud was Jewish, his books were among the first to be burned by the Nazis following Hitler's annexation of Austria.

importance beyond science – where his influence was more complex – lay in providing a new mythology. It was to prove highly corrosive.

The message people took from Freud suggested that the unconscious was the real source of most significant behaviour, that moral values and attitudes were projections of the influences which had moulded this unconscious, that, therefore, the idea of responsibility was at best a myth and probably a dangerous one, and that perhaps rationality itself was an illusion. It did not matter much that Freud's own assertions would have been nonsense had this been true or that this left out the subtlety and science of his work. This was what many people believed he had proved – and still believe. Such a bundle of ideas called in question the very foundation of liberal civilization itself, the idea of the rational, responsible, consciously motivated individual, and this was its general importance.

Freud's teaching was not the only intellectual force contributing to the loss of certainty and the sense that human beings had little firm ground beneath their feet. But it was the most apparent in the intellectual life of the interwar period. From grappling with the insights he brought, or with the chaos of the arts, or with the incomprehensibility of a world of science which seemed suddenly to have abandoned Laplace and Newton, men and women plunged worriedly into the search for new mythologies and standards to give them bearings. Politically, this led to fascism, Marxism, and the more irrational of the old certainties, extreme nationalism, for example. People did not feel inspired or excited by tolerance, democracy, and the old individual freedoms.

THE GERMAN PROBLEM

THE SWING AWAY FROM the old liberal assumptions made it all the more difficult to deal with the deepening uncertainty and foreboding clouding international relations in the 1930s. The heart of this lay in Europe, in the German problem which threatened a greater upheaval than could Japan. Germany had not been destroyed in 1918; it was a logical consequence, therefore, that she would one day again exercise her due weight. Geography, population and industrial power all meant that in one way or another a united Germany must dominate Central Europe and overshadow France. What was at issue at bottom was whether this could be faced without war; only a few cranks thought it might be disposed of by dividing again the Germany united in 1871.

Germans soon began to demand the revision of the settlement of Versailles. This demand eventually became unmanageable, though in the 1920s it was tackled in a hopeful spirit. The real burden of reparations was gradually whittled away and the Treaty of Locarno was seen as a great landmark because by it Germany gave her consent to

The German delegation, lead by Dr Gustav Streseman, leaves Berlin to join the representatives of other European governments for the signing of the Treaty of Locarno in 1925. The treaty represented a high point in the successful use of diplomacy to solve international conflicts peacefully.

Friedrich Ebert (1871–1925), the first president of Germany's Weimar Republic, is pictured delivering an address to the National Constituent Assembly in March 1919.

the Versailles territorial settlement in the west. But it left open the question of revision in the east and behind this loomed the larger question: how could a country potentially so powerful as Germany be related to its neighbours in a balanced, peaceful way, given the particular historical and cultural experience of the Germans?

THE FRAGILE WEIMAR REPUBLIC

Most people hoped the German issue had been settled by the creation of a democratic German republic whose institutions would gently and benevolently reconstruct German society and civilization. It was true that the constitution of the Weimar Republic (as it was called from the place where its constituent assembly met) was very liberal, but too many Germans were out of sympathy with it from the start. That Weimar had

solved the German problem was revealed as an illusion when economic depression shattered the narrow base on which the German republic rested and set loose the destructive nationalist and social forces it had masked.

When this happened, the containment of Germany again became an international problem. But for a number of reasons, the 1930s were a very unpromising decade for containment to be easy. To begin with, some of the worst effects of the world economic crisis were felt in the relatively weak and agricultural economies of the new eastern countries. France had always looked for allies against a German revival there, but such allies were now gravely weakened. Furthermore, their very existence made it doubly difficult to involve Russia, again an indisputable (if mysterious) great power, in the containment of Germany. Her ideological distinction presented barriers enough to cooperation with the United Kingdom and

The 1929 Wall Street Crash

By the 1920s, the United States had become an industrialized nation. In the post-war years of economic boom, an atmosphere of optimism and complete confidence in the country's financial security reigned in America. Many investors believed that the time had come in which they could make their fortunes by investing in Wall Street. Even for those who were not familiar with the stock exchange, it was more profitable to speculate on the stock market than to wait for a particular company to pay dividends.

In spring 1928, the New York Stock Exchange rose by 25 points owing to highly optimistic forecasts made by influential figures in industry and agriculture. Speculation on the stock exchange pushed the index up another 30 points in January 1929. During that summer, millions of investors bought shares, often on credit, in the hope of selling them on at a higher price. However, in October, crisis struck. People began to

sell their shares and prices started to sink at an alarming speed. The worst came on 29 October, when the general index dropped 43 points. Panic-selling led to 16 million shares being sold on that day, for a fraction of their original value. On 13 November, the industrial index was worth half its value of two months earlier.

The stock exchange crash triggered a series of repercussions. Many banks were not able to cover the loans their ruined clients had taken out and closed one by one as their funds ran out: in 1929 642 banks closed; in 1930 there were 1,945 closures; and in 1931, 2,298. This brought about similar disasters in Europe, where many banks were closely linked to the North American system through war loans and money lent for reconstruction in the post-war period. When American capital was urgently recalled, the crisis spread across Europe.

After the Wall Street Crash, those who had bought shares on credit during the stock market boom had to pay for their lost shares in cash. Many speculators, such as this man in New York in October 1929, were forced to sell their possessions. The newspapers were full of tales of the resounding ruin of seemingly indestructible fortunes and there was more than a touch of truth in comedian Will

Rogers' quip about having to queue for a hotel window from which to jump (11 financiers committed suicide on 29 October, known as "Black Thursday"). Haunting images of the ensuing Great Depression – the long lines of the unemployed queueing at soup kitchens in the American cities and starving people in rural areas – were soon seen around the world.

France, but there was also her strategic remoteness. No Soviet force could reach Central Europe without crossing one or more of the east European states whose short lives were haunted by fear of Russia and communism: Romania, Poland and the Baltic states, after all, were built from, among other things, former Russian lands.

PRE-WAR AMERICA

THE AMERICANS, like the USSR, could not be relied upon to help contain Germany. The whole trend of American policy since Wilson failed to get his countrymen to join the League had been back towards a self-absorbed isolation which was, of course, suited to traditional ideas. Americans who had gone to Europe as soldiers did not want to repeat the experience. Justified apparently by boom in the 1920s, isolation was paradoxically confirmed by slump in the 1930s. When Americans did not confusedly blame Europe for their troubles – the question of debts from the war years had great psychological impact because it was believed to be tied up with international financial problems (as indeed it was, though not quite as Americans thought) – they felt distrustful of further entanglement. Anyway, the depression left them with enough on their plate. With the election of a Democratic president in 1932 they were, in fact, at the beginning of an era of important change which would in the end sweep away this mood, too, but this could not be foreseen.

FRANKLIN ROOSEVELT

The next phase of American history was to be presided over by Democrats for five successive presidential terms, the first four of them after elections won by the same man,

Franklin Roosevelt. To stand four successive times as presidential candidate was almost unprecedented (only the unsuccessful socialist, Eugene Debs, also did so); to win, astonishing. To do so with (on each occasion) an absolute majority of the popular vote was something like a revolution. No earlier Democratic candidate since the Civil War had ever had one at all (and no other was to have one until 1964). Moreover, Roosevelt was a rich, patrician figure. It is all the more surprising, therefore, that he should have emerged as one of the greatest leaders of the early twentieth century. He did so in an electoral contest which was basically one of hope versus despair. He offered confidence and the promise of action to shake off the blight of

President Franklin D. Roosevelt (1882–1945) (right) is seen on board the electoral train in 1932. It would take his Republican Party opponents another 20 years to recover from the loss of credibility the Great Depression had brought them.

economic depression. A political transformation followed his victory, the building of a Democratic hegemony on a coalition of neglected constituencies – the South, the poor, the farmer, the black American, the progressive liberal intellectual – which then attracted further support as it seemed to deliver results.

THE NEW DEAL

There was some degree of illusion in Roosevelt's success. The "New Deal" on which the Roosevelt administration embarked was still not grappling satisfactorily with the economy by 1939. None the less it changed the emphasis of the working of American capitalism and its relations with government. A huge programme of unemployment relief with insurance was started, millions were poured into public works, new regulation of finance was introduced, and a great experiment in public ownership was launched in a hydroelectric scheme in the Tennessee valley.

The Tennessee Valley Authority emblem is displayed in 1934 shortly after its approval by President Roosevelt. The ambitious government project to develop the enormous Tennessee river basin resulted in the creation of thousands of jobs and significantly increased the national level of electricity production.

This in the end gave capitalism a new lease of life, in a new governmental setting. The New Deal brought the most important extension of the power of the Federal authorities over American society and the states that had ever occurred in peacetime and it has proved irreversible. Thus American politics reflected the same pressures towards collectivism which affected other countries in the twentieth century. In this sense, too, the Roosevelt era was historically decisive. It changed the course of American constitutional and political history as nothing had done since the Civil War and incidentally offered to the world a democratic alternative to fascism and communism by providing a liberal version of large-scale governmental intervention in the economy. This achievement is all the more impressive in that it rested almost entirely on the interested choices of politicians committed to the democratic process and not on the arguments of economists, some of whom were already advocating greater central management of the economy in capitalist nations. It was a remarkable demonstration of the ability of the American political system to deliver what people felt they wanted.

DIPLOMATIC PROBLEMS IN EUROPE

The American political machinery, of course, could also only deliver as a foreign policy what most Americans would tolerate. Roosevelt was much more aware than the majority of his fellow citizens of the dangers of persistent American isolation from Europe's problems. But he could reveal his own views only slowly. With Russia and the United States unavailable, only the Western European great powers remained to confront Germany if she revived. Great Britain and France were badly placed to act as the police-

Italian troops invaded the ancient African kingdom of Ethiopia (then called Abyssinia) in October 1935. In this photograph taken by an Italian soldier, natives of a captured province salute a portrait of Mussolini, whom they knew as the "Great White Father". By May 1936, the Italian annexation of Ethiopia was complete. The kingdom was part of Italian East Africa until 1941.

men of Europe. They had memories of their difficulties in dealing with Germany even when Russia had been on their side. Furthermore, they had been much at odds with one another since 1918. They were also militarily weak. France, conscious of her inferiority in manpower should Germany ever rearm, had invested in a programme of strategic defence by fortification which looked impressive but effectively deprived her of the power to act offensively. The Royal Navy was no longer without a rival, nor, as in 1914, safe in concentrating its resources in European waters. British governments long pursued the reduction of expenditure on armaments at a time when worldwide commitments were a growing strain on her forces. Economic depression reinforced this tendency; it was feared that the costs of rearmament would cripple recovery by causing inflation. Many British voters, too, believed that Germany's grievances were just. They were disposed to make concessions in the name of German nationalism and self-determination, even by handing back German colonies. Both Great Britain and France were also troubled by a joker in the European pack, Italy. Under Mussolini, hopes that she might be enlisted against Germany had disappeared by 1938.

ITALY INVADES ETHIOPIA

The realization that Mussolini would not ally his country with Britain and France arose from a belated attempt by Italy to participate in the Scramble for Africa when, in 1935, her forces invaded Ethiopia. Such action posed the question of what should be done by the League of Nations; it was clearly a breach of its Covenant that one of its members should attack another. France and Great Britain were in an awkward position. As great powers, Mediterranean powers and African colonial powers, they were bound to take the lead against Italy at the League. But they did so feebly and half-heartedly, for they did not want to alienate an Italy they would like to have with them against Germany. The result was the worst possible one. The League failed to check aggression and Italy was alienated. Ethiopia lost its independence, though, it later proved, only for six years.

IDEOLOGY AND INTERNATIONAL RELATIONS

The League's failure to prevent Italy's invasion of Ethiopia was one of several moments at which it later looked as if a fatal error was committed. But it is impossible to say in retrospect at what stage the situation which developed from these facts became unmanageable. Certainly the emergence of a much more radical and ferociously opportunist régime in Germany was the major turning-point. But the depression preceded this and made it possible. Economic collapse also had another important effect. It made plausible an ideological interpretation of events in the 1930s and thus further embittered them. Because of the intensification of class conflict which economic collapse brought with it, interested politicians sometimes interpreted the development of international relations in terms of Fascism versus Communism, and even of Right versus Left or Democracy versus Dictatorship. This was easier after Mussolini, angered by British and French reactions to his invasion of Ethiopia, came to ally Italy to Germany and talked of an anti-Communist crusade. But this was misleading, too. All ideological interpretations of international affairs in the 1930s tended to obscure the central nature of the German problem – and, therefore, to make it harder to tackle.

RUSSIA BETWEEN THE WARS

Russian propaganda was important, too. During the 1930s her internal situation was precarious. The industrialization programme was imposing grave strains and sacrifices. These were mastered – though perhaps also exaggerated – by a savage intensification of dictatorship which expressed itself not only in the collectivization struggle against the peasants, but in the turning of terror against the cadres of the régime itself from 1934 onwards. In five years millions of Russians were executed, imprisoned or exiled, often to forced labour. The world looked on amazed as batches of defendants grovelled with

When Stalin took power in 1924, Leon Trotsky's persistent criticism of the Communist Party's increasingly undemocratic organization won him many enemies. He was eventually exiled from the Soviet Union in 1929. During the following decade, Stalin's régime would similarly exile, imprison or execute thousands of Soviet citizens for alleged political dissent. Trotsky was murdered by a Stalinist assassin in Mexico in 1940.

Voters gather in Saint-Denis in Paris at the end of the French election day in 1936. The election was won by the leftist-liberal Popular Front coalition government led by Léon Blum, which governed until 1938. Although the French Communist Party supported Blum's government, they did not join it – they knew that further unrest among the French workers would wreak chaos and leave the country exposed to a Fascist invasion.

grotesque "confessions" before Soviet courts. Nine out of ten generals in the army went, and, it has been estimated, half the officer corps. A new Communist élite replaced the old one in these years; by 1939 over half the delegates who had attended the Party Congress of 1934 had been arrested. It was very difficult for outsiders to be sure what was happening, but it was clear to them that Russia was by no means either a civilized, liberal state nor necessarily a very strong potential ally.

More directly, this affected the international situation because of the propaganda which accompanied it. Much of this, no doubt, arose from the deliberate provocation inside Russia of a siege mentality; far from being relaxed, the habit of thinking of the world in terms of Us versus Them which had been born in Marxist dogma and the interventions of 1918–22 was encouraged in the 1930s. As this notion took hold, so, outside, did the preaching of the doctrine of international class-struggle by the Comintern. The

reciprocal effect was predictable. The fears of conservatives everywhere were intensified. It became easy to think of any concession to left-wing or even mildly progressive forces as a victory for the Bolsheviks. As attitudes thus hardened on the Right, so communists were given new evidence for the thesis of inevitable class-conflict and revolution.

THE REJECTION OF COMMUNISM IN EUROPE

In spite of the communists' hopes, though, there was not one successful left-wing revolution. The revolutionary danger had subsided rapidly after the immediate post-war years. Labour governments peacefully and undramatically ruled Great Britain for part of the 1920s. The second ended in financial collapse in 1931, to be replaced by conservative coalitions which had overwhelming electoral support and proceeded to govern with remarkable fidelity to the tradition of progressive and piecemeal social and administrative reform which had marked Great Britain's advance into the "welfare state". This direction had been followed even further in the Scandinavian countries, often held up for admiration for their combination of political democracy and practical socialism, and as a contrast to communism. Even in France, where there was a large and active Communist Party, there was no sign that its aims were acceptable to the majority of the electorate even after the depression. In Germany the Communist Party before 1933 had been able to get more votes, but it was never able to displace the Social Democrats in control of the working-class movement. In less advanced countries than these, communism's revolutionary success was even smaller. In Spain it had to compete with socialists and anarchists; Spanish conservatives certainly feared it and may have been right to fear also the tendency to slide towards social revolution felt under the republic which was established in 1931, but they had better grounds for seeing else-

Hitler's *Mein Kampf*

"To win the masses for a national resurrection, no social sacrifice is too great. Whatever economic concessions are made to our working class today, they stand in no proportion to the gain for the entire nation if they help to give the broad masses back to their nation. Only pig-headed short-sightedness, such as is often unfortunately found in our employer circles, can fail to recognize that in the long run there can be no economic upswing for them and hence no economic profit, unless the inner national solidarity of our people is restored.

"If during the War the German unions had ruthlessly guarded the interests of the working class, if even during the War they had struck a thousand times over and forced approval of the demands of the workers they represented on the dividend-hungry employers of those days; but if in matters of national defence they had avowed their Germanism with the same fanaticism; and if with equal ruthlessness they had given to the fatherland that which is the fatherland's, the War would not have been lost."

An extract from *Mein Kampf* by Adolf Hitler, 1929, translated by Ralph Manheim.

The German dictator Adolf Hitler (1889–1945) delivers a speech at the opening ceremony of a new Volkswagen car factory in Fallersleben, Germany, in 1936.

where than in Spanish communism the real danger facing them.

ADOLF HITLER

THE IDEOLOGICAL interpretation had great appeal, even to many who were not communists. It was much strengthened by the accession to power of a new ruler in Germany, Adolf Hitler, whose success makes it very difficult to deny him political genius despite the pursuit of goals which make it difficult to believe him wholly sane. In the early 1920s he was only a disappointed agitator, who had failed in an attempt to overthrow a government (the Bavarian) and

Crowds at the 1936 Olympic Games in Berlin greet the Führer. The Nazi régime was determined that the games would be a showcase for Hitler's Germany. The competing German athletes were put under enormous pressure to win the maximum number of medals in order to demonstrate to the world the superiority of the Aryan race. This aim was thwarted, much to Hitler's disgust, by the black American athlete Jesse Owens (1913–1980), who won four gold medals and was declared "Athlete of the Games".

who poured out his obsessive nationalism and anti-Semitism not only in hypnotically effective speeches but in a long, shapeless, semi-autobiographical book which few people read. In 1933, the National Socialist German Workers Party which he led ("Nazi" for short) was strong enough for him to be appointed chancellor of the German republic. Politically, this may have been the most momentous single decision of the century, for it meant the revolutionizing of Germany, its redirection upon a course of aggression which ended by destroying the old Europe and Germany too, and that meant a new world.

Though Hitler's messages were simple, his appeal was complex. He preached that Germany's troubles had identifiable sources. The Treaty of Versailles was one. The international capitalists were another. The supposedly anti-national activities of German Marxists and Jews were others. He also said that the righting of Germany's political wrongs must be combined with the renovation of German society and culture, and that this was a matter of purifying the biological stock of the German people, by excising its non-Aryan components.

THE NAZIS IN POWER

In 1922 Hitler's message took him very little way. In 1930 it won him 107 seats in the German parliament – more than the Communists, who had 77. The Nazis were already the beneficiaries of economic collapse, and it was to get worse. There are several reasons why the Nazis reaped its political harvest, but one of the most important was that the Communists spent as much energy fighting the socialists as their other opponents. This had

Berlin's Reichstag (parliament) building went up in flames on 27 February, 1933. Marinus van der Lubbe, a mentally disturbed Dutchman and an ex-Communist, was later accused of starting the fire. The Nazis claimed that the fire was intended to signal the start of a Communist revolution. On 28 February, Chancellor Hitler persuaded President Hindenburg to declare a temporary state of emergency (which was to last until 1945). Historians disagree about the true cause of the Reichstag fire. Some believe that Hitler's bodyguards, the SS, had started it and then deliberately implicated van der Lubbe in the crime; others think that van der Lubbe, who was later found guilty and exe-cuted, acted alone and that the Nazis merely seized the opportunity to take power.

fatally handicapped the Left in Germany all through the 1920s. Another reason was that under the democratic republic anti-Semitic feeling had grown. It, too, was exacerbated by economic collapse. Anti-Semitism, like nationalism, had an appeal which cut across classes as an explanation of Germany's trou-bles, unlike the equally simple Marxist explanation in terms of class war which, naturally, antagonized some as well as (it was hoped) attracting others.

By 1930 the Nazis showed they were a power in the land. They attracted more support, and won backers from those who saw in their street-fighting gangs an anti-Communist insurance, from nationalists who sought re-armament and revision of the Versailles peace settlement and from conservative politicians who thought that Hitler was a party leader like any other who might now be valuable in their own game. The manoeuvres were com-plicated, but in 1932 the Nazis became the biggest party in the German parliament, though without a majority. In January 1933 Hitler was called to office legally and consti-tutionally by the head of the republic. There followed new elections, in which the régime's monopoly of the radio and use of intimida-tion still did not secure the Nazis a majority of seats; none the less, they had one when supported by some right-wing members of parliament who joined them to vote special enabling powers to the government. The most important was that of governing by emer-gency decree. This was the end of parliament and parliamentary sovereignty. Armed with these powers, the Nazis proceeded to carry out a revolutionary destruction of democratic institutions. By 1939, there was virtually no sector of German society not controlled or intimidated by them. The conservatives, too, had lost. They soon found that Nazi inter-ference with the independence of traditional authorities was likely to go very far.

HITLER'S AMBITIONS UNLEASHED

Like Stalin's Russia, the Nazi régime rested in large measure on terror used mercilessly against its enemies. It was also unleashed against the Jews and an astonished Europe

found itself witnessing revivals in one of its most advanced societies of the pogroms of medieval Europe or tsarist Russia. This was indeed so amazing that many people outside Germany found it difficult to believe that it was happening. Confusion over the nature of the régime made it even more difficult to deal with. Some saw Hitler simply as a nationalist leader bent, like an Atatürk, upon the regen-eration of his country and the assertion of its rightful claims. Others saw him as a crusader against Bolshevism. Even when people only thought he might be a useful barrier against it, that increased the likelihood that politi-cians of the Left would see him as a tool of capitalism. But no simple formula will con-tain Hitler or his aims – and there is still great disagreement about what these were – and probably a reasonable approximation to the truth is simply to recognize that he expressed the resentments and exasperations of German society in their most negative and destruc-tive forms and embodied them to a mon-strous degree. When his personality was given scope by economic disaster, political cynicism and a favourable arrangement of interna-tional forces, he could release these negative

Nazi soldiers in 1935 hold banners warning "Don't buy from Jews". The Nuremberg Laws of 1935 deprived the German Jews (defined as anyone who had at least one Jewish grand-parent) of citizenship, barred them from practising a profession, isolated them socially and banned mixed marriages. This was Hitler's first step on the road to his "Final Solution" – the Nazi attempt to exterminate all the Jews in Europe.

qualities at the expense of all Europeans in the long run, his own countrymen included.

THE SPANISH CIVIL WAR

The path by which Germany came to be at war again in 1939 is complicated. There is still much argument about when, if ever, there was a chance of avoiding the final outcome. One important moment, clearly, was when Mussolini, formerly wary of German ambitions in Central Europe, became Hitler's ally. After he had been alienated by British and French policy over his Ethiopian adventure, a civil war broke out in Spain when a group of generals mutinied against the left-wing republic. Hitler and Mussolini both sent contingents to support the man who emerged as the rebel leader, General Franco. This, more

German war planes, at General Franco's behest, carried out a devastating aerial attack on the small Basque town of Guernica in April 1937. Picasso's depiction of the event expresses his emotional reaction to the bombing and his horror at the terrible human cost of military action, small though the slaughter was by comparison with what was soon to follow.

than any other single fact, gave an ideological colour to Europe's divisions. Hitler, Mussolini and Franco were all now identified as "Fascist" and Russian foreign policy began to coordinate support for Spain within Western countries by letting local Communists abandon their attacks on other left-wing parties and encouraging "Popular Fronts". Thus Spain came to be seen as a conflict between Right and Left in its purest form; this was a distortion, but it helped to accustom people to think of Europe as divided into two camps.

RENEWED GERMAN AGGRESSION

BRITISH AND FRENCH GOVERNMENTS were by this time well aware of the difficulties of dealing with Germany. Hitler had already in

Hitler and Mussolini meet in 1940. Their decision to join forces had major implications for international relations.

1935 announced that her rearmament (forbidden at Versailles) had begun. Until their own rearmament was completed, they remained very weak. The first consequence of this was shown to the world when German troops re-entered the "demilitarized" zone of the Rhineland from which they had been excluded by the Treaty of Versailles. No attempt was made to resist this move. After the civil war in Spain had thrown opinion in Great Britain and France into further

disarray, Hitler then seized Austria. The terms of Versailles which forbade the fusion of Germany and Austria seemed hard to uphold; to the French and British electorates this could be presented as a matter of legitimately aggrieved nationalism. The Austrian republic had also long had internal troubles. The Anschluss (as union with Germany was called) took place in 1938. In the autumn came the next German aggression, the seizure of part of Czechoslovakia. Again, this was justified by the specious claims of self-determination; the areas involved were so important that their loss crippled the prospect of future Czechoslovak self-defence, but they were areas with many German inhabitants. Memel would follow, on the same grounds, the next year. Hitler was gradually fulfilling the old dream which had been lost when Prussia beat Austria – the dream of a united Great Germany, defined as all lands of those of German blood.

In the Sudetenland, a largely German-speaking area of Czechoslovakia, pro-Nazi feelings were running high by 1938, particularly after the Anschluss with Austria. Here, Sudetenland women salute the German troops as they arrive to take power in the region on 12 October, 1938.

The dismemberment of Czechoslovakia was something of a turning-point. It was achieved by a series of agreements at Munich in September 1938 in which Great Britain and Germany took the main parts. This was the last great initiative of British foreign policy to try to satisfy Hitler. The British prime minister was still too unsure of rearmament to resist, but hoped also that the transference of the last substantial group of Germans from alien rule to that of their homeland might deprive Hitler of the motive for further revision of Versailles – a settlement which was now somewhat tattered in any case.

WAR OVER POLAND

But the dismemberment of Czechoslovakia did not satisfy Hitler, who went on to inaugurate a programme of expansion into Slav lands. The first step was the absorption of what was left of Czechoslovakia, in March 1939. This brought forward the question of the Polish settlement of 1919. Hitler resented the "Polish Corridor" which separated East Prussia from Germany and contained Danzig, an old German city given an internationalized status in 1919. At this point the British government, though hesitatingly, changed tack and offered a guarantee to Poland and other East European countries against aggression. It also began a wary negotiation with Russia.

Russian policy remains hard to interpret. It seems that Stalin kept the Spanish Civil War going with support to the republic as long as it seemed likely to tie up German attention, but then looked for other ways of buying time against the attack from the West which he always feared. To him, it seemed likely that a German attack on Russia might be encouraged by Great Britain and France who would

---

The German–Soviet Pact of Non-Aggression

By spring 1939, Stalin had probably come to the conclusion that he could not trust France and Great Britain actually to confront Germany and that, when they sought cooperation from the Soviet Union, they were merely hoping to implicate Russia in a war against Germany in which they themselves would not take part. Soviet diplomats therefore began to negotiate separately with both sides, hoping to force them to continue supporting their initial positions: the

Western powers should continue to believe that they could rely on Soviet aid, while Germany was to believe it could count on Russia to remain neutral.

In August 1939, while the French and British delegations were in Moscow, Hitler showed great interest in reaching an immediate agreement with the USSR. This sudden eagerness on the part of the Germans convinced Stalin that attack was imminent. He knew that his own country was not in immediate danger – it had no shared frontier with Germany and it was too late in the year to attack Russia herself. In fact, Germany was planning to attack Poland. Stalin met with Hitler's foreign minister Joachim von Ribbentrop on 23 August and signed the German–Soviet pact. A secret protocol established that Finland, Estonia, Lithuania, a large part of Poland and Bessarabia would become areas of Russian influence. This was the price Germany paid to keep Russia neutral, leaving Hitler free to attack Poland.

Molotov, the Soviet commissar for foreign affairs, signs the German–Soviet Pact of Non-Aggression. Ribbentrop is standing in the centre with Stalin by his side.

German troops in Paris parade along the Champs Elysées towards the Arc de Triomphe in August 1940, two months after Hitler's conquest of France.

see with relief the trouble they had so long faced turning on the workers' state. No doubt they would have done. There was little possibility of working with the British or French to oppose Hitler, however, even if they were willing to do so, because no Russian army could reach Germany except through Poland – and this the Poles would never permit. Accordingly, as a Russian diplomat remarked to a French colleague on hearing of the Munich decisions, there was now nothing for it but a fourth partition of Poland. This was arranged in the summer of 1939. After all the propaganda each had directed against Bolshevik-Slav barbarism and fascist-capitalist exploitation, Germany and Russia made an agreement in August which provided for the division of Poland between them; authoritarian states enjoy great flexibility in the conduct of diplomacy. Armed with this, Hitler went on to attack Poland. He thus began the Second World War on 1 September, 1939. Two days later the British and French honoured their guarantee to Poland and declared war on Germany.

BRITISH AND FRENCH RELUCTANCE

The British and French governments were not very keen on declaring war, for it was obvious that they could not help Poland. That unhappy nation disappeared once more, divided by Russian and German forces about a month after the outbreak of war. But not to have intervened would have meant acquiescing to the German domination of Europe, for no other nation would have thought British or French support worth having. So, uneasily and without the excitement of 1914, the only two constitutional great powers of Europe found themselves facing a totalitarian régime. Neither their peoples nor their governments had much enthusiasm for this role, and the decline of liberal and democratic forces since 1918 put them in a position much inferior to that of 1914, but exasperation with Hitler's long series of aggressions and broken promises made it hard to see what sort of peace could be made which would reassure them. The basic cause of the war

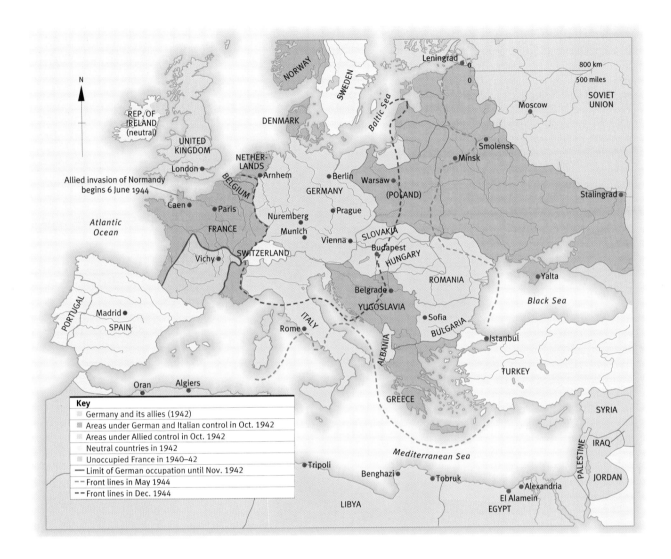

Allied invasion of Normandy
begins 6 June 1944

*Atlantic
Ocean*

Key
▪ Germany and its allies (1942)
▪ Areas under German and Italian control in Oct. 1942
▪ Areas under Allied control in Oct. 1942
▪ Neutral countries in 1942
▪ Unoccupied France in 1940–42
— Limit of German occupation until Nov. 1942
- - Front lines in May 1944
- - Front lines in Dec. 1944

was, as in 1914, German nationalism. But whereas then Germany had gone to war because *she* felt threatened, now Great Britain and France were responding to the danger presented by her expansion. *They* felt threatened this time.

BRITAIN IS ISOLATED

To the surprise of many observers, and the relief of some, the first six months of the war were almost uneventful once the short Polish campaign was over. It was quickly plain that mechanized forces and air power were to play

a much more important part than between 1914 and 1918. The memory of the slaughter of the Somme and Verdun was too vivid for the British and French to plan anything but an economic offensive; the weapon of blockade, they hoped, would be effective. Hitler was unwilling to disturb them, because he was anxious to make peace. This deadlock was only broken when the British sought to intensify the blockade in Scandinavian waters. This coincided, remarkably, with a German offensive to secure ore supplies which conquered Norway and Denmark. Its launching on 9 April, 1940 opened an astonishing period of fighting. Only a month later

The German army arrives in the Danish town of Horsens in May 1940.

there began a brilliant German invasion first of the Low Countries and then of France. A powerful armoured attack through the Ardennes opened the way to the division of the Allied armies and the capture of Paris. On 22 June France signed an armistice with the Germans. By the end of the month, the whole European coast from the Pyrenees to the North Cape was in German hands. Italy had joined in on the German side ten days before the French surrender. A new French government at Vichy broke off relations with Great Britain after the British had seized or destroyed French warships they felt might fall into German hands. The Third Republic effectively came to an end with the installation of a French marshal, a hero of the First World War, as head of state. With no ally left on the continent, Great Britain faced a worse strategical situation by far than that in which she had struggled against Napoleon.

ANTI-GERMAN FORCES UNITE

The French armistice was followed by a capitulation which marked a huge change in the nature of the war. Great Britain was not quite alone. There were the dominions, all of which had entered the war on her side, and a number of governments in exile from the overrun continent. Some of these commanded forces of their own and Norwegians, Danes, Dutchmen, Belgians, Czechs and Poles were to fight gallantly, often with decisive effect, in the years ahead. The most important exiled contingents were those of the French, but at this stage they represented a faction within France, not its legal government. A general who had left France before the armistice and was condemned to death *in absentia* was their leader: Charles de Gaulle. He was recognized by the British as "leader of the Free French". He saw himself as constitutional legatee of the Third Republic and the custodian of France's interests and honour. He soon began to show an independence which was in the end to make him the greatest servant of France since Clemenceau.

De Gaulle's position was important because of uncertainties about what might happen to parts of the French Empire where he hoped to find sympathizers who wished to join him to continue the fight. This was one way in which the war was now extended geographically. Another resulted from Italy's entry into the war, since her African possessions and the Mediterranean sea-lanes then became operational areas. Finally, the availability of Atlantic and Scandinavian ports meant that what was later called the "Battle of the Atlantic", the German struggle to sever British sea communications by submarine, surface, and air attack, was now bound to become much fiercer.

WINSTON CHURCHILL

Mounting German aggression in the Atlantic meant that the British Isles immediately faced direct attack. The hour had already found the

The Free French Forces, founded by General Charles de Gaulle (1890–1970), originally consisted of 7,000 exiled French volunteers funded by Great Britain. By 1942, under the new name of the Fighting French, and boosted by soldiers from French colonies, the organization had 400,000 troops. Here General de Gaulle is shown on his triumphant return to France after the liberation in June 1944.

man to brace the nation against such a challenge. Winston Churchill, after a long and chequered political career, had become prime minister when the Norwegian campaign collapsed, because no other man commanded support in all parties in the House of Commons. To the coalition government which he immediately formed he gave vigorous leadership, something hitherto felt to be lacking. More important than this, he called forth in his people, whom he addressed frequently by radio, qualities they had forgotten they possessed. It was soon clear that only defeat after direct assault was going to get the British out of the war.

This was even more certain after a great air battle over southern England in August and September had been won by British science and the Royal Air Force. For a moment, the British knew the pride and relief of the Greeks after Marathon. It was true, as Churchill said in a much-quoted speech, that "never in the field of human conflict was so much owed by so many to so few". This victory made a German seaborne invasion impossible (though a successful one was always unlikely). It also established that Great Britain could not be defeated by air bombardment alone. The islands had a bleak outlook ahead, but this victory changed the direction of the war, for it was the beginning of a period in which a variety of influences

The British prime minister Winston Churchill (1874–1965) demonstrates his "V for Victory" sign during a visit to the United States in 1946. Throughout the Second World War, Churchill personified the British determination to fight Hitler to the end.

THE GERMAN INVASION OF RUSSIA

BY THE END OF 1940, Russia had made further gains in the west, apparently with an eye to securing a glacis against a future German attack. A war against Finland gave her important strategic areas. The Baltic republics of Latvia, Lithuania and Estonia were swallowed in 1940. Bessarabia, which Romania had taken from Russia in 1918, was now taken back, together with the northern Bukovina. In the last case, Stalin was going beyond tsarist boundaries. The German decision to attack Russia arose in part because of turned German attention in another direction. In December 1940 planning began for a German invasion of Russia.

disagreements about the future direction of Russian expansion: Germany sought to keep Russia away from the Balkans and the Straits. It was also aimed at demonstrating, by a quick overthrow of Russia, that further British war-making was pointless. But there was also a deep personal element in the decision. Hitler had always sincerely and fanatically detested Bolshevism and maintained that the Slavs, a racially inferior group, should provide Germans with living-space and raw materials in the east. This was a last, perverted vision of the old struggle of the Teuton to impose Western civilization on the Slav East. Many Germans responded to such a theme. It was to justify more appalling atrocities than any earlier crusading myth.

BARBAROSSA

In a brief spring campaign, which provided an overture to the holocaust ahead, the Germans overran Yugoslavia and Greece, with which Italian forces had been unhappily engaged since October 1940. Once again British arms were driven from the mainland of Europe. Crete, too, was taken by a spectacular German airborne assault. Now all was ready for "Barbarossa", as the great onslaught on Russia was named, after a crusading German emperor of the Middle Ages.

The attack was launched on 22 June, 1941 and had huge early successes. Vast numbers of prisoners were taken and the Russian armies fell back hundreds of miles. The German advance guard came within a narrow margin of entering Moscow. But that margin was not quite eliminated and by Christmas the first successful Russian counter-attacks had announced that in fact Germany was pinned down. German strategy had lost the initiative. If the British and Russians could hold on and if they could keep in alliance

Winston Churchill and Franklin D. Roosevelt on board the British battleship *Prince of Wales* on 14 August, 1941, where the conference that produced the Atlantic Charter was held. The two leaders met nine times during the war and the mutual admiration and close friendship that developed between them were to have a major impact on the course of events, in spite of their profound differences over some important questions.

with one another then, failing a radical technical modification of the war by the discovery of new weapons of great power, their access to American production would inexorably increase their strength. This did not, of course, mean that they would inevitably defeat Germany, only that they might bring her to negotiate terms.

JAPAN AND THE UNITED STATES ENTER THE WAR

THE AMERICAN PRESIDENT had believed since 1940 that in the interests of the United States Great Britain had to be supported up to the limits permitted by his own public and the law of neutrality. In fact, he went well beyond both at times. By the summer of 1941, Hitler knew that to all intents and purposes the United States was an undeclared enemy. A crucial step had been the American Lend-Lease Act of March that year which provided production and services to the Allies without immediate payment. Soon afterwards, the American government extended naval patrols and the protection of its shipping further eastward into the Atlantic. After the invasion of Russia came a meeting between Churchill and Roosevelt which resulted in a statement of shared principles – the Atlantic Charter – in which a nation at war and another formally at peace spoke of the needs of a post-war world "after the final destruction of the Nazi tyranny". This was a long way from isolationism and was the background to Hitler's second fateful but foolish decision of 1941, a declaration of

The American battleships *West Virginia* and *Tennessee* are pictured in flames in Pearl Harbor. President Roosevelt later referred to the surprise Japanese attack on the US naval base in Hawaii as "a day which will live in infamy". During the same month, the Japanese took Hong Kong, Guam, Luzon and Borneo, threatening the other American garrisons in the Philippines, the British in the Moluccas, and even Australia.

war on the United States on 11 December, after a Japanese attack on British and American territories four days earlier. Hitler had earlier promised the Japanese to do this. The war thus became global. The British and American declarations of war on Japan might have left two separate wars to rage, with only Great Britain engaged in both; Hitler's action threw away the chance that American power might have been kept out of Europe and deployed only in the Pacific. Few single acts have so marked the end of an epoch, for this announced the eclipse of European affairs. Europe's future would now be settled not by her own efforts but by the two great powers on her flanks, the United States and Soviet Russia.

The Japanese decision was also a rash

one, though the logic of Japanese policy had long pointed towards conflict with the United States. Japan's ties with Germany and Italy, though they had some propaganda value for both sides, did not amount to much in practice. What mattered in the timing of Japanese policy was the resolution of debates in Tokyo about the danger, or lack of it, of a challenge to the United States which must involve war. The crux of the matter was that Japan's needs for a successful conclusion of the war in China included oil which she could only obtain with the tacit consent of the United States that Japan was to destroy China. This no American government could have given. Instead, in October 1941 the American government imposed an embargo on all trade by United States citizens with Japan.

PEARL HARBOR

After the imposition of the trade embargo, there followed the last stages of a process which had its origins in the ascendancy established in Japan by reactionary and militant forces in the 1930s. The question had by this time become for the Japanese military planners purely strategic and technical; since they would have to take the resources in Southeast Asia which they needed by force, all that had to be settled was the nature of the war against the United States and its timing. Such a decision was fundamentally irrational, for the chances of ultimate success were very small; once arguments of national honour had won, though, the final calculations about the best point and moment of attack were carefully made. The choice was made to strike as hard a blow as possible against American sea-power at the outset in order to gain the maximum freedom of movement in the Pacific and South China Sea. The result was the onslaught of 7 December, whose centre-piece was an air attack on the American fleet at Pearl Harbor which was one of the most brilliantly conceived and executed operations in the history of warfare. By mischance it fell just short of complete success, for it did not destroy American naval air power, though it gave the Japanese for months the strategical freedom they sought. This failure was fatal; after it the Japanese faced a prolonged war they were bound to lose in the end. Pearl Harbor united Americans as little else could have done. Isolationism could be virtually ignored after 8 December; Roosevelt had a nation behind him as Wilson never had.

GLOBAL CONFLICT

When a few Japanese bombs were reported to have fallen on the American mainland, it was obvious that this was much more truly a world war than the first had been. The German operations in the Balkans had by the time of Pearl Harbor left Europe with only four neutral countries – Spain, Portugal, Sweden and Switzerland. The war in North Africa raged back and forth between Libya and Egypt. It was extended to Syria by the

American marines, killed during the Battle of Midway in 1943, are buried at sea. They died when a Japanese kamikaze, or suicide plane, crashed onto the US aircraft-carrier *Lexington*.

Japanese tanks are paraded through the streets of Tokyo in April 1940 as a demonstration to the world of the nation's military might.

arrival there of a German mission and to Iraq when a nationalist government supported by German aircraft was removed by a British force. Iran had been occupied by the British and Russians in 1941. In Africa, Ethiopia was liberated and the Italian colonial empire destroyed.

With the opening of the Far Eastern war the Japanese wrought destruction on the colonial empires there, too. Within a few months they took Indonesia, Indo-China, Malaya, the Philippines. They pressed through Burma towards the Indian border and were soon bombing the north Australian port of Darwin from New Guinea. Meanwhile, the naval war was fought by German submarine forces, aircraft and surface raiders all over the Atlantic, Arctic, Mediterranean and Indian oceans. Only a tiny minority of countries were left outside this struggle. Its demands were colossal and carried much further the mobilization of whole societies than

had the First World War. The role of the United States was decisive. Her huge manufacturing power made the material preponderance of the "United Nations" (as the coalition of states fighting the Germans, the Italians and the Japanese was called from the beginning of 1942) incontestable.

A TURNING-POINT FOR THE UNITED NATIONS

In spite of the United Nations' advantages, the way ahead was still a hard one. The first part of 1942 was still very bleak for them. Then came the turning-point, in four great and very different battles. In June a Japanese fleet attacking Midway Island was broken in a battle fought largely by aircraft. Japanese losses in carriers and aircrews were such that Japan never regained the strategical initiative and the long American counter-attack in the

The Allied invasion of Normandy

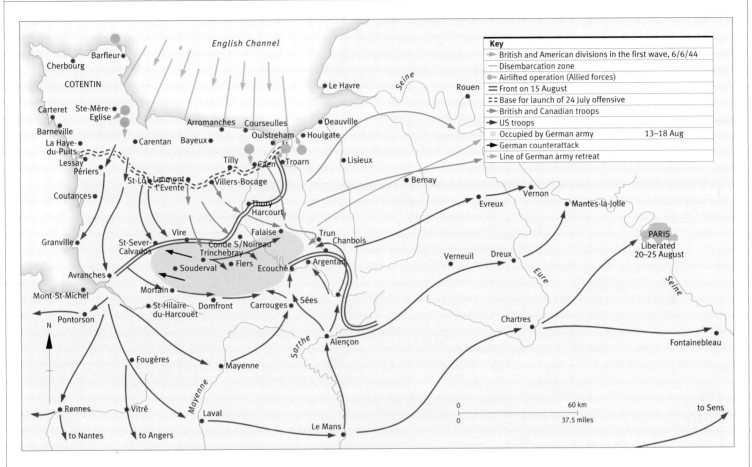

D-Day, which took place on 6 June, 1944, was the largest military operation in history. Some 3 million Allied soldiers had been assembled in Britain, together with large numbers of aircraft, battleships, tanks, armaments and troop carriers. Allied aircraft carried out extensive air raids over northern France, devastating communications networks. Attacks from the sea breached the Atlantic wall. By evening, the German defences had been fatally weakened and the Allies' Normandy Campaign was well under way.

Pacific now began to unroll. Then, at the beginning of November, the British army in Egypt decisively defeated the Germans and Italians and began a march west which was to end with the eviction of the enemy from all North Africa. The battle of El Alamein had coincided with landings by Anglo-American forces in French North Africa. They subsequently moved eastwards and by May 1943 German and Italian resistance on the continent had ceased. Six months earlier, at the end of 1942, the Russians had bottled up at Stalingrad on the Volga a German army rashly exposed by Hitler. The remnants surrendered in February in the most demoralizing defeat yet suffered by the Germans in Russia, and yet one which was only part of three splendid months of winter advance which marked the turning-point of the war on the Eastern Front.

THE END OF THE WAR IN EUROPE

The other great Allied victory has no specific date, but was as important as any of these.

The use of the atomic bomb

Although German scientists had discovered the potential to build atom bombs in 1938 it was then widely believed that such weapons would take a long time to develop and would be too heavy to be carried by aircraft. After the outbreak of the Second World War, however, two physicists exiled from Germany in Great Britain prepared a report in which they stated that it may be possible to manufacture portable atom bombs in a relatively short time. Research began in Britain. After its entry into the war in December 1941 the United States concentrated all its scientific might on the construction of atomic bombs under the "Manhattan Project". The first nuclear test was carried out on 16 July, 1945 in New Mexico, when a plutonium bomb was exploded.

On 6 August, a B-29 bomber dropped a uranium atom bomb on the Japanese city of Hiroshima. The explosion completely flattened the city, killing around 80,000 people instantly and injuring 70,000. Thousands who survived the initial blast died in the following days of burns, injuries and radiation sickness. Thousands more died in later years from cancer and other radiation-related illnesses.

Three days later, another bomb, made of plutonium, was dropped on Nagasaki, where 40,000 people were killed and 25,000 injured. In the face of this devastating atomic power, Japan surrendered.

Pictured are the ground crew and pilot (centre) of the American bomber that dropped the atom bomb on Hiroshima.

This was the Battle of the Atlantic. Its peak came in the early months of 1942. In March nearly 850,000 tons of shipping were lost and six U-boats were sunk; six months later, the figures were 560,000 tons and eleven U-boats. The tide had turned, though there was still hard fighting ahead. At the end of the year nearly eight million tons of shipping had been lost for eighty-seven U-boats sunk. In 1943 the figures were three and a quarter million tons and 237 U-boats. This was the most crucial battle of all for the United Nations, for on it depended their ability to draw on American production.

Command of the sea also made possible re-entry to Europe. Roosevelt had agreed to give priority to the defeat of Germany, but the mounting of an invasion of France to take the strain off the Russian armies could not in the end be managed before 1944, and this angered Stalin. When it came, the Anglo-American invasion of northern France in June 1944 was the greatest seaborne expedition in history. Mussolini had by then been overthrown by Italians and Italy had already been invaded from the south; now Germany was fighting on three fronts. Soon after the landings in Normandy, the Russians entered Poland. Going faster than their allies, it still took them until next April to reach Berlin. In the west, Allied forces had broken out of Italy into central Europe and from the Low Countries into northern Germany. Almost incidentally, terrible destruction had been inflicted on German cities by a great air offensive which, until the last few months of the war, exercised no decisive strategic effect. When, on 30 April, the man who had ignited this conflagration killed himself in a bunker in the ruins of Berlin, historic Europe was literally as well as figuratively in ruins.

JAPAN SURRENDERS

The war in the Far East took a little longer. At the beginning of August 1945 the Japanese government knew it must be defeated. Many of Japan's former conquests had been retrieved, her cities were devastated by American bombing and her sea-power, on which communications and safety from invasion rested, was in ruins. At this moment two nuclear weapons of a destructive power hitherto unapproached were dropped with terrible effect on two Japanese cities by the Americans. Between the explosions, the Russians declared war on Japan. On 2 September the Japanese government abandoned its plan of a suicidal last-ditch stand and signed an instrument of surrender. The Second World War had come to an end.

THE HORRORS OF NAZISM REVEALED

In the immediate aftermath of the war it was difficult to measure the colossal extent of what happened. Only one clear and unambiguous good was at once visible, the overthrow of the Nazi régime. As the Allied armies advanced into Europe, the deepest evils of a system of terror and torture were revealed by the opening of the huge prison camps and the revelations of what went on in them. It was suddenly apparent that Churchill had spoken no more than the bare truth when he told his countrymen that "if we fail, then the whole world, including the United States, including all that we have known and cared for, will sink into the abyss of a new Dark Age made more sinister, and perhaps more protracted, by the lights of perverted science". The reality of this threat could be seen in Belsen and Buchenwald. Distinctions could hardly be meaningful between degrees of atrocity inflicted on political prisoners, slave labourers from other countries, or some prisoners of war. But the world's imagination was most struck by the systematic attempt which had been made to wipe out European Jewry, the so-called "Final Solution" sought by

Germans, an attempt which was carried far enough to change the demographic map: the Polish Jews were almost obliterated, and Dutch Jews, too, suffered terribly in proportion to their numbers. Overall, though complete figures may never be available, it is probable that between five and six million Jews were killed, whether in the gas chambers and crematoria of the extermination camps, by shootings and extermination on the spot in east and southeast Europe, or by overwork and hunger.

THE MEANING OF VICTORY

FEW PEOPLE AND NO NATIONS had engaged in the war because they saw it as a struggle against such wickedness, though no doubt many of them were heartened as it proceeded by the sense that the conflict had a moral dimension. Propaganda contributed to this. Even while Great Britain was the only nation in Europe still on her feet and fighting for her survival, a democratic society had sought to see in the struggle positive ends which went

The American soldiers who liberated the Nazis' Buchenwald concentration camp in 1945 were horrified to discover piles of unburied corpses and crude huts packed with starving prisoners. Millions of Jews and other "undesirables" had been forced into slave labour, used as the subjects of macabre medical experiments or simply sent to the gas chambers in death camps such as this.

On 13–15 February, 1943, 800 Allied planes dropped more than 3,500 tons of bombs on the German city of Dresden, seen here after the attacks. In those raids, and in others that followed over the next two months, thousands of civilians were killed and the city's unique Baroque architecture was completely destroyed. Militarily, the Allied attack achieved little.

beyond survival and beyond the destruction of Nazism. Hopes of a new world of cooperation between great powers and social and economic reconstruction were embodied in the Atlantic Charter and United Nations. They were encouraged by sentimental goodwill towards allies and a tragic blurring of differences of interest and social ideals which were only too quickly to re-emerge. Much wartime rhetoric boomeranged badly with the coming of peace; disillusionment followed inspection of the world after the guns were silent. Yet for all this, the war of 1939–45 in Europe remains a moral struggle in a way, perhaps, in which no other has ever been. It is important to emphasize this. Too much has been heard of the regrettable consequences of Allied victory, and it is too easily forgotten that it crushed the worst challenge to liberal civilization which has ever arisen.

A SHATTERED EUROPE

Some far-sighted observers could see a deep irony in the anti-liberal nature of the Nazi régime. In many ways, Germany had been one of the most progressive countries in Europe; the embodiment of much that was best in its civilization. That Germany should fall prey to collective derangement on this scale suggested that something had been wrong at the root of that civilization itself. The crimes of Nazism had been carried out not in a fit of barbaric intoxication with conquest, but in a systematic, scientific, controlled, bureaucratic (though often inefficient) way about which there was little that was irrational except the appalling end which it sought. In this respect the Asian war was importantly different. Japanese imperialism replaced the old Western imperialisms for a time, but often the subject peoples did not much regret the change. Propaganda during the war attempted to give currency to the notion of a "fascist" Japan, but this was a distortion of so traditional a society's character. No such appalling consequences as faced European nations under German rule would have followed from a Japanese victory.

The second obvious result of the war was its unparalleled destructiveness. It was most visible in the devastated cities of Germany and Japan, where mass aerial bombing, one of the major innovations of the Second World War, proved much more costly to life and buildings than had been the bombing of Spanish cities in the Spanish Civil War. Yet even those early essays had been enough to convince many observers that bombing alone could bring a country to its knees. In fact, although often invaluable in combination with other forms of fighting, the huge strategic bombing offensive against Germany built up by the British Royal Air Force from tiny beginnings in 1940 and steadily supplemented by the United States Air Force from 1942 onwards up to the point at which their combined forces could provide a target with continuous day and night bombing, achieved very little until the last few months of the war. Nor was the fiery destruction of the Japanese cities strategically so important as the elimination of her sea-power.

EAST AND WEST

Not only cities had been shattered. The economic life and communications of Central Europe had also been grievously stricken. In 1945, millions of refugees were wandering about in it, trying to get home. There was a grave danger of famine and epidemic because of the difficulty of supplying food. The tremendous problems of 1918 were upon Europe again, and this time confronted nations demoralized by defeat and occupation; only the neutrals and Great Britain had escaped those scourges. There were abundant arms in private hands, and a revolutionary

threat could be feared. These conditions could also be found in Asia, but there the physical destruction was less severe and prospects of recovery better.

In Europe, too, the revolutionary political impact of the war was obvious. The power structure which had been a reality until 1914 and had an illusory prolongation of life between the two world wars, was doomed in 1941. Two great peripheral powers dominated Europe politically and were established militarily in its heart. This was evident at a meeting of the Allied leaders at Yalta in February 1945 which provided a basis for agreement, and the nearest thing to a formal peace settlement in Europe for decades. Its outcome was that old Central Europe would disappear. Europe would be divided into eastern and western halves. Once again a

The "Big Three", Churchill (left), an ailing Roosevelt (centre) and Stalin (right), pose for the camera during the Yalta Conference on 9 February, 1945.

Trieste–Baltic line became a reality, but now new differences were to be layered on top of old. At the end of 1945 there lay to the east a Europe of states which, with the exception of Greece, all had Communist governments or governments in which Communists shared power with others. The Russian army which had overrun them had proved itself a far better instrument for the extension of international Communism than revolution had ever been. The pre-war Baltic republics did not emerge from the Soviet state, of course, and the Soviet Union now also absorbed parts of pre-war Poland and Romania.

THE NEW BALANCE OF THE WORLD ECONOMY

Germany, the centre of the old European power structure, had effectively ceased to exist. A phase of European history which she had dominated was at an end, and Bismarck's creation was partitioned into zones occupied by the Russians, Americans, British and French. The other major political units of Western Europe had reconstituted themselves after occupation and defeat, but were feeble; Italy, which had changed sides after Mussolini had been overthrown, had, like France, a much strengthened and enlarged Communist Party which, it could not be forgotten, was still committed to the revolutionary overthrow of capitalism. Only Great Britain retained her stature of 1939 in the world's eyes; it was even briefly enhanced by her stand in 1940 and 1941. She remained for a while the recognized equal of Russia and the United States. (Formally, this was true of France and China, too, but less attention was paid to them.) Yet Great Britain's moment was past. By a huge effort of mobilizing her resources and social life to a degree unequalled outside Stalin's Russia, she had been able to retain her standing. But she had been let out of a strategic impasse only by the German attack on Russia, and kept afloat only by American Lend-Lease. And this aid had not been without its costs: the Americans had insisted on the sale of British overseas assets to meet the bills before it was forthcoming. Moreover, the sterling area was dislocated. American capital was now to move into the old dominions on a large scale. Those countries had learnt new lessons both from their new wartime strength and, paradoxically, from their weakness in so far as they had relied upon the mother country for their defence. From 1945, they more and more acted with full as well as formal independence.

THE END OF AN ERA

It only took a few years for this huge change in the position of the greatest of the old imperial powers to become clear. Symbolically, when Great Britain made her last great

The British army's "Desert Rats", who had fought in North Africa during the war, parade through Berlin in July 1945 after the Allied victory.

military effort in Europe, in 1944, the expedition was commanded by an American general. Though British forces in Europe for a few months afterwards matched the Americans, they were by the end of the war outnumbered. In the Far East, too, though the British reconquered Burma, the defeat of Japan was the work of American naval and air power. For all Churchill's efforts, Roosevelt was by the end of the war negotiating over his head with Stalin, proposing *inter alia* the dismantling of the British Empire. Great Britain, in spite of her victorious stand alone in 1940 and the moral prestige it gave her, had not escaped the shattering impact of the war on Europe's political structure. Indeed, she was in some ways the power which, with Germany, illustrated it best.

Thus was registered in Europe the passing of the European supremacy also evident at its periphery. British forces secured Dutch and French territories in Asia in time to hand them back to their former overlords and prevent the seizure of power by anti-colonial régimes. But fighting with rebels began almost immediately and it was clear that the imperial powers faced a difficult future. The war had brought revolution to the empires, too. Subtly and suddenly, the kaleidoscope of authority had shifted, and it was still shifting as the war came to an end. The year 1945 is not, therefore, a good place at which to pause; reality was then still masked somewhat by appearance and many Europeans still had to discover, painfully, that the European age of empire was over.

4 THE SHAPING OF A NEW WORLD

This aerial view of the United Nations headquarters in New York City was taken in 1950, when the organization symbolized post-war hopes for lasting peace.

AFTER THE FIRST WORLD WAR, it had still been possible to embrace the illusion that an old order might be restored. In 1945, no one in authority could believe

such a thing. This was one great and healthy contrast between the circumstances of the two great attempts of this century to re-order international life. The victory could not, of course, start with a clean sheet on which to plan. Events had closed off many roads, and even during the war crucial decisions had already been taken, some by agreement, some not, about what should follow victory. One of the most important had been that an international organization should be set up to maintain international peace. The fact that the great powers saw such an organization in different ways, the Americans as a beginning to the regulation of international life by law and the Russians as a means of maintaining the Grand Alliance, did not prevent them pressing forward. So the United Nations Organization (UNO) came into being at San Francisco in 1945.

THE UNITED NATIONS

MUCH THOUGHT, naturally, had been given to the League of Nations' failure to come up to expectations. One of its great defects was remedied in 1945: the United States and Russia belonged to the new organization from the start. Apart from this, the

Time chart (1945–1948)

	1945 The Yalta and Potsdam conferences Surrender of Germany and Japan Proclamation of independence in Vietnam		1948 Gandhi is assassinated Birth of the state of Israel First Arab-Israeli war
1900			1950
	1946 Definitive phase of the civil war in China begins	1947 Independence of India and Pakistan The Marshall Plan is drawn up	

The United Nations

At the meetings of the world powers held at Dumbarton Oaks mansion in Washington, DC in 1944 and in Yalta in 1945, it was agreed that an international organization should be set up in order to help maintain world balance and peace. The 51 states that signed the San Francisco Charter in 1945 made up the first General Assembly of the United Nations Organization. Its inaugural session was held in two parts: in London in February 1946 and in New York in November and December of the same year.

The UN is made up of the General Assembly, the Security Council, the Economic and Social Council, the Secretariat General, the International Tribunal of Justice and other subsidiary organizations, comprising a busy network of commissions, conferences, committees and other specialized groups. The General Assembly is made up of representatives of all the member countries and is the UN's highest deliberative organ. It is a kind of world parliament – a forum for debate and recommendation – which also encourages research into methods of improving international cooperation on a political level. The Security Council has five permanent members with the right to veto out of a total of fifteen. Its jurisdiction is limited to peacekeeping and matters of international security. The Economic and Social Council is a consultative body that depends on the General Assembly, whose mission is to prepare reports and research on economic, social, cultural, educational and other matters. The General Assembly also has the capacity to convoke international conferences on matters under its jurisdiction.

A representative of the Netherlands addresses one of the committees at the San Francisco Conference of 1945.

The International Tribunal is based in The Hague; the magistrates who sit on it are elected independently of their nationality. Its main tasks are to provide voluntary arbitration between countries in conflict and to consult on issues of international law.

---

basic structure of the United Nations resembled that of the League in outline. Its two essential organs were a small Council and a large Assembly. Permanent representatives of all member states were to sit in the General Assembly. The Security Council had at first eleven members, of whom five were permanent; these were the representatives of the United States, Russia, Great Britain, France (at the insistence of Winston Churchill) and China. The Security Council was given greater power than the old League Council and this was largely the doing of the Russians. They saw that there was a strong likelihood that they would always be outvoted in the General Assembly – where, at first, fifty-one nations were represented – because the United States could rely not only on the votes of its allies, but also on those of its Latin American satellites. Naturally, not all the smaller powers liked this. They were uneasy about a body on which at any one moment any of them was likely not to sit, which would have the last word and in which the great powers would carry the main weight. Nevertheless, the structure the great powers wanted was adopted, as, indeed, it had to be if any organization was to work at all.

A NEW ERA IN INTERNATIONAL POLITICS

The other main issue which caused grave constitutional dispute when the UN was founded was the veto power given to the permanent members of the Security Council. This was a necessary feature if the great powers were to accept the organization, though in the end the veto was restricted somewhat, in that a permanent member could not prevent investigation and discussion of matters which especially affected it unless they were likely to lead to action inimical to its interests.

In theory the Security Council possessed very great powers, but, of course, their operation was bound to reflect political reality. In its first decades, the importance of the United Nations proved to lie not in its power to act, but rather in the forum it provided for discussion. For the first time, a world public linked as never before by radio and film – and later,

A 1990 session of the United Nations Security Council is pictured.

by television – would have to be presented with a case made at the General Assembly for what sovereign states did. This was something quite new. The United Nations at once gave a new dimension to international politics; it took much longer to provide effective new instrumentation for dealing with its problems. Sometimes, the new publicity of international argument led to feelings of sterility, as increasingly bitter and unyielding views were set out in debates which changed no one's mind. But an educational force was at work. It was important, too, that it was soon decided that the permanent seat of the General Assembly should be in New York; this drew American attention to it and helped to offset the historic pull of isolationism.

The United Nations General Assembly met for the first time, none the less, in London in 1946. Bitter debates began at once; complaints were made about the continued presence of Russian soldiers in Iranian Azerbaijan, occupied during the war, and the Russians promptly replied by attacking Great Britain for keeping her forces in Greece. Within a few days the first veto was cast, by the Soviet delegation. There were to be many more. The instrument which the Americans and British had regarded and continued to use as an extraordinary measure for the protection of special interests became a familiar piece of Soviet diplomatic technique. Already in 1946 the United Nations was an arena in which the USSR contended with a still inchoate Western bloc which its policies were to do much to solidify.

RUSSIAN AND AMERICAN POWER

THOUGH THE ORIGINS OF CONFLICT between the United States and Russia are often traced back a very long way, in the later years of the war the British government had tended to feel that the Americans made too many concessions and were over-friendly to the Soviet Union. Of course, there was always a fundamental ideological division; if the Russians had not always had a deep preconception about the roots of behaviour of capitalist societies, they would certainly have behaved differently after 1945 towards their wartime ally. It is also true that some Americans never ceased to distrust Russia and saw her as a revolutionary threat. But this did not mean that they had much impact on the making of American policy. In 1945, when the war ended, American distrust of Russian intentions was much less than it later became. Of the two states the more suspicious and wary was the Soviet Union.

At that moment, there were no other true great powers left. For all the legal fictions expressed in the composition of the Security Council, Great Britain was gravely over-strained, France barely risen from the living death of occupation and stricken by internal divisions (a large Communist Party threatened her stability), while Italy had discovered new quarrels to add to old ones. Germany was in ruins and under occupation. Japan was occupied and militarily powerless, while China had never yet been a great power in modern times. The Americans and Russians therefore enjoyed an immense superiority over all possible rivals. They were the only real victors. They alone had made positive gains from the war. All the other victorious states had, at the most, won survival or resurrection. To the United States and the USSR, the war brought new empires.

THE SOVIET UNION IN 1945

Though the Soviet Union's new empire had been won at huge cost, she now had greater

After two months of meetings, held in San Francisco in 1945, the United Nations Charter was passed unanimously and signed by all the representatives. Here the Earl of Halifax, the United Kingdom's ambassador to the United States, is pictured signing the charter during a ceremony held at the Veterans' War Memorial Building on 26 June, 1945.

strength than she had ever known under the tsars. Her armies dominated a vast European glacis, much of which was sovereign Soviet territory; the rest was organized in states which were by 1948 in every sense satellites, and one of them was East Germany, a major industrial entity. Beyond the glacis lay Yugoslavia and Albania, the only Communist states to emerge since the war without the help of Russian occupation; in 1945 both seemed assured allies of Moscow. This advantageous Soviet position had been won by the fighting of the Red Army, but it also owed something to decisions taken by Western governments and to their commander in Europe during the closing stages of the war, when General Eisenhower had resisted pressure to get to Prague and Berlin before the Russians. The resulting Soviet strategical preponderance in Central Europe was all the more menacing because the old traditional barriers to Russian power had gone: in 1914 the Habsburg empire, and now a united Germany. An exhausted Great Britain and slowly reviving France could not be expected to stand up to the Red Army, and no other conceivable counterweight on land existed if the Americans went home.

Russian armies also stood in 1945 on the borders of Turkey and Greece – where a Communist rising was under way – and occupied northern Iran. In the Far East they had held much of Sinkiang, Mongolia, northern Korea and the naval base of Port Arthur as well as liberating the rest of Manchuria, though the only territory they actually took from Japan was the southern half of the island of Sakhalin and the Kuriles. The rest of these gains had been effectively at China's expense. Yet in China there was already visible at the end of the war the outline of a new Communist state which could be expected to be friendly to Moscow. Stalin might have backed the wrong horse there in the past, but the Chinese Communists could not hope for moral and material help from anyone else. So it seemed that in Asia, too, a new Russian satellite might be in the making.

THE UNITED STATES IN 1945

The new world power of the United States rested much less on occupation of territory than that of the USSR. She, too, had at the end of the war a garrison in the heart of Europe, but American electors in 1945 wanted it brought home as soon as possible. American naval and air bases round much of the Eurasian land mass were another matter. Though Russia was a far greater Asian power than ever, the elimination of Japanese naval power, the acquisition of island airfields and technological changes which made huge fleet trains possible had together turned the Pacific Ocean into an American lake. Above all, Hiroshima and Nagasaki had demonstrated the power of the new weapon which the

United States alone possessed, the atomic bomb. But the deepest roots of American empire lay in her economic strength. Apart from the land-power of the Red Army, the overwhelming industrial power of the United States had been the decisive material factor behind the Allied victory. America had equipped not only her own huge forces but those of her allies. Moreover, by comparison with them, victory had cost her little. American casualties were fewer than theirs; even those of the United Kingdom were heavier and those of Russia colossally so. The home base of the United States had been immune to enemy attack in any but a trivial sense and was undamaged; her fixed capital was intact, her resources greater than ever. Her citizens had seen their standard of living actually rise during the war; the armament programme ended a depression which had not been mastered by Roosevelt's New Deal. She was a great creditor country, with capital to invest abroad in a world where no one else could supply it. Finally, America's old commercial and political rivals were staggering under the troubles of recovery. Their economies drifted into the ambit of the American because of their own lack of resources. The result was a worldwide surge of indirect American power, its beginnings visible even before the war ended.

SOVIET–AMERICAN RELATIONS

Something of the future implicit in the great power polarization could dimly be seen before the fighting stopped in Europe. It was made clear, for example, that the Russians would not be allowed to participate in the occupation of Italy or the dismantling of her colonial empire, and that the British and Americans could not hope for a Polish settlement other than the one wanted by Stalin. Yet (in spite of their record in their own hemisphere) the Americans were not happy about

The photograph shows the remains of Hiroshima after the atom bomb explosion of 6 August, 1945. Hundreds of thousands of people died in the Japanese city on that day and in the weeks, months and years that followed from the effects of the blast. Horrified as the Americans were by the terrible destruction that had been wrought by the bomb, they also believed that its deployment had been necessary to bring a swift end to the war.

explicit spheres of influence; the Russians were readier to take them as a working basis. There is no need to read back into such divergences assumptions which became current a few years after the war, when conflict between the two powers was presumed to have been sought from the start by one or other of them. Appearances can be deceptive. For all the power of the United States in 1945, there was little political will to use it; the first concern of the American military after victory was to achieve as rapid a demobilization as possible. Lend-Lease arrangements with allies had already been cut off even before the Japanese surrender. This further reduced America's indirect international leverage; it simply weakened friends she would soon be needing who now faced grave recovery problems. They could not provide a new security system to replace American strength. Nor could the use of the atomic bomb be envisaged except in the last resort; it was too powerful.

THE USSR ACQUIRES NUCLEAR WEAPONS

It is difficult to be sure of what was going on in Stalin's Russia after the war. Her peoples had clearly suffered appallingly from the conflict, more, certainly, than even the Germans. No one has been able to do more than provide estimates, but it seems likely that over twenty million Soviet citizens may have died. Stalin may well have been less aware of Soviet strength than of Soviet weakness when the war ended. True, his governmental methods relieved him of any need, such as faced Western countries, to demobilize the huge land forces which gave him supremacy on the spot in Europe. But the USSR had no atomic bomb nor a significant strategic bomber force, and Stalin's decision to develop nuclear weapons put a further grave strain on the Soviet economy at a time when general economic reconstruction was desperately needed. The years immediately after the war were to prove

Russian refugees return to their home town in 1944 to find that their house has been obliterated by German bombers.

After the liberation of France, those who had collaborated with the Nazis were subjected to public humiliation. Hundreds of women accused of sleeping with German soldiers had their heads shaved and were paraded through the streets of French towns.

as grim as had been those of the industrialization race of the 1930s. Yet in September 1949 an atomic explosion was achieved. In the following March it was officially announced that the USSR had an atomic weapon. By then much had changed.

THE DEVASTATED EUROPEAN ARENA

Piecemeal, relations between the two major world powers had deteriorated very badly by 1949. This was largely the result of what happened in Europe, the area most in need of imaginative and coordinated reconstruction in 1945. The cost of the war's destruction there has never been accurately measured. Leaving out the Russians, about fourteen and a quarter million Europeans were dead. In the

most-stricken countries those who survived lived amid ruins. One estimate is that about seven and a half million dwellings were destroyed in Germany and Russia. Factories and communications were shattered. There was nothing with which to pay for the imports Europe needed and currencies had collapsed; Allied occupation forces found that cigarettes and bully-beef were better than money. Civilized society had given way not only under the horrors of Nazi warfare, but also because occupation had transformed lying, swindling, cheating and stealing into acts of virtue; they were not only necessary to survival, but they could be glorified as acts of "resistance". The struggles against German occupying forces had bred new divisions; as countries were liberated by the advancing Allied armies, the firing squads got to work in their wake and old scores were wiped out. It was said that in France more perished in the "purification" of liberation than in the great Terror of 1793.

Above all, more finally than in 1918, the economic structure of Europe had disintegrated. The flywheel of much of European economic life had once been industrial Germany. But even if the communications and the productive capacity to restore the machine had been there, the Allies were at first bent on holding down German industrial production to prevent her recovery. Furthermore, Germany was divided. From the start the Russians had been carrying off capital equipment as "reparations" to repair their own ravaged lands – as well they might; the Germans had destroyed 39,000 miles of railway track alone in their retreat in Russia. The Soviet Union may have lost a quarter of her gross capital equipment.

THE EAST–WEST DIVIDE

A POLITICAL DIVISION between Eastern and Western Europe was coming to be evident before the end of the war. The British, in particular, had been alarmed by what happened to Poland. It seemed to show that Russia would only tolerate governments in Eastern Europe which were subservient. This was hardly what the Americans had envisaged as freedom for Eastern Europeans to choose their own rulers, but until the war was over neither government nor public in the United States was much concerned or much doubted they could come to reasonable agreement with the Russians. Broadly speaking, Roosevelt had been sure that America could get on with the Soviet Union; they had common ground in resisting a revival of German power and supporting anti-colonialism. Neither he nor the American public showed any awareness of the historic tendencies of

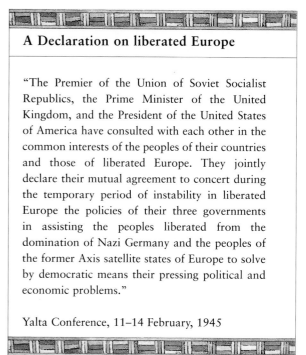

A Declaration on liberated Europe

"The Premier of the Union of Soviet Socialist Republics, the Prime Minister of the United Kingdom, and the President of the United States of America have consulted with each other in the common interests of the peoples of their countries and those of liberated Europe. They jointly declare their mutual agreement to concert during the temporary period of instability in liberated Europe the policies of their three governments in assisting the peoples liberated from the domination of Nazi Germany and the peoples of the former Axis satellite states of Europe to solve by democratic means their pressing political and economic problems."

Yalta Conference, 11–14 February, 1945

Russian policy. They disapproved strongly of British intervention in Greece against the Communist guerrillas who sought to overthrow the monarchy after the German withdrawal. (Stalin did not object: he agreed with Churchill that Great Britain should have a virtually free hand in Greece in return for letting him have one in Romania.)

A DIVIDED GERMANY

President Truman (who succeeded Roosevelt on his death in April 1945) and his advisers came to change American policies largely as a result of their experience in Germany. At first, the Russians had been punctilious in carrying out their agreement to admit British and American (and later French) armed forces to Berlin and share the administration of the city they had conquered. There is every indication that they wished Germany to be governed as a unit (as envisaged by the victors at Potsdam in July 1945), for this would give them a hand in controlling the Ruhr, potentially a treasure-

From November 1944, Germany was divided into four sectors, ruled by France, Britain, the United States and the Soviet Union. This scene from occupied Berlin gives an impression of the ruined condition of the city at the end of the war.

house of reparations. Yet the German economy soon bred friction between West and East. Russian efforts to ensure security against German recovery led to the increasing practical separation of her zone of occupation from those of the three other occupying powers. Probably this was at first intended to provide a solid and reliable (that is, Communist) core for a united Germany, but it led in the end to a solution by partition to the German problem which no one had envisaged. First, the western zones of occupation were for economic reasons integrated, without the eastern zone. Meanwhile Russian occupation policy aroused increasing distrust. The entrenchment of Communism in the Soviet zone of Germany seemed to repeat a pattern seen elsewhere. In 1945 there had been Communist majorities only in Bulgaria and Yugoslavia, and in other East European countries the Communists only shared power in coalition governments. None the less, it increasingly looked as if those governments could, in fact, do little more than behave as Russian puppets. Something like a bloc was already appearing in Eastern Europe in 1946.

POST-WAR SOVIET FOREIGN POLICY

It is rash to dogmatize about Soviet motives. Stalin obviously feared any reunification of Germany except under a government he could control; Russia had too many memories of attacks from the west to trust a united Germany. It would always have a potential for aggression which a satellite could not have. This would have been true whatever the ideological character of the Russian régime; it only made it worse that a united Germany might be capitalist. Elsewhere, though, Soviet policy showed more flexibility. While anxiously organizing eastern Germany on the Russian side of a line slowly appearing across Europe, it was still in China officially supporting the KMT. In Iran, on the other hand, there was an obvious reluctance to withdraw Soviet forces as had been agreed. Even when they finally departed they left behind a satellite Communist republic in Azerbaijan – to be later obliterated by the Iranians, to whom, by 1947, the Americans were giving military aid. In the Security Council the Soviet veto was more and more employed to frustrate her former allies and it was clear that the communist parties of Western Europe were manipulated in Russian interests. Yet Stalin's calculations remain in doubt; perhaps he was waiting, expecting or even relying upon economic collapse in the capitalist world.

AN IRON CURTAIN

There had been and still was much goodwill for the USSR among her former allies. When Winston Churchill had drawn attention in 1946 to the increasing division of Europe by an "iron curtain" he by no means spoke either for all his countrymen or for his American audience; some condemned him. Yet though the British Labour Government elected in 1945 was at first hopeful that "Left could speak to Left", it quickly became more sceptical. British and American policy began to converge during 1946, as it became clear that the British intervention in Greece had in fact made possible free elections and as American officials had more experience of the tendency of Russian policy. Nor did President Truman have any prejudices in favour of Russia to shed. The British, moreover, were by now clearly embarked upon a deliberate policy of leaving India; that counted with American official opinion.

THE TRUMAN DOCTRINE

Truman took a momentous decision in February 1947. It was occasioned by a communication from the British government which, perhaps more than any other, conceded the long-resisted admission that Great Britain was no longer a world power. The British economy had been gravely damaged by the huge efforts made during the war;

The Marshall Plan

On 5 June, 1947, the US secretary of state, General George Marshall declared that it was imperative for the European countries to draw up a plan for economic recovery, which the United States would whole-heartedly support.

Although the Soviet Union and its satellites refused to participate in the plan, Austria, Belgium, Denmark, France, Great Britain, Greece, Iceland, Ireland, Italy, Luxembourg, the Netherlands, Norway, Portugal, Sweden, Switzerland and Turkey reacted favourably to the scheme. The Organization for European Economic Cooperation was set up to put the Marshall Plan into practice. It took from 15 September, 1947 to 1 April, 1948 to set up the European Reconstruction Programme, as the Marshall Plan was officially called.

George Marshall (1880–1959) was awarded the Nobel peace prize in 1953.

there was urgent need for investment at home. The first stages of decolonialization, too, were expensive. One outcome was that by 1947 the British balance of payments could only be maintained if forces were withdrawn from Greece. President Truman at once decided that the United States must fill the gap. Financial aid was given to Greece and Turkey, to enable them to survive the pressure they were under from Russia. He deliberately drew attention to the implication; much more than propping up two countries was involved. Although only Turkey and Greece were to receive aid, he deliberately offered the "free peoples" of the world American leadership to resist, with American support, "attempted subjugation by armed minorities or by outside pressures". This was a reversal of the apparent return to isolation from Europe which the United States had seemed to pursue in 1945, and an enormous break with the historic traditions of American foreign policy. The decision to "contain" Russian power, as it was called, was possibly the most important in American diplomacy since the Louisiana Purchase. Ultimately, it was to lead to unrealistic assessments of the effective limits of American power, and, critics were to say, to a new American imperialism, as the policy was extended outside Europe, but this could not be seen at the time. It was provoked by Russian behaviour and the growing fears Stalin's policy had aroused over the previous eighteen months as well as by British weakness.

THE MARSHALL PLAN

A few months after the president's offer of support to the "free peoples" of the world, the "Truman Doctrine" was completed by another much more pondered step, an offer of American economic aid to European

nations which would come together to plan jointly their economic recovery. This was the Marshall Plan, named after the American secretary of state who announced it. Its aim was a non-military, unaggressive form of containment. It surprised everyone. The British foreign secretary, Ernest Bevin, was the first European statesman to grasp its implications. With the French, he pressed for the acceptance of the offer by Western Europe. It was made, of course, to all Europe. But the Russians would not participate, nor did they allow their satellites to do so. Instead, they bitterly attacked the plan. When, with obvious regret, the Czechoslovakian coalition government also declined to adhere, that country, the only one in Eastern Europe still without a fully Communist government and not regarded as a Russian satellite, was visibly having to toe the Soviet line. Any residual belief in Czechoslovakia's independence was removed by a Communist coup in February 1948. Another sign of Russian intransigence was an old pre-war propaganda device, the Comintern, revived as the Cominform in September 1947. It at once began the

Armed workers' units march across Prague's Charles Bridge in 1948 in a show of force which ended in a mass demonstration in support of Communism. The Communist coup had been carefully prepared, with Czechoslovakia's administration, police and army neutralized in advance. The president, desperate to avoid a civil war, accepted the formation of a Communist government.

denunciation of what it termed a "frankly predatory and expansionist course ... to establish the world supremacy of American imperialism". Finally, when Western Europe set up an Organization for European Economic Cooperation to handle the Marshall Plan, the Russians replied by organizing their own half of Europe in Comecon, a Council for Mutual Economic Assistance which was window-dressing for the Soviet integration of the command economies of the East.

THE ADVENT OF THE COLD WAR

By 1947, THE COLD WAR (as it came to be called) had begun. The first phase of Europe's post-war history was over. The next, a phase in global history, too, was to continue well into the 1960s. In it, two groups of states, one led by the United States and one by Soviet Russia, strove throughout a succession of crises to achieve their own security by all means short of war between the principal contenders. Much of what was said was put into ideological terms. In some countries of what came to be a Western bloc, the Cold War therefore also appeared as civil war or near-war, and as moral debate about values such as freedom, social justice and individualism. Some of it was fought in marginal theatres by propaganda and subversion or by guerrilla movements sponsored by the two great states. Fortunately, they always stopped short of the point at which they would have to fight with nuclear weapons whose increasing power made the notion of a successful outcome more and more unrealistic. The Cold War was also an economic competition by example and by offers of aid to satellites and uncommitted nations. Inevitably, in the process much opportunism got mixed up with doctrinaire rigidity. Probably it was

On 23 October, 1956, an uprising against the Communist régime took place in Budapest. A dissident who had been expelled from Hungary's Communist Party claimed to head the new government, demanding the withdrawal of the Russian troops from the city and the dismantling of the Warsaw Pact. The Soviet Union reacted swiftly: Russian tanks, seen in this photograph, were sent in to Budapest, and the rebellion was quashed within 24 hours.

unavoidable, but it was a blight which left little of the world untouched, and a seeping source of crime, corruption and suffering for more than thirty years.

THE EFFECTS OF THE COLD WAR

In retrospect, for all the simple brutalities of the language it generated, the Cold War now looks somewhat like the complex struggles of religion in sixteenth- and seventeenth-century Europe, when ideology could provoke violence, passion, and even, at times, conviction, but could never wholly accommodate the complexities and cross currents of the day. Above all, it could not contain those introduced by national interest. Like the religious struggles of the past, too, though, there was soon every sign that although specific quarrels might die down and disaster be avoided, its rhetoric and mythology could go rolling on long after they ceased to reflect reality.

The first important complication to cut across the Cold War was the emergence of a growing number of states which did not feel committed to one side or the other. Many new nations came into existence within a few years of 1945 as a result of decolonization, which caused just as great an upheaval in international relations as the Cold War. The United Nations General Assembly was much more important as a platform for anti-colonial than for Cold War propaganda (though they were sometimes confused).

POST-WAR ASIA

THERE WERE MANY DIFFERENCES of circumstance and timing, but by and large the Asian nationalist movements had been guaranteed eventual success when the war flattened the card castle of European imperi-

alism. This was first obvious in Southeast Asia and Indonesia, but its repercussions were great even in areas (such as the Indian subcontinent) where the imperial power was not displaced by the Japanese. The surrender of sixty thousand British, Indian and dominion troops at Singapore in 1942 had been the signal that European empire in Asia was doomed. No efforts could retrieve a disaster far worse than Yorktown. The loss of face had compromised the confidence and prestige of every European in the Far East. It did not matter that the Japanese often behaved badly to their new conquests. Parachuting arms to formerly subject peoples to resist the conquerors only made it likely that they would be used in due course against their former rulers in London, Paris or The Hague. Furthermore, though (by comparison with the upheavals caused by bombing, fighting, labour conscription, starvation and disease in Europe) life went on in most Asian villages undisturbed, there were notable side-effects. By 1945 there was a big potential for change in the East.

In the end, the former Asian empires were all but swept away within a few years. Yet territorial rule was not all that was at stake.

This Soviet Cold War propaganda cartoon, which dates from 1953, mock's "Washington's Dove" of peace. Similar anti-Soviet cartoons were common in the American press.

Japanese brutality towards prisoners of war aroused great indignation in Great Britain and the United States, where propaganda such as this was used to spur on the war effort. In the Asian colonies, administrative and economic posts left vacant by the colonists (who had been withdrawn or taken prisoner) were taken over by native local élites.

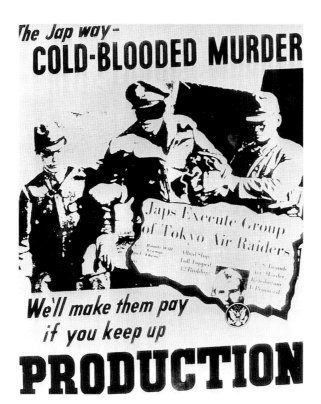

Though Russian and American spheres of influence in Europe were (with the possible exception of Berlin) clearly enough demarcated in 1948 to remain unchanged for forty years, the settlement of great power relationships in the Far East was to be in doubt for much longer.

INDIA

Some had always thought India might become a dominant Asian power once she achieved self-government. Even before 1939 it was plain that the survival of imperial rule in India was no longer in question. What was being discussed was the timetable and form of its replacement. Those among the British who favoured Indian independence hoped to keep it linked to the British Commonwealth of Nations, the name usually given to the empire since the Imperial Conference of 1926, which produced the first official definition of "dominion status" as independent association to the Commonwealth in allegiance to the Crown, with complete control of internal and external affairs. This set a conceivable goal for India, though not one which British governments could concede as an immediate aim before 1940. Yet though unevenly, some progress was made before this, and this in part explains the absence in India of so complete a revulsion of anti-Western feeling as had occurred in China.

INDIA BETWEEN THE WARS

The Indian politicians had been deeply disappointed after the First World War. They had for the most part rallied loyally to the Crown; India had made big contributions of men and money to the imperial war effort, and Gandhi, later to be seen as the father of the Indian nation, had been one of those who had worked for it in the belief that this would bring a due reward. In 1917, the British government had announced that it favoured a policy of steady progress towards responsible government for India within the empire – Home Rule, as it were – though this was short of the dominion status some Indians were beginning to ask for. Reforms introduced in 1918 were none the less very disappointing, though they satisfied some moderates, and even such limited success as they had was soon dissipated. Economics came into play as international trading conditions worsened. In the 1920s the Indian government was already supporting Indian demands to put an end to commercial and financial arrangements favouring the United Kingdom, and soon insisted on the imperial government paying a proper share of India's contribution to imperial defence. Once into the world slump, it became clear that London could no longer be allowed to settle Indian tariff policy so as to suit British industry.

GANDHI AND INDIAN NATIONALISM

One influential factor hindering progress was the continuing isolation of the British community in India. Convinced that Indian nationalism was a matter of a few ambitious intellectuals, its members pressed merely for strong measures against conspiracy, a course not unattractive to administrators confronted with the consequences of the Bolshevik revolution (though the Indian Communist Party was not founded until 1923). The result, against the wishes of all the Indian members of the legislative council, was the suspension of normal legal safeguards in order to deal with conspiracy. This provoked Gandhi's first campaign of strikes and pacifist civil disobedience. In spite of his efforts to avoid violence there were riots. At Amritsar in 1919, after some Englishmen had been killed and others attacked, a foolish general decided, as an example of his countrymen's determination, to disperse a crowd by force. When the firing stopped, nearly four hundred Indians had been killed and over a thousand wounded. An irreparable blow to British prestige was made worse when British residents in India and some Members of Parliament loudly applauded what had been done.

DIVISIONS BETWEEN THE NATIONALISTS

A period of boycott and civil disturbance followed the Amritsar massacre, in which Gandhi's programme was adopted by Congress. Although Gandhi himself emphasized that his campaign was non-violent there was nevertheless much disorder and he was arrested and imprisoned for the first time in 1922 (and was soon released because of the danger that he might die in prison). This was

the end of significant agitation in India for the next few years. In 1927 British policy began to move slowly forward again. A commission was sent to India to look into the working of the last series of constitutional changes (though this caused more trouble because no Indians had been included in it). Much of the enthusiasm which had sustained unity among the nationalists had by now evaporated and there was a danger of a rift bridged only by Gandhi's efforts and prestige between those who stuck to the demand for complete independence and those who wanted to work

In 1930, Gandhi attacked the British government's high tax and production monopoly on salt – an issue that appealed to India's poor. Gandhi is pictured here during his 240 mile (385 km) march from Satarmati to the shore at Dandi, where he illegally extracted salt by boiling sea water. He was later arrested for this breach of the law.

for dominion status. Congress was, in any case, not so solid a structure as its rhetoric suggested. It was less a political party with deep roots in the masses than a coalition of local bigwigs and interests. Finally, a more grievous division still was deepening between Hindu and Muslim. The leaders of the two communities had watched the relations between their followers deteriorate rapidly in the 1920s into communal rioting and bloodshed. By 1930 the president of the

Muslim political league was proposing that the future constitutional development of India should include the establishment of a separate Muslim state in the northwest.

THE ROLE OF THE CONGRESS PARTY

Nineteen-thirty was a violent year. The British viceroy had announced that a conference was to take place with the aim of achieving dominion status, but this undertaking was made meaningless by opposition in Great Britain. Gandhi would not take part, therefore. Civil disobedience was resumed after a second conference foundered on the question of minorities' representation, and intensified as distress deepened with the world economic depression. The rural masses were now more ready for mobilization by nationalist appeals; although this alienated some elements in Congress, who saw their movement changing to take account of mass interests, it made Gandhi the first politician to be able to claim an India-wide following.

The wheels of the India Office were by now beginning to turn as they absorbed the lessons of the discussions and the 1927 commission. A real devolution of power and patronage came in 1935, when a Government of India Act was passed which took still further the establishment of representative and responsible government, leaving in the viceroy's sole control only such matters as defence and foreign affairs. Though the transfer of national power proposed in the Act was never wholly implemented, this was the culmination of legislation by the British. They had by now effectively provided a framework for a national politics. It was increasingly clear that at all levels the decisive struggles between Indians would be fought out within the Congress party, but it was already under

A scene from the aftermath of Hindu–Muslim riots at Cawnpore (Kanpur), India, in 1931. On the right are the ruins of the private residence of a rich Hindu banker, demolished and looted by Muslims.

The key figures in the fight for Indian independence, Mahatma Gandhi (1869–1948) and Jawarhal Nehru (1889–1964), are seen in discussion during a meeting of the Indian Congress in Bombay in 1946.

grave strain. The 1935 Act once more affirmed the principle of separate communal representation and almost immediately its working provoked further hostility between Hindu and Muslim. Congress was by now to all intents and purposes a Hindu organization (though it refused to concede that the Muslim League should therefore be the sole representative of Muslims). But Congress had its internal problems, too, divided as it was between those who still wished to press forward to independence and those – some of them beginning to be alarmed by Japanese aggressiveness – who were willing to work the new institutions in cooperation with the imperial government. The evidence that the British were in fact devolving power was bound to be a divisive force. Different interests began to seek to insure themselves against an uncertain future.

THE BRITISH RESPONSE

Under the surface, the tide was running fast by 1941. Nearly two decades of representative institutions in local government and the progressive Indianization of the higher civil service had already produced a country which could not be governed except with the substantial consent of its élites. It was also one which had undergone a considerable preparatory education in self-government, if not democracy. Though the approach of war made the British increasingly aware of their need of the Indian army, they had already given up trying to make India pay for it and were by 1941 bearing the cost of its modernization. Then the Japanese attack forced the hand of the British government. It offered the nationalists autonomy after the war and a right of secession from the Commonwealth,

Gandhi is pictured with Lord Mountbatten (1900–1979), the last viceroy of India, and his wife, in 1947.

but this was too late; they now demanded immediate independence. Their leaders were arrested and the British Raj continued. A rebellion in 1942 was crushed much more rapidly than had been the Mutiny nearly a century earlier, but the sands were running out if the British wanted to go peacefully. One new factor was pressure from the United States. President Roosevelt discussed confidentially with Stalin the need to prepare for Indian independence (as well as that of other parts of Asia, and the need for trusteeship for French Indo-China); the involvement of the United States implied revolutionary change in other people's wars as it had done in 1917.

PARTITION

In 1945 the Labour Party, which had long had the independence of India and Burma as part of its programme, came to power at Westminster. On 14 March, 1946, while India was torn with Hindu–Muslim rioting and its politicians were squabbling over the future, the British government offered full independence. Nearly a year later, it put a pistol to the head of the Indians by announcing that it would hand over power not later than June 1948. Thus the tangle of communal rivalries was cut, and the partition of the subcontinent followed. The only governmental unity it had ever enjoyed was ended and on 15 August, 1947 two new dominions appeared within it, Pakistan and India. The first was Muslim and was itself divided into two slabs of land at the extremities of northern India; the second was officially secular but was overwhelmingly Hindu in composition and inspiration.

Perhaps Partition was inevitable. India had never been ruled directly as one entity, even by the British, and Hindu and Muslim had been increasingly divided since the Mutiny. Nevertheless, its cost was enormous. The psychic wound to many nationalists was symbolized when Gandhi was murdered by a Hindu fanatic for his part in it. Huge massacres occurred in areas where there were minorities. Something like two million people fled to where their co-religionists were in control. Almost the only clear political gain on the morrow of independence was the solution, a bloody one, of the communal problem for the immediate future. Apart from this, the assets of the new states were the goodwill (arising from very mixed motives) shown to them by great powers, the inheritance of a civil service already largely native before independence, and an important infrastructure of institutions and services. These inheritances were not, however, equally shared, India tending to enjoy more of them than Pakistan.

POPULATION GROWTH

In spite of their advantages, the new states could not do much to deal with the grave problems of the subcontinent's economic and social backwardness. The worst problem was demographic. A steady rise in population had begun under British rule. Sometimes it was briefly mitigated by Malthusian disasters like the great influenza epidemic at the end of the First World War which struck down five million Indians or a famine in Bengal during the Second World War which carried off millions more. But in 1951 there was famine again in India, and in 1953 in Pakistan. The spectre of it lingered into the 1970s.

The subcontinent's industrialization, which had made important strides in the twentieth century (notably in the Second World War), did not offset this danger. It could not provide new jobs and earnings fast enough for a growing population. Though the new India had most of what industry there was, her problems were graver in this respect than those of Pakistan. Outside her huge cities, most Indians were landless peasants, living in villages where, for all the

egalitarian aspirations of some of the leaders of the new republic, inequality remained as great as ever. The landlords who provided the funds for the ruling Congress Party and dominated its councils stood in the way of any land reform which could have dealt with this. In many ways, the past lay heavy on a new state proclaiming the Western ideals of democracy, nationalism, secularism and material progress, and it was to encumber the road of reform and development.

CHINA

CHINA HAD FOR A LONG TIME been engaged in fighting off a different sort of imperialism. Success against the Japanese and completion of her long revolution was made possible by the Second World War. The political

Gandhi is among the participants at the India Conference, which was held in London in 1947 and resulted in the declaration of the terms of Indian independence.

phase of this transformation began in 1941, when the Sino-Japanese War merged in a world conflict. This gave China powerful allies and a new international standing. Significantly, the last vestiges of the "unequal treaties" with Great Britain, France and the United States were then swept away. This was more important than the military help the Allies could give; for a long time they were too busy extricating themselves from the disasters of early 1942 to do much for China. A Chinese army, indeed, came instead to help to defend Burma from the Japanese. Still hemmed in to the west, though supported by American aircraft, the Chinese had for a long time to hold out as best they could, in touch with their allies only by air or the Burma Road. None the less a decisive change had begun.

China had at first responded to Japanese attacks with a sense of national unity long desired but never hitherto forthcoming except, perhaps, in the May 4th Movement. In spite of friction between the Communists and the Nationalists, sometimes breaking out into open conflict, this unity survived, broadly speaking, until 1941. Then, the new fact that the United States was now Japan's major enemy, and would eventually destroy her, subtly began to transform the attitude of the Nationalist government. It came to feel that as ultimate victory was certain, there was no point in using up men and resources in fighting the Japanese when they might be husbanded for the struggle against the Communists after the peace. Some of its members went further. Soon the KMT was fighting the Communists again.

NATIONALIST AND COMMUNIST CHINA

Two Chinas appeared. Nationalist China increasingly displayed the lethargy, self-seeking and corruption which had from the early 1930s tainted the KMT because of the

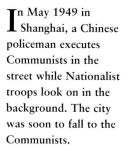

In May 1949 in Shanghai, a Chinese policeman executes Communists in the street while Nationalist troops look on in the background. The city was soon to fall to the Communists.

nature of the support on which it drew. The régime was repressive and stifled criticism. It alienated the intellectuals. Its soldiers, sometimes badly officered and undisciplined, terrorized the peasant as much as did the Japanese. Communist China was different. In large areas controlled by the Communists (often behind the Japanese lines) a deliberate attempt was being made to ensure the support of as wide a spectrum of interests as possible by moderate but unambiguous reform and disciplined behaviour. Outright attacks on landlords were usually avoided, but peasant goodwill was cultivated by enforcing lower rents and abolishing usury. Meanwhile, Mao published a series of theoretical writings designed to prepare the new Communist cadres for the task that lay ahead. There was a need for political education as the Party and the army grew steadily in numbers; when the Japanese collapsed in 1945 there were about a million Chinese Communist soldiers.

The suddenness of victory was the second factor which shaped the last stage of the Chinese Revolution. Huge areas of China had suddenly to be reoccupied and reincorporated in the Chinese state. But many of them were already under Communist control before 1945 and others could not possibly be reached by Nationalist forces before the Communists dug themselves in there. The Americans did what they could by sending soldiers to hold some of the ports until the Nationalists could take them over. In some places the Japanese were told to hold on until the Chinese government could re-establish its authority. But when the final and military phase of the revolution opened, the Communists held more territory than they had ever done before and held it in the main with the support of the population who found that Communist rule was by no means as bad as they had heard.

THE DEMISE OF THE KMT

All unwittingly, the Japanese, by launching their attack on the KMT régime, had in the end brought about the very triumph of the Chinese Revolution they had long striven to avoid. It is at least possible that if the Nationalists had been undistracted by foreign invasion and had not suffered the crippling damage it inflicted, they might have been able to master Chinese Communism in the short run. In 1937 the KMT could still draw heavily on patriotic goodwill; many Chinese believed that it was the authentic carrier of the revolution. The war destroyed the chance of exploiting this, if it were true, but also enabled China to resume for the last time her long march towards world power from which she had been deflected first by Europeans and then by fellow Asians. The long frustration of Chinese Nationalism was about to end, and the beneficiary would be Communism.

The defeat of the KMT took three years. Although the Japanese usually sought to surrender to the KMT or Americans, the Communists had acquired authority in new areas and often large stocks of arms when they gave in. The Russians, who had invaded

Chiang K'ai-shek, president of the Republic of China until 1947, is pictured in front of a huge portrait of Sun Yat-sen. Chiang claimed to be Sun's natural successor.

Manchuria in the last days before the Japanese surrender, helped them by giving them access to the Japanese arms there. Mao made deliberately moderate policy pronouncements and continued to push forward with land reform. This conferred a further great advantage on the Communists in the Civil War which continued until 1949; victory in that war was essentially a victory of the countryside over a city-based régime.

THE PEOPLE'S REPUBLIC OF CHINA

American policy was increasingly disillusioned by the revealed inadequacy and corruption of the Chiang K'ai-shek government. In 1947 American forces were withdrawn from China and the United States abandoned the efforts it had hitherto made to mediate between the two Chinas. In the following year, with most of the north in Communist hands, the Americans began to cut down the amount of financial and military aid given to the KMT. From this time, the Nationalist government ran militarily and

politically downhill; it became obvious, and more and more employees of government and local authorities sought to make terms with the Communists while they might still do so. The conviction spread that a new era was dawning. By the beginning of December, no important Nationalist military force remained intact on the mainland and Chiang withdrew to Formosa (Taiwan). The Americans cut off their aid while this withdrawal was under way and publicly blamed the inadequacies of the Nationalist régime for the débâcle. Meanwhile, on 1 October, 1949, the People's Republic of China was officially inaugurated at Peking and the largest Communist state in the world had come into existence. Once again, the Mandate of Heaven had passed.

SOUTHEAST ASIA AND INDONESIA

IN SOUTHEAST ASIA AND INDONESIA the Second World War was as decisive as elsewhere in ending colonial rule, though the pace was faster in Dutch and French colonies than British. The grant of representative institutions by the Dutch in Indonesia before 1939 had not checked the growth of a Nationalist party, and a flourishing Communist movement had appeared by then, too. Some nationalist leaders, among them one Achmed Sukarno, collaborated with the Japanese when they occupied the islands in 1942. They were in a favourable position to seize power when the Japanese surrendered, and did so by proclaiming an independent Indonesian republic before the Dutch could return. Fighting and negotiation followed for nearly two years until agreement was reached for an Indonesian republic still under the Dutch Crown; this did not work. Fighting went on again, the Dutch pressing forward vainly with their "police operations" in one

Chinese Communist troops advance to liberate the people of the province of Guanxi from the Japanese at the end of the Second World War.

of the first campaigns by a former colonial power to attract the full blast of Communist and anti-colonial stricture at the United Nations. Both India and Australia (which had concluded that she would be wise to conciliate the independent Indonesia which must eventually emerge) took the matter to the Security Council. Finally the Dutch gave in. The story begun by the East India Company of Amsterdam three and a half centuries before thus came to an end in 1949 with the creation of the United States of Indonesia, a mixture of more than a hundred million people scattered over hundreds of islands, of scores of races and religions. A vague union with the Netherlands under the Dutch Crown survived, but was dissolved five years later.

Ho Chi Minh (1892–1969) is pictured during his first year as president of North Vietnam in 1954. Ho Chi Minh was re-elected in 1960 and played a leading role in the war with South Vietnam and the United States during the following decade.

HO CHI MINH AND THE VIETNAM REPUBLIC

For a time the French in Indo-China seemed to be holding on better than the Dutch. That area's wartime history had been somewhat different from that of Malaysia or Indonesia because although the Japanese had exercised complete military control there since 1941 French sovereignty was not formally displaced until early 1945. The Japanese had amalgamated Annam, Cochin China and Tongking to form a new state of Vietnam under the emperor of Annam and as soon as the Japanese surrendered, the chief of the local Communist Party, the Viet Minh, installed himself in the government place at Hanoi and proclaimed the Vietnam republic. This was Ho Chi Minh, a man with long experience in the Communist Party and also in Europe. The revolutionary movement quickly spread. It was soon evident that if the French wished to re-establish themselves it would not be easy. A large expeditionary force was sent to Indo-China and a concession was made in that the French recognized the republic of Vietnam as an autonomous state within the French Union. But now there arose the question of giving Cochin China separate status and on this all attempts to agree broke down. Meanwhile, French soldiers were sniped at and their convoys were attacked. At the end of 1946 there was an attack on residents in Hanoi and many deaths. Hanoi was relieved by French troops and Ho Chi Minh fled.

WAR

With the flight of Ho Chi Minh began a war in which the Communists were to struggle essentially for the nationalist aim of a united country, while the French tried to retain a diminished Vietnam which, with the other Indo-Chinese states, would remain inside the French Union. By 1949 they had come round to including Cochin China in Vietnam and recognizing Cambodia and Laos as "associate states". But new outsiders were now becoming interested. The government of Ho Chi Minh was recognized in Moscow and Peking, that of the Annamese emperor whom the French had set up by the British and Americans.

Thus in Asia decolonialization quickly burst out of the simple processes envisaged by Roosevelt. As the British began to liquidate their recovered heritage, this further complicated things. Burma and Ceylon had become independent in 1947. In the following year, Communist-supported guerrilla war began in Malaya; though it was to be unsuccessful and not to impede steady progress towards independence in 1957, it was one of the first of several post-colonial problems which were to torment American policy. Growing antagonism with the Communist world soon cut across the simplicities of anti-colonialism.

THE MIDDLE EAST

ONLY IN THE MIDDLE EAST did things still seem clear-cut for the United States in 1948. In May that year, a new state, Israel, came into existence in Palestine. This marked the end of forty years during which only two great powers had needed to agree in order to

A scene from the 1949 "Song Thao" campaign in Vietnam shows a French colonialist military post that has been overrun by troops from the Vietnam People's Army.

manage the area. France and Great Britain had not found this too difficult. In 1939 the French still held mandates in Syria and the Lebanon (their original mandate had been divided into two), and the British retained theirs in Palestine. Elsewhere in the Arab lands the British exercised varying degrees of influence or power after negotiation with the new rulers of individual states. The most important were Iraq, where a small British force, mainly of air force units, was maintained, and Egypt, where a substantial garrison still protected the Suez Canal. The latter had become more and more important in the 1930s as Italy showed increasing hostility to Great Britain.

ANTI-COLONIAL FEELING

The war of 1939 was to release change in the Middle East as elsewhere, though this was not at first clear. After Italy's entry to the war, the Canal Zone became one of the most vital areas of British strategy and Egypt suddenly found herself with a battlefront for a western border. She remained neutral almost to the end, but was in effect a British base and little else. The war also made it essential to assure the supply of oil from the Gulf and especially from Iraq. This led to intervention when Iraq threatened to move in a pro-German direction after another nationalist coup in 1941. A British and Free French invasion of Syria to keep it, too, out of German hands led in 1941 to an independent Syria. Soon afterwards the Lebanon proclaimed its independence. The French tried to re-establish their authority at the end of the war, but unsuccessfully, and during 1946 these two countries saw the last foreign garrisons leave. The French also had difficulties further west, where fighting broke out in Algeria in 1945. Nationalists there were at that moment asking only for

Crowds of Jewish refugees throng the deck of a ship in the port of Haifa, northwestern Israel, in 1948. During the war with Palestine that followed the foundation of the state of Israel, Haifa was one focus of fighting between the Arabs and the Jewish defence force, the Hagana.

autonomy in federation with France and the French went some way in this direction in 1947, but this was far from the end of the story.

Where British influence was paramount, anti-British sentiment was still a good rallying-cry. In both Egypt and Iraq there was much hostility to British occupation forces in the post-war years. In 1946 the British announced that they were prepared to withdraw from Egypt, but negotiations on the basis of a new treaty broke down so badly that Egypt referred the matter (unsuccessfully) to the United Nations. By this time the whole question of the future of the Arab lands had been diverted by the Jewish decision to establish a national state in Palestine by force.

THE GROWING CRISIS OVER PALESTINE

The Palestine question has been with us ever since. Its catalyst had been the Nazi revolution in Germany. At the time of the Balfour Declaration 600,000 Arabs had lived in Palestine beside 80,000 Jews – a number already felt by Arabs to be threateningly large. In some years after this, though, Jewish emigration actually exceeded immigration and there was ground for hope that the problem of reconciling the promise of a "national home" for Jews with respect for "the civil and religious rights of the existing non-Jewish communities in Palestine" (as the Balfour Declaration had put it) might be resolved. Hitler changed this.

From the beginning of the Nazi persecution the numbers of those who wished to come to Palestine rose. As the extermination policies began to unroll in the war years, they made nonsense of British attempts to restrict immigration which were the side of British policy unacceptable to the Jews; the other side – the partitioning of Palestine – was rejected by the Arabs. The issue was dramatized as soon as the war was over by a World Zionist Congress demand that a million Jews should be admitted to Palestine at once. Other new factors now began to operate. The British, in 1945, had looked benevolently on the formation of an "Arab League" of Egypt, Syria, Lebanon, Iraq, Saudi Arabia, the Yemen and Transjordan. There had always been in British policy a strand of illusion – that pan-Arabism might prove the way in which the Middle East could be persuaded to settle down and that the coordination of the policies of Arab states would open the way to the solution of its problems. In fact the Arab League was soon preoccupied with Palestine to the virtual exclusion of anything else.

SUPPORT FOR THE ZIONISTS

The other novelty was the Cold War. In the immediate post-war era, Stalin seems to have been impressed still with the old Communist view that Great Britain was the main imperialist prop of the international capitalist system. Attacks on her position and influence therefore followed, and in the Middle East this, of course, coincided with traditional Russian interests, though the Soviet govern-

---

The Palestinian refugee crisis of 1949

With the foundation of Israel in 1948, the Arabs born in Palestine found themselves in a terrible position. The Jews not only colonized but expanded the areas they had seized, as a direct result of the war launched against them by the Arab states that had bitterly opposed the partition of Palestine.

The conflict, together with the fresh wave of Jewish immigration that began in 1948, created well over half a million Arab refugees. At the end of the war, in 1949, barely 160,000 Arabs remained in the Israeli-occupied areas of the country in which they had previously been the predominant population. The land that the UN had granted to the Palestinians in the partition of their territory had vanished: some areas, especially in the Negev desert, had been absorbed by Israel, while others were taken over by the Arab states who had fought on the side of the Palestinians. Egypt kept Gaza, and the West Bank (Samaria and Judaea) was annexed by Jordan.

The first problem the displaced Palestinians faced was of where to go. Those who had families in Judaea, Samaria or Gaza moved there. The rest sheltered in improvised refugee camps, where conditions were so appalling that the UN created an organization to guarantee survival in the Palestinian camps (the Aid and Re-adaptation Organization for Arab Refugees). Some Palestinians managed to improve their lot by finding work in Jordan, Egypt, Syria, Iraq and the United Arab Emirates.

To prevent their disappearance as a people, Palestinians do not take the nationality of any other Arab country: Palestinian nationality is passed on from one generation of refugees to the next. Many of the ever-growing numbers of Palestinian refugees, such as those pictured here in 1993, live in atrocious conditions in camps in Gaza.

ment had shown little interest in the area between 1919 and 1939. Pressure was brought to bear on Turkey at the Straits, and ostentatious Soviet support was given to Zionism, the most disruptive element in the situation. It did not need extraordinary political insight to recognize the implications of a resumption of Russian interest in the area of the Ottoman legacy. Yet at the same moment American policy turned anti-British, or, rather, pro-Zionist. This could hardly have been avoided. In 1946 mid-term congressional elections were held and Jewish votes were important. Since the Roosevelt revolution in domestic politics, a Democratic president could hardly envisage an anti-Zionist position.

THE FOUNDATION OF ISRAEL

The British sought to disentangle themselves from the Holy Land. From 1945 they faced both Jewish and Arab terrorism and guerrilla warfare in Palestine. Unhappy Arab, Jewish and British policemen struggled to hold the ring while the British government still strove to find a way acceptable to both sides of bringing the mandate to an end. American help was sought, but to no avail; Truman wanted a pro-Zionist solution. In the end the British took the matter to the United Nations. It recommended partition, but this was still a non-starter for the Arabs. Fighting between the two communities grew fiercer and the British decided to withdraw without more ado. On the day that they did so, 14 May 1948, the state of Israel was proclaimed. It was immediately recognized by the United States (sixteen minutes after the foundation act) and Russia, who were to agree about little else in the Middle East for the next quarter-century.

Israel was attacked almost at once by

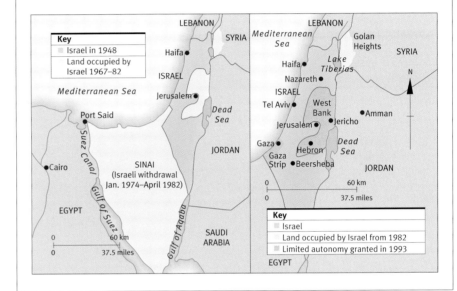

Israel 1948–1967 (left) and 1982–1993 (right)

From 1948 to 1967, despite hundreds of Palestinian assaults on Israelis, Israel consolidated its presence in the region and won important foreign support. In the Six Day War of 1967, Israel won major victories against Egypt, Jordan and Syria, gaining new territories. During the Yom Kippur War of 1973, Israel took yet more land from Egypt and Syria. In 1982 Israel invaded Lebanon and defeated PLO troops there. After six years of Palestinian rebellion (the *intifada*) in Gaza and the West Bank, an Israeli–PLO treaty gave limited self-rule to the Palestinians in the occupied territories.

Egypt, whose armies invaded a part of Palestine which the United Nations proposal had awarded to Jews. Jordanian and Iraqi forces supported Palestinian Arabs in the territory proposed for them. But Israel fought off her enemies, and a truce, supervised by the United Nations, followed (during which a Zionist terrorist murdered the United Nations mediator). In 1949 the Israeli government moved to Jerusalem, a Jewish national capital again for the first time since the days of imperial Rome. Half of the city was still occupied by Jordanian forces, but this was almost the least of the problems left to the future. With American and Russian diplomatic support and American private money, Jewish energy and initiative had successfully established a new national state where no basis for one had existed twenty-five years before. Yet the cost

Israel's first prime minister, David Ben-Gurion, watches British troops preparing to leave the newly established state from the port of Haifa in 1948.

ing were it true (as some students believe) that the first president of Israel quickly began to encourage his country's scientists to work on a nuclear energy programme.

AGE-OLD PROBLEMS

Many currents flowed together in a curious and ironical way to swirl in confusion in an area always a focus of world history. Victims for centuries, the Jews were in their turn now seen by Arabs as persecutors. The problems with which the peoples of the area had to grapple were poisoned by forces flowing from the dissolution of centuries of Ottoman power, from the rivalries of successor imperialisms (and in particular from the rise of two new world powers which dwarfed these in their turn), from the interplay of nineteenth-century European nationalism and ancient religion, and from the first effects of the new dependence of developed nations on oil. There are few moments in the twentieth century so soaked in history as the establishment of Israel. It is a good point at which to pause before turning to the story of the second half of the twentieth century.

was to prove enormous. The disappointment and humiliation of the Arab states assured their continuing hostility to it and therefore opportunities for great power intervention in the future. Moreover, the action of Zionist extremists and the far from conciliatory behaviour of Israeli forces in 1948–9 led to an exodus of Arab refugees. Soon there were 750,000 of them in camps in Egypt and Jordan, a social and economic problem, a burden on the world's conscience, and a potential military and diplomatic weapon for Arab nationalists. It would hardly be surpris-

A Jew casts his vote in the first general election to be held in the new state of Israel, in January 1949. One month later, the elected constituent assembly decreed that Israel's legislature was to be a one-chamber parliament, which would be known as the Knesset.

5 POPULATION, ECONOMY AND THE MANAGEMENT OF NATURE

The Long Duration Exposure Facility (LDEF) satellite, which was deployed from the space shuttle *Challenger* on 7 April, 1984, was designed to test the long-term effects of exposure to space conditions on electronic systems. The recent development of communications satellites has revolutionized global communications.

WHETHER WE THINK 1917 a more important turning-point than 1919, or that the start of Japanese aggression in Manchuria in 1931 registers more of a new departure than the invasion of Poland in 1939, does not much matter; during the twentieth century history moved into a new phase. Politically, we could call it post-European, in that after 1945 no sensible person could deny that the days of political or military domination of the world by the great powers of Europe were over. But something else has also become clear: the world is one as never before. Events and trends interact more than ever; communications tie human beings together with a new closeness and rapidity. This partly explains and partly exemplifies a common human civilization, now shared more widely than any civilization hitherto, but still bearing the marks of its European origins.

WORLD HEGEMONY

GLOBAL INTERACTION ought by now to be merely a commonplace, yet it can still surprise us. Motorists may have got used to sudden rises in the price of petrol if there is an emergency in the Middle East, but not long ago it would still have been incredible that – say – Indians should demonstrate about something going on in the South Pacific, or that a Chinese government should feel concerned by an Arab-Israeli war. Yet now almost anything that happens anywhere in the world may very rapidly produce effects elsewhere, and most of our leaders seem to recognize this, whether they do so because of ideology, calculation, or just simple fear.

Some of the world's new interconnectedness arises from greater economic and technological interdependence, and the faster exchange of information which goes with that. At a more fundamental level, there is a worldwide, still unrolling, change of attitudes. It marks a reversal of what went on for most of the thousands of years of prehistory and history already dealt with in this book. Once humanity was liberated in prehistoric times by its first primitive technologies from the simplest and most crushing restraints, it

wandered for thousands of years along paths which diverged into increasingly different ways of life. The paths started slowly to converge again, a few centuries ago, when there began to spread from Europe a process which has various names and has been interpreted in many ways, but which is often called modernization. Since 1945, it looks as if it is the dominant theme of world history. The paths have come together again, and people are beginning to act accordingly.

MODERNIZATION

Of course no absolute statements can be made in general terms. We must not exaggerate the extent of change in many parts of the world. The richest and the poorest societies are now more obviously different than they have ever been. Great cultures and traditions still cling to their own values and ways of life, sensing threats in the individualism and hedonism which came from Europe even when often they were cloaked in otherwise desirable change. They seek, often successfully, to preserve social disciplines which, however harsh, they still find acceptable. Yet, when all is said and done, it remains true that because of the political supremacy Europeans established in the eighteenth and nineteenth centuries, and the technological advances, especially in communications, which followed, more common experiences and assumptions are now shared more widely than ever before.

In defiance of the homogenizing effect of the global mass media, many countries are now experiencing a reaffirmation of cultural traditions. The geishas in Japan, who are currently enjoying a resurgence in popularity, are a good example of this phenomenon.

Modernization has usually looked attractive because it promised wealth. Optimism about material progress and the possibility of improvement has now spread worldwide from its origins in eighteenth-century Europe, thanks to a golden age of wealth creation in the last couple of centuries. An immense increase in the consumption of resources provided unambiguous evidence of humanity's material betterment; there were more human beings, and most of them were living longer, than ever before. For all the notorious pockets of degradation and poverty which remained (or were created), the human race seemed to be able to make a greater success

Time chart (1900–1969)

		1903 First flight of the Wright brothers' aeroplane	1905 Einstein's special theory of relativity	1916 Einstein's general theory of relativity	1953 Discovery of the structure of DNA	1957 The USSR launches Sputnik I
	1900				1950	
		1900 Quantum theory, Planck	1904 Pavlov is awarded Nobel prize for physiology or medicine		1938 Discovery of nuclear fission	1969 The first manned moon landing

than ever before of the business of living on this planet. Only in the last couple of decades has anyone begun to worry much about the costs of this and what it might portend.

CONFLICT AND PEACE AROUND THE WORLD

For most of the last half-century, issues other than those we now call "environmental" have been far more worrying. One is the fragility of peace. Yet since 1945 the major powers have avoided fighting one another openly, unlikely though this sometimes seemed. On the other hand, for all the hopes and rhetoric swirling about the infant United Nations Organization, nations belonging to it went to war many times. There has been no return to what from this distance seems the Augustan calm of late nineteenth-century international relations. We have frequent enough reminders, moreover, of persistent divisions within humanity, and

enough evidence of new ones appearing, to make the world still appear dangerously unstable. Nationality, ideology and economic interest still fragment it. Yet this, too, is a view from a particular perspective. There are others. The Second World War released many currents and some of them have yet to run their full course. Judgments in the last quarter-century have sometimes had to change almost day by day. The war in the Middle East in 1973 was from one point of view just another of many indecisive conflicts following the collapse of Ottoman Empire; in another perspective, it was the first to reveal a reversal of the relations of some great industrial societies to the Islamic world because of dependence on its oil. After another decade, that reversal again seemed less permanent and important; the view had changed once more. Then came the Gulf crisis of 1990 and the most recent war of the Ottoman succession. All we can do in looking at near-contemporary history is to try to understand its changes historically. That

From the Second World War weapons scientists have worked for governments around the world to create ever more powerful arms guided by increasingly sophisticated control systems. Here, anti-aircraft and tracer bullets fired by Iraq illuminate the skies of Baghdad during the Gulf War in 1991. During this conflict American missiles pin-pointed specific targets with unprecedented accuracy.

Hungry children wait to receive food from foreign aid agencies in Somalia, where civil war and famine brought immense suffering to the country's population of seven million during the last decade of the 20th century.

may help to make the overwhelming rush of events just a little more comprehensible.

THE GROWTH OF THE WORLD POPULATION

IN 1974 THE FIRST WORLD CONFERENCE on population ever held met in Romania; uneasiness about its future had for the first time persuaded the human race to unite to consider the demographic outlook. The unwilled, seemingly uncontrollable and accelerating rise in world population which has gone on for the last couple of centuries is now seen to be a global problem, even if much about its exact nature remains uncertain.

Accuracy in computing populations is still a highly relative business. We can only estimate to within one or two hundred millions how many people are now alive. None the

less, the likely degree of error is not such that our estimates significantly distort what has happened. In round numbers, a world population of about seven hundred and twenty million in 1750 more than doubled by 1900, when it stood at about sixteen hundred million. Thus about eight hundred and fifty million had been added to it over a century and a half. It then took fifty years to add the next eight hundred and fifty million and somewhat more; by 1950 the population of the world stood at about two thousand five hundred million. Even more striking, the next eight hundred and fifty million were added by the middle of the 1960s, in less than twenty years. Now the total is over five thousand million. Though it had taken at least fifty thousand years for *Homo sapiens* to number one thousand million (a figure reached in 1840 or thereabouts) the last one thousand million of the species has been added in only

A government propaganda poster in Chengdu, China, advocates family planning and endorses the state's one-child-per-family policy, which was launched to control the growth of the country's huge population.

fifteen years or so to a total which has grown faster and faster. Though growth rates in some countries have fallen since the 1960s, up-to-date estimates still say the human race is growing by 1.63 per cent per year; that means it will probably number just under six thousand million before the end of the twentieth century.

ATTEMPTS TO LIMIT POPULATION GROWTH

The current rapid rate of population growth is alarming. The spectre of Malthusian disaster has been revived. Fortunately, as Malthus himself observed, "no estimate of future population or depopulation, formed from any existing rate of increase or decrease, can be depended upon". We cannot be sure what might change or modify such an acceleration. Some societies have now accepted the possibility of conscious control of their shape and size, for instance. Strictly, this is not a new idea; in some places murder and abortion have long been customary ways of keeping down demands on scarce resources. Babies were exposed to die in medieval Japan; female infanticide was widespread in India a century and a half ago and has emerged again (or perhaps been acknowledged again) in recent years in China. What is new is that in some countries governments are now putting resources and authority behind more humane means of population control. Their aim is new: positive economic improvement instead of just the avoidance of family and personal disaster.

DIFFERENCES IN GROWTH RATES

Not all governments make efforts to control population. This is a negative aspect of the complex truth that population growth, though worldwide, does not everywhere take the same form nor produce the same effects. Though many non-European countries have followed the pattern of nineteenth-century Europe (in first showing a fall in death rates without a corresponding fall in birth rates) it would be rash to prophesy that they will go on to repeat the next phase of the population history of developed countries. We cannot simply expect a pattern of declining natality shown in one place or one society to be repeated elsewhere. But nor can we expect that it will not be. The dynamics of population growth or decline are exceedingly complex. They reflect limits set by ignorance, and by social and personal attitudes, and these are hard to measure, let alone manipulate.

At present it looks as if there is plenty of scope in many countries for things to go on for some time much as at present. At the very least, some poor countries cannot for a long time hope to achieve demographic equilibrium. Natality only began to drop in the last century when prosperity in a few countries made it attractive to large numbers of men and women to have smaller families; few of today's fast-growing countries are yet anywhere near that point. Further medical, nutritional and sanitary progress may make things much worse. The advances have been colossal since the nineteenth century, yet there are many places where they have yet to cut into mortality as dramatically as they did in Europe between 1800 and 1900. When they do so, humanity's numbers will probably rise faster still.

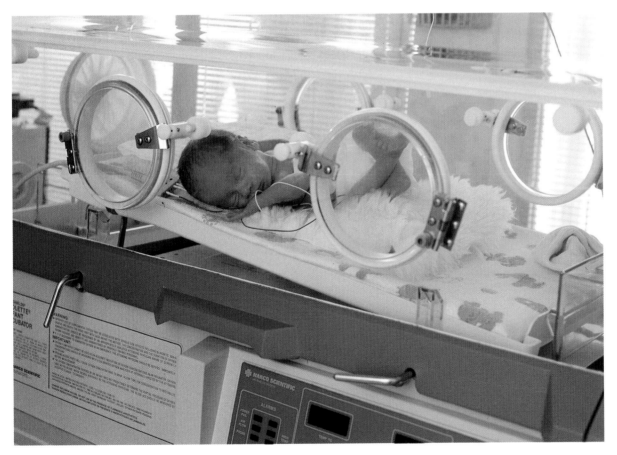

Technological advances in post-natal care have contributed to the fall in the infant mortality rate in the developed world. This premature baby is being kept alive in an incubator in a modern intensive care unit. Between 5 and 10 per cent of all babies born in developed countries are now born before 37 weeks' gestation. Of babies born at 28 weeks' gestation and given specialist care, around 80 per cent survive.

Infant mortality is one of the most expressive indicators of the socio-economic level of a country. In the least developed countries, particularly in central Africa, infant death rates are as high as 126 per thousand. This child, suffering from dehydration, was photographed in a refugee camp in drought-ridden Somalia, Africa, in 1995.

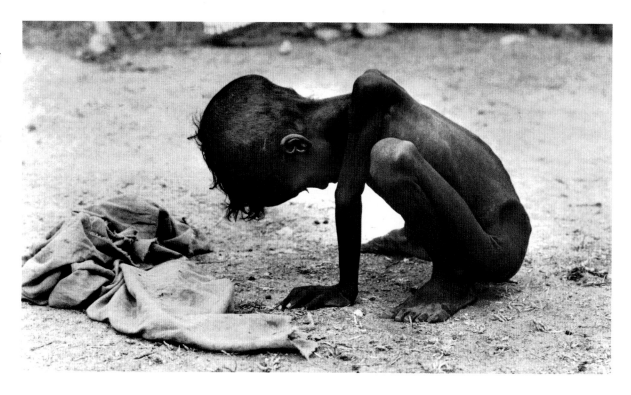

LIFE EXPECTANCY PATTERNS

One rough indicator of potential for future growth is infant mortality. In the century before 1970 this fell dramatically from an average of about 225 per thousand live births to under 20 in developed countries; in 1988 the comparative figures for Bangladesh and Japan were 118 and 5. Such discrepancies continue to exist – and they are much greater than in the past – between poor and rich countries. There are comparable differences in life expectancy, too. In developed countries, life expectancy at birth rose from rather more than 40 in 1870 to slightly over 70 a hundred years later. It now shows a remarkable evenness. Life expectancy at birth in the United States, Great Britain and the USSR in 1987, for example, was 76, 75 and 70 years respectively; the differences were negligible by comparison with Ethiopia (41), or even India (58). Yet even the Indian baby faces prospects enormously better than those of Indian babies at the beginning of this century – let alone those of French babies in 1789. It is unlikely that the steam will go out of population growth while there are still such good prospects of improvement.

In the immediate future, this will present different problems in different places. For most of human history, all societies resembled pyramids, with very large numbers of young people and a few old. Now, developed societies are beginning to look like slowly tapering columns; the proportion of older people is bigger than in the past. The reverse is true in poorer countries. Over half Kenya's

Population distribution

At the beginning of 1990, world population was distributed roughly as follows:

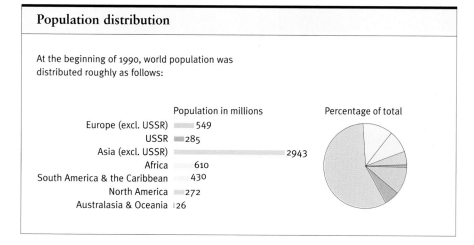

	Population in millions	Percentage of total
Europe (excl. USSR)	549	
USSR	285	
Asia (excl. USSR)	2943	
Africa	610	
South America & the Caribbean	430	
North America	272	
Australasia & Oceania	26	

population is under 15, and two-thirds of China's is under 33. What this implies is too complicated for discussion here, but it shows that overall population growth is a somewhat obscuring notion. Although the world's population goes on growing mightily, it does so in ways which have different origins and produce very different historical effects.

POPULATION DISTRIBUTION

Among the various historical effects of population growth are big changes in the way population is shared. The fall from Europe's mid-nineteenth century quarter-share of world population is striking. Until the 1920s moreover, Europe was still exporting a lot of manpower overseas, notably to the Americas. This emigration was cut down by restrictions on entry to United States in the 1920s, dwindled even more during the world depression, and has never since recovered its former importance. On the other hand, immigration to the United States from the Caribbean, Central and South America, and Asia has surged upwards in the last two decades. Meanwhile, though some European countries still sent out many emigrants (in the early 1970s more Britons still left their country each year than were needed to balance an inflow from abroad), they also began from the 1950s onwards to attract North Africans, Turks, Asians and West Indians seeking work they could not find at home.

AREAS WITH THE FASTEST GROWTH

Present world patterns are not likely to be unchanged for long. Asia now contains over half of humanity and China one-fifth of it, but huge as are the growth rates which have

produced these populations, others leave them behind. If world population increase averages out at about 1.6 per cent per annum, that of Brazil, for example, was running at more than twice this rate in the early 1960s. In other Latin American countries, though standards of living and life expectancy are

Population density

The world's most heavily populated region is Asia, with the highest population density occurring on the islands of Macao, Singapore and Hong Kong. Life expectancy is highest in wealthy, industrialized countries, where infant mortality rates are also the lowest. Life expectancy is shortest in developing countries, which have the highest infant mortality rates.

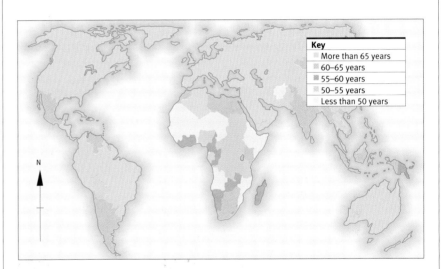

Worldwide life expectancy in 1900–1995: the average lifespan in years is given.

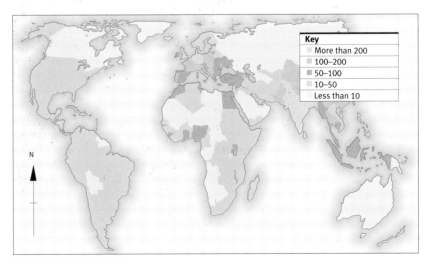

Worldwide population density in 1993: the number of people per square km is given.

still not very much better than the European levels early in this century, high growth has continued. Birth-rates have kept up, and so have multiplied the effect of even modest falls in death-rates. The long resistance of the Roman Catholic Church to contraception and legal abortion is not the whole explanation. The attitudes of Latin American males and the social disciplines which impose large families on Latin American women – who are, because of these same disciplines, often unquestioningly complaisant – have very

complex historical sources. The most threatening growth rates of all are to be found in the Islamic world; Jordan's annual rate is 3.9 per cent and present projections imply a doubling of population in sixteen years, while Iran grows at 3.5 and the much smaller Saudi population at 5.6 per cent.

POPULATION CONTROL THROUGH CONTRACEPTION

Where conscious attempts are made by governments to stem population growth it is hard (and perhaps too soon) to guess at the likely outcome. For a long time, Communist states did not warm to the ideas of population stabilization or reduction, but, though with very different historical backgrounds, both China and the Soviet Union began in the 1960s to try to control population growth by encouraging people to delay marriage and have smaller families. China has had some success, using legal regulation, tax incentives and social pressure, but found the unacceptable practice of female infanticide reappearing as a result. In some other poor countries propaganda for contraception, the Western answer to overpopulation, has been tried but no general conclusions emerge about results. In India large sums have been spent, but seemingly not to much effect. Neither revolutionized by industrialization (as was Japan) nor by a political attack on its traditional institutions (as was China), India is still a predominantly agrarian society. Both British and later Indian government has long been respectful of its social traditions. This has protected a conservatism in ideas and institutions which makes population control very difficult. One example is the survival, outside a tiny minority among India's élites, of a vast and traditional inequality in the status and employment prospects of men and women.

Contraception

For centuries, because infant mortality rates were generally high, governments never saw a need to lower the birth-rate through artificial means.

After the Second World War, when more Western women were working, the average number of children per family began to fall. Medical advances have since widened the range of contraceptive methods available, mainly for women. Among others, the contraceptive pill, intrauterine devices (IUD), diaphragms and spermicidal creams have allowed couples to chose when to start a family and how many children they want to have. The use of these methods has caused a marked fall in the birth-rate in several countries in the developed world. However, in some developing countries, such as India or China, the birth-rate remains extremely high, in spite of government campaigns to limit the number of children born and attempts to make family planning advice and contraception available to everyone.

This maternity hospital in Shanghai, China, provides women with information about family planning methods.

Were attitudes towards women which are taken for granted in Europe or North America (and frequently denounced there as inadequate) even slightly more prevalent in India, they would be likely to raise dramatically the average age of women at marriage, and therefore to reduce the number of children in the average family. But such a change would presuppose fundamental and improbable revolution in Indian life, in the provision of new opportunities of employment and in the redistribution of authority inside the family and village, a much more radical break with India's past than independence in 1947. No country should be expected easily to shake off so much. No great tradition of civilization can be got rid of painlessly.

Perhaps, though, we need not be too gloomy. A solution to population growth may after all be found along the lines of Western experience, where mortality has tended to fall as economic well-being improved. India, unfortunately, has not been able to generate much improvement in the economic lot of her peoples since independence, but even in Latin America, there is evidence that economic growth has been followed by at least the beginning of a decline in natality. There is still a huge revolutionary power in the expanding, developing civilization of the European tradition; however it is packaged, it is the most powerful solvent of traditional structures history can show. A change in population structure in one way or another seems as unavoidable a concomitant of that civilization as the weakening of religious culture, the building of factories or the liberation of women – and the list can be hugely extended.

POPULATION AND POWER

Differences of population, and changes in those differences, affect the comparative

strengths of nations. They are not, of course, simply translatable into differences of power. Resources and culture also come into the matter, and power for one purpose is not always power for another. None the less, population and power are related. At the end of 1988, West Germany, with 61 million, was the most populous European country. On any reckoning, the list of the ten most populous states at that time contains the three most

In many parts of the Indian subcontinent, the status of women has remained practically unchanged for centuries. Age-old traditions govern expectations of behaviour. This young Indian dancer is from Jaipur.

India was the second most populous state in the world in the late 1980s and, according to UN forecasts, it will remain so until at least the year 2000. Pictured here are some of the millions of Hindu pilgrims who travel to the Ganges and Yamuna rivers each year to purify their souls by bathing in the sacred waters.

powerful countries in the world. China, now again part of a world which she long shunned, is bound to be a great power on grounds of population alone, for in a sense she is militarily unbeatable. Her social revolution has begun to increase her wealth, too, whereas the obstacle to some other highly populated countries becoming very powerful is a poverty which looks unsurmountable, whether it is absolute, in the sense that natural resources are poor (Bangladesh), or relative, in that they are swallowed by population growth which is too fast (India and, until recently, Indonesia) and has overtaken the cashing of the cheque of aid from abroad and the reaping of the reward of improved technology and planned investment. Newly generated wealth has simply been consumed. It is not easy, though, to generalize. In the early 1970s India was thought to be about to enter a period of self-sufficiency in food. Her agricultural output had doubled between 1948 and 1973. Yet this increase in wealth only just succeeded in holding the line for a population growing by a million a month.

WORLD RESOURCES

Rapid population growth is itself revealing of another fact: greater world resources. The

The ten most populous states in 1988

At the end of 1988 the ten most populous states were roughly as shown:

Population in millions

State	Population
China	1104
India	796
USSR	283
USA	246
Indonesia	175
Brazil	144
Japan	123
Pakistan	105
Nigeria	105
Bangladesh	104

world's gross output of food has risen dramatically. Though many have starved, more have lived. Though millions have died in local famines, there has been (so far) no worldwide disaster. If the world had not been able to feed a growing population human numbers would be smaller. Whether this can continue is another matter. Yet experts have concluded that we shall be able for a considerable time to come to feed our growing numbers. Some hope that population policies could be effectively introduced to stabilize demand in relation to sustainable levels of supply while there is still time. In such matters, we enter the realms of speculation. Only the very existence of such hopes and aspirations should concern the historians, for they say something about what is – about the present and actual state of the world, where what is believed to be possible is a very important factor in determining what can happen. In considering how those hopes and aspirations have come to be we can direct our attention to another phenomenon of the last half-century: it was an age of unprecedented economic growth.

ECONOMIC GROWTH

MANY READERS OF THIS BOOK will have seen, perhaps often, television pictures of harrowing details of famine and deprivation. Yet since 1945, at least in the developed world, economic growth has come to be taken for granted. It has there become the "norm", in spite of hiccups and interruptions along the way, and the result is that even a slowing-down in its rate now occasions alarm. What is more, as population growth shows, there has been real economic growth in gross terms in much of the "underdeveloped" world, too. Against the background of the 1930s, this can be considered a revolution, though the story does not in fact begin

Worldwide daily calorie intake in 1992

Africa and South America, which contain the world's largest areas of arable land, also have, proportionally, the smallest areas of land under cultivation. If present economic and socio-political obstacles could be removed in those regions – and if suitable farming methods were applied – the land available would be capable of providing 4,000–5,000 calories per person per day to ten times the world's present population.

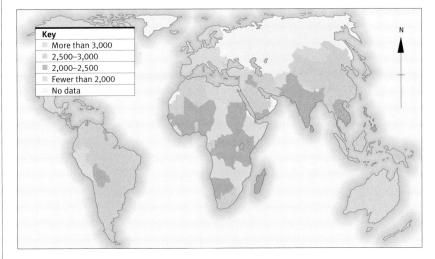

This map shows the average daily calorie intake per person.

at the end of the Second World War. The decades since 1950 have been a golden age of growth, but the appropriate context in which to understand the unprecedented wealth production which has so far successfully carried the burden of world population growth is the whole twentieth century. Since 1900, there has been an increase in the world's wealth only briefly and locally interrupted by two world wars and, between them, a major worldwide setback, above all in the world economic depression of the 1930s. In 1945 wealth creation was resumed and has since barely ceased (though it greatly slowed in some countries after 1975), even under the impact of the most serious tests and even allowing for notable contrasts between different economies in the developed world. The overall rate of growth has now slowed from its peaks in the 1950s and 1960s, but the trend has continued upward.

THE DIFFERENTIATION OF WEALTH

In spite of huge disparities and setbacks affecting some countries more than others, this growth has been widely shared. Gross Domestic Product (GDP) has risen almost everywhere since 1960, and often it has risen per capita, too. The world has become much richer, whatever the differential rates at which new wealth has been created and distributed. Some countries remain woefully poor. In 1988, Afghanistan, Madagascar, Laos, Tanzania, Ethiopia, Cambodia and Mozambique all had a GDP per capita of less than $150.

The major fact none the less remains that of wealth creation. The beginnings of a general explanation of a growing abundance must be the long peace between major industrial powers. The fact that the decades since 1945 have been studded by smaller-scale or incipient conflicts, that men and women have

been killed in warlike operations on every day of them, that great powers have often had surrogates to do their fighting for them, and that there have been long periods of international tension, does not affect this. No such destruction of human and material capital as that of 1914–18 and 1939–45 has taken place. International rivalry, instead, has in fact sustained economic activity in many countries, provoked it in others. It has provided much technological spin-off, and has led to major capital investments and transfers for political motives, many of which have provided increased real wealth.

THE WORLD ECONOMIC ORDER

The first transfers of capital came about in the later 1940s, when American aid made possible the recovery of Europe as a major world centre of industrial production. For this to be successful, of course, the American

In countries such as Somalia and Rwanda in Africa, tribal warfare has compounded food shortages, created thousands of displaced refugees and destroyed the already fragile national economies. This Rwandan child, whose parents lie dead behind him, was photographed in a refugee camp in neighbouring Zaire in 1994.

dynamo had to be there to power recovery. The enormous wartime expansion of the American economy which had brought it out of the pre-war depression, together with the immunity of the American home base from physical damage by war, had ensured that it would be. They had rebuilt American economic strength. Explanation for its deployment as aid has to be sought in a complex of other factors. They include the international circumstances (of which the Cold War was an important part) which made it seem in America's interest to behave as she did; an imaginative grasp of opportunities by many of her statesmen and businessmen, the absence for a long time of any alternative source of capital on such a scale, and the wisdom of many men of different nations who, even before the end of the war, had tried to set in place institutions for cooperation in regulating the international economy. They were determined to avoid a return to the near-fatal economic anarchy of the 1930s. Their efforts produced the International Monetary Fund, the World Bank and the General Agreement on Tariffs and Trade (GATT). Much of the successful recovery of the non-Communist world after 1945 (and therefore of the remarkable growth which followed) is attributable to

Worldwide Gross Domestic Product

Defined as the total market value of the final goods and services produced per year, GDP is a useful estimate of a country's prosperity. While most world trade remains that in manufactured goods (57 per cent in 1992), since 1960 the fastest growing section of GDP is the service sector (21 per cent), almost equivalent to the volume of trade in food and raw materials (22 per cent).

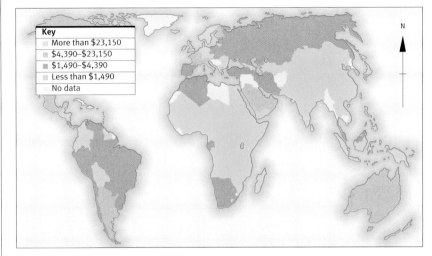

Key
- More than $23,150
- $4,390–$23,150
- $1,490–$4,390
- Less than $1,490
- No data

This map shows worldwide Gross Domestic Product per capita in US dollars in 1993.

these institutions. The economic stability which they provided underpinned two decades of growth in world trade at nearly 7 per cent per annum in real terms. Between 1945 and the 1980s the average level of tariffs on manufactured goods fell from 40 per cent to 5 per cent, and world trade multiplied

Changes in GDP in the 20th century

Recent calculations provide the following examples of the change in GDP per capita (in terms of 1988 US dollars) over this century:

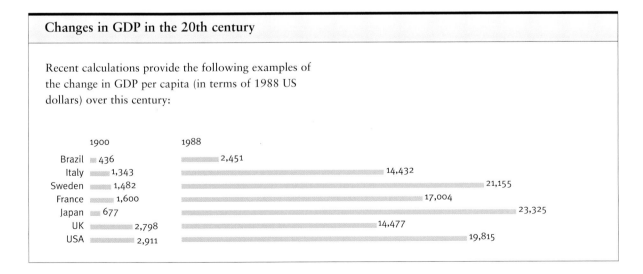

	1900	1988
Brazil	436	2,451
Italy	1,343	14,432
Sweden	1,482	21,155
France	1,600	17,004
Japan	677	23,325
UK	2,798	14,477
USA	2,911	19,815

Pictured are the logos of the World Bank (top) and the International Monetary Fund.

more than fivefold. These institutions have substituted a degree of management and regulation for the reliance on "natural" economic harmony which was the basis of the pre-1914 economic order, and for the virtual absence of order between 1914 and 1945. This does not mean they can solve all the world's economic problems, but that economic order can at least be improved.

SCIENTIFIC PROGRESS

ANOTHER DECISIVE CONTRIBUTION of human agency to economic growth was less formal, often less visible, and has been made over a much longer term. It was provided by scientists and engineers. The continued application of scientific knowledge through technology, and the improvement and rationalization of processes and systems in the search for greater efficiency, were all visible before 1939. They came dramatically to the fore and began to exercise a quite new order of influence after 1945.

ADVANCES IN AGRICULTURE

Agriculture, where improvement had begun long before industrialization itself was a recognizable phenomenon, may well be the best example of the successful application of scientific knowledge. For thousands of years farmers edged their returns upwards almost entirely by clearing and breaking in new land. There is still a lot left which, with proper investment, can be made to raise crops (and much has been done in the last twenty-five years to use such land, even in a crowded country like India). Yet it is not by such means that world agriculture output has recently risen so dramatically. The root explanation is a continuation of the

agricultural revolution which began in early modern Europe, and has been visible at least from the seventeenth century. Two hundred and fifty years later, it was speeding up at an accelerating rate.

Well before 1939, wheat was being successfully introduced to lands in which, for climatic reasons, it had not been grown hitherto. This was increasingly thanks to work by plant geneticists who evolved new strains of cereals, one of the first twentieth-century scientific contributions to agriculture comparable in effect to the trial-and-error "improvement" of earlier times. Even greater contributions to world food supplies were to come from existing grain-growing areas, thanks to better chemical fertilizers. An unprecedented rate of replacement of nitrogen in the soil is the basic explanation of the huge yields which have now become commonplace in countries with advanced agriculture. They have their costs. A huge energy input is now needed to sustain the productivity of advanced Western agriculture, and some other ecological consequences are only just beginning to emerge.

Fertilizers are only one theme in the story of continuing agricultural innovation. Effective herbicides and insecticides began to be available commercially in the 1940s and 1950s. At the same time the use of machinery in agriculture grew enormously in developed countries. England had in 1939 the most mechanized farming in the world in terms of horsepower per acre cultivated. English farmers none the less then still did much of their work with horses, while combine harvesters (already common in the United States) were rare. Working horses are now preserved only as interesting curiosities in countries of advanced agriculture – though there has been some reintroduction of them for certain types of work where the rising cost of fuel does not justify the use of a tractor as a prime mover.

But the fields are not the only part of the farm to be mechanized. The coming of electricity has brought automatic milking, grain-drying, threshing, the heating of animal sheds in winter. Now, the computer and automation have begun to reduce dependence on human labour even more; in both the United States and Western Europe the agricultural workforce has continued to fall while production per acre has risen.

DISPARITIES IN AGRICULTURAL PRODUCTION LEVELS

Paradoxically, there are probably more subsistence farmers in the world today than in 1900. This is because there are more people. Their relative share of cultivated land and of the value of what is produced has fallen. In Europe, peasants – cultivators of tiny farms –

are fast disappearing, as they disappeared in Great Britain two hundred years ago. But this change is unevenly spread and easily disrupted. Russia was traditionally one of the great agricultural economies, but as recently as 1947 suffered famine so severe as once more to provoke outbreaks of cannibalism. Local disasters are not likely to cease in countries with large and rapidly growing populations where subsistence agriculture is the norm and productivity remains low. Just before the First World War, the British yield of wheat per acre was already more than two and a half times that of India; by 1968 it was roughly five times. Over the same period the Americans raised their rice yield from 4.25 to nearly 12 tons an acre, while that of Burma, the "rice bowl of Asia", rose only from 3.8 to 4.2. Another way of looking at these facts is to consider how many families can be provided for by one agricultural worker in

An aerial view of a farm in the Lancaster region of Pennsylvania, which boasts the most productive farming land in the United States. Most North American commercial farms are highly mechanized. Reliance on improved irrigation techniques, fertilizers, seed selection and crop rotation have all contributed to a considerable increase in productivity, while enabling farmers to prevent soil erosion.

Bolivian Aymara women are pictured working in the fields. The Aymara live in the Titicaca plateau in the central Andes, where the soil is poor and the climate harsh. Hard labour in difficult conditions is required to raise their staple crops, which include potatoes, maize, beans and wheat.

Water shortage is one of the basic causes of suffering in many developing countries, where drought, for example, can easily cause famine. The creation of water distribution systems can radically improve the lives of people in villages such as this one in Ethiopia.

different countries. In 1968 the answer for Egypt was slightly more than one, while for New Zealand the figure was over forty.

The most advanced agricultural practice is found in countries advanced in other ways. Unless they have a special mineral resource (like oil) or a particular agricultural speciality, countries where there is most need to improve agricultural productivity have often found it very difficult to produce crops more cheaply than can the leading industrial countries. Ironic paradoxes result; the Russians, Indians and Chinese, big grain and rice producers, have found themselves buying American and

Canadian wheat. Disparities between developed and undeveloped countries have widened in the decades of plenty.

THE USE OF RESOURCES

The most striking measure of the difference between developed and undeveloped countries is relative consumption of the world's resources. Roughly half of humanity consumes about six-sevenths of the world's production; the other half shares the rest. Moreover, even among the wealthy nations there are wide disparities. In 1970 there were about six Americans in every hundred human beings, but they used about forty of every hundred barrels of oil produced in the world. They each consumed roughly a quarter-ton of paper products a year; the corresponding figure for China was about twenty pounds. The electrical energy used by China for all purposes in a year at that time would (it was said) just sustain the supply of power to the United States' air conditioners. Electricity production, indeed, is one of the best ways of making the point, since relatively little electrical power is traded internationally and most of it is consumed in the country where it is generated. At the end of the 1980s, the United States produced nearly 40 times as much electricity per capita as India, 23 times as much as China, but only 1.3 times as much as Switzerland.

RICH AND POOR

In all parts of the world the disparity between rich and poor nations has grown more and more marked since 1945, not usually because the poor have grown poorer, but because the rich have grown much richer. Almost the only exception to this was to be found in the

This timber processing plant, in Port Angeles in the United States, produces wood chips, wood pulp and paper from logs. North America is one of the world's largest consumers of wood and paper products. Only recently has public awareness of the environmental cost of deforestation led to the creation of large-scale paper-recycling projects in Western countries.

comparatively rich (by poor world standards) economies of the USSR and Eastern Europe where mismanagement and the exigencies of a command economy held back growth and so narrowed the gap between those economies and poorer but developing countries. With these exceptions, even spectacular accelerations of production (some Asian countries, for example, pushed up their agricultural production between 1952 and 1970 proportionately more than Europe and much more than North America) have rarely succeeded in improving the position of poor countries in relation to that of the rich, because of the problems posed by rising populations – and rich countries, in any case, began at a higher level. As a result, though their ranking in relation to one another may have changed, those countries which enjoyed the highest standards of living in 1950 still, by and large, enjoy them today, though they

The Asian–African Conference, 1955

"The Asian–African Conference recommended: the early establishment of the Special United Nations Fund for Economic Development; the allocation by the International Bank for Reconstruction and Development of a greater part of its resources to Asian–African countries; the early establishment of the International Finance Corporation which should include in its activities the undertaking of equity investment, and encouragement to the promotion of joint ventures among Asian–African countries in so far as this will promote their common interest."

Para. A3 of the Final Communiqué of the Asian–African Conference, which was held in Bandung, Indonesia, 18–24 April, 1955.

World energy resources

Of world production of raw minerals, 80 per cent is concentrated in just 20 countries. The main importers are Japan, the USA and Western Europe, the latter importing more than two-thirds of what it consumes. The main exporters are in Latin America, Africa, the Middle East, Southeast Asia and Russia. Exported products include crude oil, iron, copper, tin, phosphates and coal.

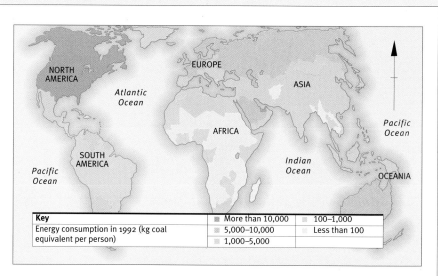

Key		
Energy consumption in 1992 (kg coal equivalent per person)	▨ More than 10,000	▨ 100–1,000
	▨ 5,000–10,000	☐ Less than 100
	▨ 1,000–5,000	

World production of fuel and energy in 1993

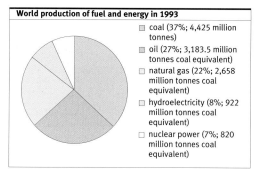

☐ coal (37%; 4,425 million tonnes)

☐ oil (27%; 3,183.5 million tonnes coal equivalent)

☐ natural gas (22%; 2,658 million tonnes coal equivalent)

☐ hydroelectricity (8%; 922 million tonnes coal equivalent)

☐ nuclear power (7%; 820 million tonnes coal equivalent)

Production and consumption of energy by region in 1992

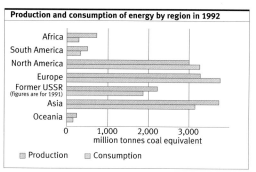

☐ Production   ☐ Consumption

The above map shows the use of the world's energy resources; the pie chart (left) shows world production of fuel and energy; the bar chart (right) shows the production and consumption of energy by region (million tonnes coal equivalent).

have been joined by Japan. These are the major industrial countries. In the great acceleration of wealth production, manufacturing industry has played the major role. The manufacturing economies are today the richest per capita, and their example spurs poorer countries to seek their own salvation in industrialization. In 1970 three of the great industrial agglomerations of the world were still, as they had been in 1939, the United States, Europe and Russia; a fourth was Japan, in 1939 already the most important Asian industrial society. By 1990, though, the picture had changed somewhat. While the USSR was still one of the big four,

it had fallen far behind the others and even behind one of the nations making up the West European industrial agglomeration, West Germany.

INDUSTRIAL CHANGE

COMPARISONS HAVE become more difficult. Major industrial economies today do not much resemble their nineteenth-century predecessors. The old heavy and manufacturing industries, which long provided the backbone of economic strength, are no longer a simple and satisfactory measure of it. Once-staple industries of leading countries have declined in importance. Of the three major steel-making countries of 1900, the first two (the USA and West Germany) were still among the first five world producers eighty years later, but in third and fifth places respectively; the United Kingdom (third in 1900) came tenth in the same world table – with Spain, Romania and Brazil close on her heels. In 1982, Poland made more steel than had the USA in 1900. What is more, newer industries often found a better environment for rapid growth in some developing countries than in the mature economies. It was in this way that the peoples of Taiwan and South Korea came by 1988 to enjoy per capita GDP of, in the first instance, nearly eighteen times that of India, and, in the second, more than fifteen times.

Modern industrial societies are much more than simple extrapolations in technology and structure from the past. Much of the economic growth of rich countries has been in industries – electronics and plastics are examples – which barely existed even in 1945. Coal, which replaced running water and wood in the nineteenth century as the major source of industrial energy, was long before 1939 joined by hydroelectricity, oil and natural gas; very recently, power generated by nuclear fission has been added to these.

THE MOTOR CAR ECONOMY

Industrial growth has raised standards of living by providing cheaper power and materials for the production of goods. Improving transport has further lowered costs indirectly. An enormous growth in the production of commodities directly for the use and pleasure of the consumer was the result. Often the ramifications were enormous and one example must suffice. In 1885 there appeared the first vehicle propelled by an internal-combustion engine – one, that is to say, in which the energy produced by heat was used directly to drive a piston inside the cylinder of an engine instead of being transmitted via steam made with an external flame. Nine years later came a four-wheeled contraption which is a recognizable ancestor of the modern car. It was the French Panhard, and France and Germany

A solar power station produces electricity in California in the United States. Wind and wave power can also now be used to generate electricity.

History of the automobile

In the 20th century, the car took the place of the train as the vital means of transport in the developed world. Once the internal combustion engine had been patented, Carl Friedrich Benz applied it, in 1885, to a tricycle with a top speed of 10 mph (15 km/h) – the design of the automobile soon followed.

Automobiles first became popular in the United States, and from the start Detroit was the headquarters of the most important automobile manufacturers. Since the appearance of early models, such as the Ford Model T in the United States, car design has undergone huge changes: ever higher speeds and increased braking power have been achieved, and the vast range of models now on the market would have been unimaginable at the beginning of the 20th century.

One of the most remarkable recent changes in the car industry is the growing concern for driver and passenger safety. Companies now compete to offer features such as air bags and automatic braking systems. Cars designed to give drivers better visibility in the dark (using special night-vision cameras combined with the latest computer technology) will soon be available.

The Ford car factory, seen here in 1913, was the world's first assembly line.

kept a lead in producing cars in the next decade or so. When the first motor show was held in London in 1896 cars were still few, and rich men's toys. This was automobile pre-history. Automobile history began in the United States when Henry Ford in 1907 set up a production line for his Model T. He deliberately planned for a mass market. His car was to be sold at an unprecedentedly low price – $950. Demand rose so rapidly that by 1915 a million Ford cars were made each year. The price came down and by 1926 the Model T sold for less than $300. An enormous success was under way, and a great social change with it. Ford had provided for the masses something previously regarded as a luxury. There are now more cars than households in the United States. Ford changed the world, and perhaps as much as had the coming of the railways in the nineteenth century. His car gave people of modest incomes a mobility unavailable even to millionaires fifty years earlier. This huge increase in amenity was to spread round the globe.

WORLDWIDE CAR MANUFACTURING

The coming of the mass motor car also changed history in other ways, and a long view is necessary to understand this. By the 1980s, a worldwide car manufacturing industry existed, in which international integration had gone very far and, in some countries, virtually dominated the manufacturing sector. Eight large producers now account for nearly three out of four of the world's cars. One country, Japan, could attribute a major part of its rise to economic ascendancy in the 1960s and 1970s to its car industry but was already, by 1990, consciously running it down at home in anticipation of new challengers abroad. The car industry stimulated major investment in other industries; today half the robots employed in the world's industry are welders in car factories (another quarter are painters in them). Meanwhile, over a much longer term, Ford's popularization of the car helped to stimulate a rising demand for oil, though this was already apparent before 1914, as more ships became oil-powered, and now transport is no longer oil's only major consumer. Huge numbers of people came to be employed in the supply of fuel and services to car owners. Investment in road-building – and later in arrangements for parking – became a major concern of government, both local and national, and profoundly affected the construction industry.

THE BIRTH OF THE ASSEMBLY LINE

Finally, Ford can be credited (if that is the word) with a social and technical revolution by showing in his factories what could be done with mass production. Like many great revolutionaries he brought other men's ideas to bear on his own. The result was the assembly line, the characteristic modern way of making consumer goods. On it, the article under manufacture is moved steadily from worker to worker, each one of them carrying out in the minimum necessary time the precisely delimited and, if possible, simple task in which he or she is skilled. Mass production's psychological effect on the worker was soon deplored, but the technique was fundamental to a wider sharing of the wealth of the industrial economy. Ford saw that such work would be very boring and paid high wages to compensate for it (thereby incidentally contributing to another revolutionary economic change, the fuelling of economic prosperity by increasing purchasing power and, therefore, demand). Since then,

Model T Ford cars roll off the assembly line in the Ford factory in Detroit in 1913. The Model T was produced until 1927, when Ford replaced it with the Model A.

good management practice has generated other solutions to this problem, and the diffusion of such practice in many countries through the automobile industries is, like the assembly line itself, a cultural force of incalculable significance in generalizing new attitudes, whether for good or ill.

THE COMPUTER AGE

Now the assembly line may well be "manned" by robots. The single greatest technological change since 1945 in the major industrial economies has come in Information Technology, the complex science of handling, managing, and devising electronically powered machines to process information. Few innovatory waves have moved so fast. Applications of work, much of which was only done during the Second World War, were diffused in a couple of decades over a huge range of services and industrial processes.

Rapid increases in the power and speed, reduction in the size, and improvement in the visual display capacity of computers only meant, in essence, that much more information could be ordered and processed than hitherto. But this was an example of a quantitative change bringing a qualitative transformation. Calculations which until recently would have required the lifetime of many mathematicians to complete can now be run through in a few minutes. Technical operations which would have had to wait decades for such calculations, or for the sorting and classifying of great masses of data, have now become possible. Intellectual advance has never been so suddenly accelerated. At the same time as there was revolutionary growth in the capacity and power of computers, their technology made it easier and easier to pack their potential into smaller and smaller machines. Within thirty years, a "microchip" the size of a credit card was doing the job which had first required a machine the size of an average British living-room. The transforming effects have been felt in every service – and, indeed, almost every human activity, from money-making to war-making.

IMPROVED COMMUNICATIONS

Computers, soon able to transact business with one another, are the end of a long chain of development and innovation in communication. In its simplest form, this development was expressed in physical and mechanical movement of messages, goods and people whose major nineteenth-century achievements were most obviously manifest in such improvements as the application of first steam to land and sea transport, and then the production of the internal-combustion engine and electric tram. There had long been

balloons, and the first "dirigibles" existed before 1900, but the first flight by a man-carrying, powered, heavier-than-air machine was only made in 1903. Eighty years later, the value of goods imported and exported through Heathrow, London's biggest airport, was greater than that of any British seaport and aeroplanes are now the normal form of long-distance travel. Flight now offers a mobility to the individual which was hardly imaginable at the start of the twentieth century.

By 1900, the communication of information had been revolutionized even more by liberating it from physical interaction between the source and the recipient of a signal. By the middle decades of the nineteenth century, poles carrying lines for the electric telegraph were already a familiar sight, but by 1900, Marconi had exploited electromagnetic theory to make possible the sending of the first "wireless" messages. Transmitters and receivers no longer needed physical connexion. The first radio message to cross the Atlantic did so, appropriately, in 1901, the first year of a century to be revolutionized by his invention. By 1930 most people who owned "wireless" receivers (and there were millions) had ceased to believe that windows had to be open to allow the broadcast "waves" to reach them. There were by then large-scale radio broadcasting services in all major countries. A few years earlier still the first demonstration had been made of the devices on which television was based. In 1936 the BBC opened the first regular television broadcasting service; twenty years later the medium was commonplace in the leading industrial countries. Speedier information transmission had been going on over the whole century and the post-war foundation and explosive success of new industries devoted to the use of electronic methods of communication must be seen in that perspective.

THE MANAGEMENT OF NATURE

TECHNICAL PROGRESS was for a long time almost the only way in which science came home to most people, and perhaps it still is. In some industrial processes the science is very obvious: the use of nuclear fission to generate energy, or of computers to control machine-tools are examples. In others – and the production of plastic materials for almost every conceivable requirement is one of the most common – the basic science still lies concealed from the layman in obscure chemical processes. But in both it is easy to accept that the scientists' role has been paramount. In fact, by 1950 modern industry was already dependent on science, directly or indirectly, whether obviously so or not. Moreover, the transformation of fundamental science into an end-product is now often very rapid. The generalization of the use of the motor car after the principle of the internal combustion engine had been grasped took about half a century; the gap between the first use of penicillin and its large-scale manufacture was only about ten years.

Television sets became common in Western homes from around 1950. Today, television plays an important role in both reflecting and creating social trends in the developed world.

Plastic products became highly fashionable in the 1950s. Advertisements such as this one emphasized plastic's versatility, colourfulness and practicality.

Plastic products became highly fashionable in the 1950s. Advertisements such as this one emphasized plastic's versatility, colourfulness and practicality.

THE REPERCUSSIONS OF SCIENCE

One explanation of the speed with which scientific knowledge is applied is the spread of the idea of purposive research, and of willingness to spend money on it. In the nineteenth century most practical results of science were by-products of scientific curiosity. Sometimes they were accidental. By 1900 a change was under way. Some scientists had seen that consciously directed and focused research was sensible. Twenty years later, large industrial companies were beginning to see research as a proper call on their investment, albeit a small one. Some industrial research departments were in the end to grow into enormous establishments in their own right as petrochemicals, plastics, electronics and biochemical medicine made their appearance later in the century. Nowadays, the ordinary citizen of a developed country cannot lead a life which does not rely on applied science. This all-pervasiveness, coupled with its impressiveness in its most spectacular achievements, was one of the great reasons for the ever-growing recognition given to science. Money is one yardstick. The Cavendish Laboratory at Cambridge, for example, in which some of the fundamental experiments of nuclear physics were carried out before 1914, had then a grant from the university of about $300 a year – roughly $1,500 at rates then current. When, during the war of 1939–45, the British and Americans decided that a major effort had to be mounted to produce nuclear weapons, the resulting "Manhattan Project" (as it was called) is estimated to have cost as much as all the scientific research previously conducted by human beings from the beginnings of recorded time.

GOVERNMENT INVESTMENT

Huge sums of money, such as that spent on the Manhattan Project – and there were to be even larger bills to meet in the post-war world – mark another momentous change, a new importance of science to government. After being for centuries the object of only occasional patronage by the state, science is now a major political concern. Only governments can provide resources on the scale needed for some of the things done since 1945. One benefit they usually sought was better weapons, which explained much of the huge scientific investment of the United States and the Soviet Union. The increasing interest and participation of governments has not, on the other hand, meant that science has grown more nationalistic; indeed, the reverse is true. The tradition of international communication among scientists is one of their most splendid inheritances from the first great age of science in the seventeenth century, but even without it, science would for theoretical and technical reasons have had to jump national frontiers.

A NEW PHYSICS

ALREADY BEFORE 1914 it was increasingly clear that boundaries between the individual sciences, some of them intelligible and usefully distinct fields of study since the seventeenth century, were tending first to blur and then to disappear. The full implications of this have only begun to appear very lately, though. In spite of the achievements of the great chemists and biologists of the eighteenth and nineteenth centuries, physics was

One of the most expensive areas of government-funded scientific research is the collection of data about space. These radio telescopes form part of the Very Large Array (VLA) in New Mexico in the United States. This array effectively forms one gigantic radio dish: the data gathered by the 27 telescopes, each of which has a diameter of 82 ft (25 m), is combined to produce a single image at the National Radio Astronomy Observatory.

A computer technician in Tokyo, Japan, carries out quality control tests on floppy disks. With the help of government subsidies for industry, Japan has become one of the world's leading producers of electronic goods.

the seed-bed of the major scientific achievements of the early twentieth century. Newtonian physics had provided a satisfying philosophical framework for a century and a half when James Clerk Maxwell, the first professor of experimental physics at Cambridge, published in the 1870s the work in electromagnetism which broke effectively into fields and problems left untouched by seventeenth-century science. Maxwell's theoretical work and its experimental investigation profoundly affected the post-Newtonian view that the universe obeyed natural, regular and discoverable laws of a somewhat mechanical kind and that it essentially consisted of indestructible matter in various combinations and arrangements. Into this picture had now to be fitted a new component, the electromagnetic fields whose technological possibilities quickly fascinated laymen and scientists alike.

SPLITTING THE ATOM

The crucial work which followed the investigation of electromagnetism and which founded modern physical theory was done between 1895 and 1914, by Röntgen who

discovered X-rays, Becquerel who discovered radioactivity, Thomson who identified the electron, the Curies who isolated radium, and Rutherford who carried out the investigation of the atom's structure. They made it possible to see the physical world in a new way. Instead of lumps of matter, the universe began to look more like an aggregate of atoms which were tiny solar systems of particles in particular arrangements. These particles seemed to behave in a way which blurred the distinction between lumps of matter and electromagnetic fields. Moreover, such arrangements of particles were not fixed, for in nature one arrangement might give way to another and thus elements could change into other elements. Rutherford's work, in particular, was decisive, when he established that atoms could be "split" because of their structure as a system of particles. This meant that matter, even at this fundamental level, could be manipulated (though as late as 1935 he said that nuclear physics would have no practical implications – and no one rushed to contradict him). Two such particles were soon identified, the proton and the electron; others not until after 1932, when Chadwick discovered the neutron. But Rutherford, together with Bohr, provided the scientific world with an experimentally validated picture of the atom's structure as a system of particles. Since then the discovery of new particles has continued as one of the main developmental lines along which physics has moved.

QUANTUM THEORY AND RELATIVITY

What this radically important experimental work did not do was supply a new theoretical framework to replace the Newtonian. This was only achieved by a long revolution in theory, beginning in the last years of the nineteenth century and coming to its culmination in the 1920s. It was focused on two different sets of problems, which gave rise to the work designated by the terms relativity and quantum theory. The pioneers were Max Planck and Albert Einstein. By 1905 they had provided experimental and mathematical demonstration that the Newtonian laws of motion were an inadequate framework for explanation of a fact which could no longer be contested. This was that energy transactions in the material world took place not in an even flow but in discrete jumps – quanta, as they came to be termed. Planck showed that radiant heat (from, for example, the sun) was not, as Newtonian physics required, emitted continuously; he argued that this was true of all energy transactions. Einstein argued that light was propagated not continuously but in particles. Though much important work was to be done in the next twenty or so years, Planck's contribution had the most profound effect and it was again unsettling.

ENTWURF EINER
VERALLGEMEINERTEN RELATIVITÄTSTHEORIE
UND EINER
THEORIE DER GRAVITATION

I. PHYSIKALISCHER TEIL
VON
ALBERT EINSTEIN
IN ZÜRICH

II. MATHEMATISCHER TEIL
VON
MARCEL GROSSMANN
IN ZÜRICH

LEIPZIG UND BERLIN
DRUCK UND VERLAG VON B. G. TEUBNER
1913

Newton's views had been found wanting, but there was nothing to put in their place.

Meanwhile, after his work on quanta, Einstein had published in 1905 the work for which he was to be most famous, his statement of the theory of relativity. This was essentially a demonstration that the traditional distinctions of space and time, and mass and energy, could not be consistently maintained. Instead of Newton's three dimensional physics, he directed his colleagues' attention to a "space–time continuum" in which the interplay of space, time and motion could be understood. This was soon to be corroborated by astronomical observation of facts for which Newtonian cosmology could not properly account, but which could find a

Albert Einstein (1879–1955), who was born to Jewish parents in Germany but later took Swiss nationality, was awarded the Nobel prize for physics in 1921. He resigned from his post in Berlin when Hitler came to power in Germany. From 1933 until his death he worked at the Institute for Advanced Study in Princeton (USA).

An early edition of Albert Einstein's *General Theory of Relativity*. In 1915, Einstein expanded his work to produce a general theory of relativity, the original manuscript of which had to be smuggled out of wartime Berlin. Then director of the city's Kaiser Wilhelm Physical Institute, Einstein was well known for his anti-militarist views.

While studying the distribution of energy in a black body, in 1900, Max Planck (1858–1947) formulated what he called the quantum theory of energy. This was to have an enormous impact on physics, particularly when its application by Albert Einstein and Niels Bohr led to further major discoveries. Planck was awarded the Nobel prize for physics in 1918.

place in Einstein's theory. One strange and unanticipated consequence of the work on which relativity theory was based was his demonstration of the relations of mass and energy which he formulated as $E = mc^2$, where E is energy, m is mass, and c is the constant speed of light. The importance and accuracy of this theoretical formulation was not to be clear until much more nuclear physics had been done; it would then be apparent that the relationships observed when mass energy was converted into heat energy in the breaking up of nuclei also corresponded to this formula.

A BREAKTHROUGH IN NUCLEAR PHYSICS

While these advances were absorbed, attempts continued to rewrite nuclear physics in the light of Planck's work. These did not get far until a major theoretical breakthrough in 1926 finally provided a mathematical framework for his observations and, indeed, for nuclear physics. So sweeping was the achievement of Schrödinger and Heisenberg, the two mathematicians mainly responsible, that it seemed for a time as if quantum mechanics might be of virtually limitless explanatory power in the sciences. The behaviour of particles in the atom observed by Rutherford and Bohr could now be accounted for. Further development of their work led to predictions of the existence of new nuclear particles, notably the positron, which was duly identified in the 1930s. Quantum mechanics seemed to have inaugurated a new age of physics.

A NEW VIEW OF THE UNIVERSE

By mid-century much more had disappeared in science than just a once-accepted set of general laws (and in any case it remained true that, for most everyday purposes, Newtonian physics was still all that was needed). In physics, from which it had spread to other sciences, the whole notion of a general law was being replaced by the concept of statistical probability as the best that could be hoped for. The idea, as well as the content, of science was changing. Furthermore, the boundaries between sciences collapsed under the onrush of new knowledge made accessible by new theories and instrumentation. Any one of the great traditional divisions of science was soon beyond the grasp of any single mind. The conflations involved in importing physical theory into neurology or mathematics into biology put further barriers in the way of attaining that synthesis of knowledge which had been the dream of the nineteenth century just as the rate of acquisition of new knowledge (some in such quantities that it could only be handled by the newly available computers) became faster than ever.

Life sciences: milestones in biotechnology and genetic engineering

1865 Mendel publishes first accounts of experiments with peas showing the presence of independent factors ("genes").

1909 First use of the term "gene", in a book by Johannsen.

1928 Fleming discovers penicillin – publication of the first paper.

1941 First mass production of antibiotics (penicillin) in the USA (UK production insufficient for demand).

1947 First use of the word "biotechnology" (USA).

1953 Crick and Watson publish paper showing the structure of DNA. Structure of insulin published (first protein structure to be determined).

1973 Cohen and Boyer discover recombinant rDNA – the basis for genetic engineering.

1975 Milstein publishes the results of cell fusion experiments which lead to the development of monocolonal antibodies.

1982 Commercial production of first genetically engineered drug (insulin).

1983 First publication of gene mapping (Huntington's disease).

1986 Jefferys publishes method of "DNA" fingerprinting", first used forensically 1987.

1989 First isolation (structure determination) of a defective gene (cystic fibrosis).

1990 Goodfellow discovers structure of testis-determining gene.

1991 First sex-reversed transgenic animal is produced (mouse).

1997 "Dolly" the sheep is the first mammal cloned from a cell taken from an adult animal.

THE BIOLOGICAL SCIENCES

THE INCREASINGLY COMPLEX nature of scientific research did nothing to diminish either the prestige of the scientists or the faith that they were humanity's best hope for the better management of its future. Doubts, when they came, arose from other sources than their inability to generate overarching theory intelligible to lay understanding as Newton's had been. Meanwhile, the flow of specific advances in the sciences continued. In some measure, the baton passed after 1945 from the physical to the biological sciences.

Louis Pasteur (1822–1895) showed that the fermentation that turns milk into cheese is accomplished by bacteria and went on to demonstrate the germ theory of infectious disease.

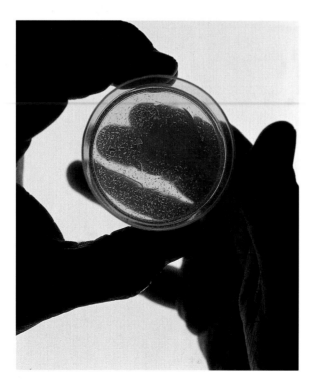

Alexander Fleming (1881–1955), shown here at work at St Mary's Hospital in London in 1943, discovered the antibiotic substance penicillin in 1928.

Some scientists have defined the end of the 20th century as the "Era of Genetics". All the progress made in this field offers enormous potential for improving human, animal and vegetable genes. Here, a scientist holds a petri dish continuing a colony of *Caenorhabditis elegans* – tiny bisexual nematode worms – which are used as subjects for genetic research.

Their current success and promise has, once again, deep roots in the origin of two paths of enquiry in nineteenth-century biology. The seventeenth-century invention of the microscope had first revealed the organization of tissue into discrete units called cells. In the nineteenth century investigators already understood that cells could divide and that they developed individually. Cell theory, widely accepted by 1900, suggested that individual cells, being alive themselves, provided a good approach to the study of life, and the application of chemistry to this became one of the main avenues of biological research. The other main line in nineteenth-century biological science was provided by a new discipline, genetics, the study of the inheritance by offspring of characteristics from parents. Darwin had invoked the principle of inheritance as the means of propagation of traits favoured by natural selection. The first steps towards understanding the mechanism which made this possible were those of an Austrian monk, Gregor Mendel. From a meticulous series of breeding experiments on pea plants Mendel concluded that there existed hereditary units controlling the expression of traits passed from parents to offspring. In 1909 a Dane gave them the name "gene".

THE DISCOVERY OF DNA

Gradually the chemistry of cells became better understood and the physical reality of genes was accepted. In 1873 the presence in the cell nucleus of a substance which might embody the most fundamental determinant of all living matter was already established. Experiments then revealed a visible location for genes in chromosomes, and in the 1940s it was shown that genes controlled the chemical structure of protein, the most important constituent of cells. In 1944 the first step was taken towards identifying the specific effective agent in bringing about changes in certain bacteria, and therefore in controlling protein structure. In the 1950s it was at last identified as "DNA", whose physical structure (the double helix) was established in 1953. The crucial importance of this substance (its full name is deoxyribonucleic acid) is that it is the carrier of the genetic information which determines the synthesis of protein molecules at the basis of life. The chemical mechanisms underlying the diversity of biological phenomena were at last accessible. Physiologically, and perhaps psychologically, this implied a transformation of human self-perception unprecedented since the general acceptance of Darwinian ideas in the last century.

THE APPLICATION OF GENETICS

The identification and analysis of the structure of DNA was the most conspicuous single step towards the manipulation of nature at the level of the shaping of life-forms. Once again, not only more scientific knowledge but new definitions of fields of study and new applications followed. "Molecular biology", "biotechnology" and "genetic engineering" quickly became familiar terms. The genes of some organisms could, it was soon shown, be altered so as to give those organisms new and desirable characteristics. By manipulating their growth processes, yeast and other microorganisms could be made to produce novel substances, enzymes or other chemicals. This was one of the first extensions of the new science; the empirical technology which had been accumulated informally by millennia of experience in the making of bread, wine and cheese was at last to be overtaken. Genetic modification of bacteria can now be carried out so as to grow chemicals or hormones. By the end of the 1980s a worldwide collaborative investi-

gation, the Human Genome Project, whose almost unimaginable aim was the mapping of the human genetic apparatus so as to identify the position, structure and function of every human gene (there are from 50,000 to 100,000 in each cell, each of them having up to 30,000 pairs of the four basic chemical units that form the genetic code) was under way. Screening for the presence of certain defective genes, and even the replacement of some of them, is already achieved; the medical implications of this are enormous. At a more obvious level, that of day-to-day police work, what is called DNA "fingerprinting" has been used to identify an individual from a blood or semen sample. Somewhat more eerily, a patent has now been acquired for a laboratory mouse genetically prone to cancer.

THE SPEED OF PROGRESS

Progress in the field of genetics has been startlingly rapid (and owes much to the availability of computers to handle very large quantities of information). It provides a remarkable instance of the accelerating tendency in scientific advance which in turn

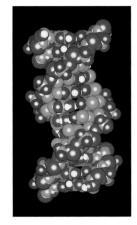

This computer-generated image represents a segment of a DNA molecule, which is formed by two chains of various atoms (represented here by the different colours). Because the chains are so long, the number of possible combinations of information in the genetic code is extremely high.

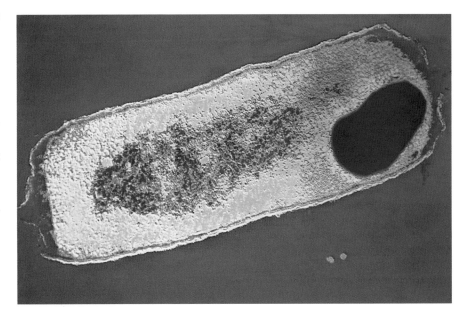

This electron micrograph shows a genetically engineered strain of the bacterium *Escherichia coli*, synthesizing human Interleukin-2, which is a naturally occurring cancer therapeutic. *E. coli* is widely used in biotechnology and molecular genetics research.

accelerates both new applications and the invasion of a world of settled assumptions and landmarks by new ideas. It is not easy to assess what this can mean. Once again, we face the old problem of establishing the level at which ideas have cultural, social, or political effect. For all the recent fundamental work in the "life sciences", it is unlikely that even their approximate importance can be assessed by most of us.

THE SPACE AGE

FOR MOST HUMAN BEINGS, the power of science is still most vividly demonstrated in its technological expression. For nearly twenty years that was above all visible in the spectacular achievements of the human exploration of space. The extension of our physical environment thus achieved may well turn out to have an ultimate significance dwarfing other historical processes which have been given more space in this book. It has been going on throughout most of the post-war era, the most exciting achievement of modern technology, suggesting that the capacity of our culture to meet unprecedented challenges is as great as ever, and perhaps the most obvious of all the manifestations of human domination of nature. Its huge psychological importance began to appear in October 1957. For most people, the space age began then, when an unmanned Soviet satellite called Sputnik I was launched by rocket and could soon be discerned in orbit around the earth emitting radio signals. The political impact was obvious: it shattered the belief that Russian technology lagged significantly behind American. The full significance of the event, though, was still obscured, because its entanglement with superpower rivalries swamped other considerations for most observers. In fact, it ended the era when the possibility of human travel in space could still be doubted, as events quickly showed. Almost incidentally and unnoticed, it marked a break in historical continuity as important as the European discovery of the

Carl Sagan on our knowledge of space

"We now have, for the first time, the tools to make contact with civilizations on planets of other stars. It is an astonishing fact that the great one-thousand-foot-diameter radio telescope of the National Astronomy and Ionosphere Center, run by Cornell University in Arecibo, Puerto Rico, would be able to communicate with an identical copy of itself anywhere in the Milky Way Galaxy. We have at our command the means to communicate not merely over distances of hundreds or thousands of light-years; we can communicate over tens of thousands of light-years, into a volume containing hundreds of billions of stars. The hypothesis that advanced technical civilizations exist on planets of other stars is amenable to experimental testing. It has been removed from the arena of pure speculation. It is now in the arena of experiment."

An extract from ch. 27 of *The Cosmic Connection: An Extraterrestrial Perspective* by Carl Sagan, 1973.

This was one of the first official photographs of the Soviet earth satellite Sputnik I, the launch of which, on 4 October, 1957, humiliated the government of the United States by beating them in the so-called "space race".

Americas, or the Industrial Revolution. One of the futures dreamed of by writers of science fiction had begun.

EARLY ACHIEVEMENTS

Space exploration had deep roots. Visions of it could be found in the last years of the nineteenth century and the early years of the twentieth, when they were brought to the notice of the Western public in fiction, notably in the stories of Jules Verne and H.G. Wells. Its technology went back almost as far. A Russian scientist, K.E. Tsolikovsky, had designed multi-staged rockets and devised many of the basic principles of space travel (and he too had written fiction to popularize his obsession) well before 1914. The first Soviet liquid-fuelled rocket went up (three miles) in 1933, and a two-stage rocket six years later. The Second World War provoked a major German rocket programme, which the United States had drawn on to begin its own in 1955. It started with more modest hardware then the Russians (who already had a commanding lead) and the first American satellite weighed only three pounds (Sputnik I weighed 184 pounds). A much-publicized launch attempt was made at the end of December 1957, but the rocket caught fire instead of taking off and a sad little bleeping from the sands near the launching site was all that resulted. The Americans would soon do much better than this, but within a month of Sputnik I the Russians had already put up Sputnik II, an astonishingly successful machine, weighing half a ton and carrying the first passenger in space, a black-and-white mongrel called Laika. For nearly six months Sputnik II orbited the earth, visible to the whole inhabited world and an outrage to thousands of dog-lovers, for Laika was not to return.

THE SPACE RACE

By early 1958, the Russian and American space programmes had already somewhat diverged. The Russians, building on their pre-war experience, had put much emphasis on the power and size of their rockets, which could lift big loads, and here their strength was to continue to lie. This had military implications more obvious than those

In April 1961, the Soviet cosmonaut Yuri Gagarin (1943–1968), shown here, orbited the earth in Vostok I. Having thus confirmed the Soviets' lead in the space race and won international fame, Gagarin was given the title Hero of the Soviet Union.

As these newspapers from 1957 show, the news that the Soviet Union had launched a new "moon" received plenty of attention in the world's press. Entire nations were caught up in the excitement of the superpower space race.

retrieving Sputnik V, a four-and-a-half-ton satellite, carrying two dogs, who thus became the first living creatures to have entered space and returned to earth safely. In the spring of following year, on 12 April, a Russian rocket took off carrying a man, Yuri Gagarin. He landed 108 minutes later after one orbit around the earth. The invasion of space by humanity had begun, four years after Sputnik I.

PRESIDENT KENNEDY'S MOON PROJECT

Possibly spurred by a wish to offset a recent publicity disaster in American relations with Cuba, President Kennedy proposed in May 1961 that the United States should try to land a man on the moon and return him safely to earth before the end of the decade. His reasons for recommending this were interestingly different from those which had led the rulers of fifteenth-century Portugal and Spain to back the Magellans and da Gamas. One was that such a project provided a good national goal, the next that it would be prestigious ("impressive to mankind" were the president's words); the third was that it was of great importance for the exploration of space; and the fourth was (somewhat oddly) that it was of unparalleled difficulty and expense. Kennedy said nothing of the advancement of science, of commercial or military advantage. Surprisingly, the project met virtually no opposition and the first money was soon allocated for the most expensive technological adventure in history.

During the early 1960s the Russians continued to make spectacular progress. The world was perhaps most struck when they sent a woman into space in 1963, but their technical competence continued to be best shown by the size of their vehicles – a three-

(equally profound but less spectacular) which flowed from American concentration on data-gathering and on instrumentation. A competition for prestige was soon under way, but although people soon spoke of a "space race" the contestants were really running towards different goals. With one great exception (the wish to be first to put a man in space) their technical decisions were probably not much influenced by one another's performance. The contrast was clear enough when Vanguard, the American satellite which failed in December 1957, was successfully launched the following March. Tiny though it was, it went much deeper into space than any predecessor and has provided more valuable scientific information in proportion to its size than any other satellite. It is likely to be going around for another couple of centuries or so.

New achievements then quickly followed; progress speeded up. At the end of 1958 the first satellite for communications purposes was successfully launched (it was American). In 1960 the Americans scored another "first" – the recovery of a capsule after re-entry. The Russians followed this by orbiting and

man machine was launched in 1964 – and in the achievement the following year of the first "space walk", when one of the crew emerged from his vehicle and moved about outside while in orbit (though reassuringly attached to it by a lifeline). The Russians were to go on to further important advances in achieving rendezvous for vehicles in space and in engineering their docking, but after 1967 (the year of the first death through space travel, when a Russian was killed during re-entry) the glamour passed to the Americans. In 1968, they achieved a sensational success by sending a three-man vehicle into orbit around the moon and transmitting television pictures of its surface. It was by now clear that "Apollo", the moon-landing project, was going to succeed.

THE FIRST MOON LANDING

In May 1969 Apollo 10, a vehicle put into orbit with the tenth rocket of the project, approached to within six miles of the moon to assess the techniques of the final stage of landing. A few weeks later, on 16 July, a three-man crew was launched. Their lunar module landed on the moon's surface four days later. On the following morning, 21 July, the first human being to set foot on the moon was Neil Armstrong, the commander of the mission. President Kennedy's goal had been achieved with time in hand. Other landings were to follow. In a decade which had opened with humiliation for the United States in the Caribbean and was ending in the morass of an unsuccessful war in Asia, it was a triumphant reassertion of what America (and, by implication, capitalism) could do. It was also a sign of the latest and greatest extension by *Homo sapiens* of his environment, the beginning of a new phase of his history, that to be lived on other celestial bodies.

The American astronaut Neil Armstrong (b.1930) is pictured in his space suit during training for his historic expedition to the moon in 1969. As he stepped from his spacecraft onto the surface of the moon, Armstrong uttered the phrase for which he will always be remembered: "That's one small step for man, one giant leap for mankind."

THE EXPLORATION AND USE OF SPACE

Even at the time, the wonderful achievement of the moon landing was decried. Its critics felt that the mobilization of resources the programme needed was unjustified, because irrelevant to the real problems of the earth. To some, the technology of space travel has seemed to be our civilization's version of the Pyramids, a huge investment in the wrong things in a world crying out for money for education, nutrition, medical research – to name only a few of its pressing needs. It is difficult not to feel immediate sympathy for such a view, but it is more difficult to sustain it. In the first place, much of the scientific and economic effect of the space effort is hardly quantifiable (and has already been very far-reaching); the use of knowledge of miniaturization needed to make control systems,

The first steps by a human being on the moon are taken on 21 July, 1969. Millions of spectators around the world were able to see this extraordinary event almost immediately on television – a fact that, as well as demonstrating the advance of space technology, showed how quickly audio-visual technology was developing.

The exploration and use of space: major steps up to 1969

1903 Konstantin Tsolikovsky publishes a paper on rocket space travel using liquid propellants.

1933 1 May: Tsolikovsky predicts that many Soviet citizens will live to see the first space flights.

1944 German V2 rockets used to bombard London and Antwerp.

1954 President Eisenhower announces that a small scientific satellite, Vanguard, will be launched 1957–8.

1957 1 October: Launch of Sputnik 1 (USSR), weight 184 lbs (83.46 kg).
3 November: Launch of Sputnik 2 (USSR), weight 1,120 lbs (508 kg), with the dog Laika as passenger.

1958 31 January: Launch of Explorer (USA) and discovery of Van Allen radiation belts.
17 March: Launch of Vanguard 1 (USA), weight 3.25 lbs (1.47 kg): the first satellite with solar batteries.

1959 13 September: Luna 2 (USSR) crashes on moon, the first man-made object to arrive there.
10 October: Luna 3 (USSR) photographs far side of moon.

1960 11 August: Discoverer 13 (USA) is recovered after first successful re-entry to atmosphere.
19 August: Sputnik 5 (USSR) orbits earth with two dogs which return unharmed.

1961 12 April: Major Yuri Gagarin (USSR) orbits the earth.
25 May: President Kennedy commits USA to landing man on the moon by 1970.
6 August: Vostok 2 (USSR) makes 17 orbits of earth.

1962 20 February: First American manned orbited space flight.
10 July: Launch of Telstar satellite (USA); first television pictures across the Atlantic.

1965 18 March: On Voskhod 2 mission (USSR) Alexey Leonov makes 10-minute "walk in space".
2 May: Early Bird commercial communications satellite (USA) first used by television.
15 December: Launch of Gemini 6 (USA), which will make rendezvous with Gemini 7, the two craft coming within a foot of one another.

1966 July–November: Gemini missions 10, 11, 12 (USA) all achieve "docking" with "Agena" vehicle.

1967 First deaths in US programme.

1968 21–27 December: Apollo 8 (USA) makes first manned voyage round the moon.

1969 14–17 January: Soyuz 4 and 5 (USSR) dock in space and exchange passengers.
21 July: Apollo 11 (USA) lands two men on the moon.

for example, rapidly spills over into application of obvious social and economic value. It cannot be said that this knowledge would necessarily have been available had not the investment in space come first. Nor, indeed, can we be confident that the resources lavished on space exploration would have been made available for any other great scientific or social goals, had they not been used in this way. Our social machinery does not operate like that.

The mythical importance of what has happened has also to be considered. However regrettable it may be, modern societies have shown few signs of being able to generate much interest and enthusiasm among their members for collective purposes except for brief periods or in war, whose "moral equivalent" (as one American philosopher put it well before 1914) is still to seek. The imagination of large numbers of people is not much spoken to by the prospect of adding marginally to the GDP or introducing one more refinement to a system of social services, however intrinsically desirable these things may be. Kennedy's identification of a national goal was shrewd; in the troubled 1960s, the Americans had much else to agitate and

divide them, but they did not turn up to frustrate launchings of the space missions.

THE SPACE SHUTTLE

It is important that space exploration became more of an international enterprise as it went on. Before the 1970s there was little cooperation between the two greatest nations concerned, the United States and Soviet Russia, and this undoubtedly led to wasteful duplication of effort and inefficiencies. Ten years before the Americans got there and planted the American flag on it, a Soviet mission had dropped a Lenin pennant on the moon. This seemed ominous; there was a basic national rivalry in the technological race itself and nationalism might provoke a Scramble for Space. But the dangers of competition were avoided; it was soon agreed that celestial objects were not subject to appropriation by any one state. In July 1975, some

hundred and fifty miles above the earth, cooperation became a startling reality in a remarkable experiment in which Soviet and American machines connected themselves so that their crews could move from one to the other. In spite of doubts, exploration continued in a relatively benign international setting. The visual exploration of further space was carried beyond Jupiter by unmanned satellite, and 1976 brought the first landing of an unmanned exploration vehicle on the surface of the planet Mars. In 1977 the space shuttle, the first reusable space vehicle, made its maiden voyage. These achievements were tremendous, yet they are now hardly noticed, so jaded are our imaginations. So rapidly did there grow up a new familiarity with the idea of space travel that in the 1980s it seemed only mildly risible that people should have begun to make commercial bookings for it – and even for space burials (if that is the word), too. As the decade drew to a close what was the last big enterprise of the Soviet space effort took place in 1988, when a satellite was launched to prepare the way for a future manned voyage to Mars.

ENVIRONMENTAL CONCERNS

BY 1988, SPACE EXPLORATION had become somewhat overshadowed by uneasiness about humanity's interference with nature. Though successful adventure in space was a supreme example of technological manipulation to achieve human goals and satisfy human desires, within only a few years of Sputnik I misgivings were increasingly expressed about what lay at the very roots of

so masterful a view of our relationship to the natural world. What is more, such uneasiness soon began to be expressed with a precision based on observed facts not hitherto considered in that light; science itself supplied the instrumentation and data which led to dismay about what was going on. There began to be perceptible a conscious recognition of the damage interference with the environment might bring. It was, of course, the recognition that was new, not the phenomenon. Centuries before, migration southwards and the adoption of dryland crops from the Americas had devastated the great forests of southwest China, bringing soil erosion and the consequential silting of the Yangtze drainage system in its train, and so culminating in

Members of the environmental action group Greenpeace hang from a bridge in Germany in 1986 as part of a campaign.

repeated flooding over wide areas. In the early Middle Ages, Islamic conquest had brought goat-herding and tree-felling to the North African littoral on a scale which destroyed a fertility once able to fill the granaries of Rome. But such great changes, though hardly unnoticed, were not then understood. The unprecedented rapidity of ecological interference initiated from the seventeenth century onwards by Europeans, however, was to bring things to a head. The unconsidered power of technology forced the dangers on the attention of human beings in the second half of this century. People began to reckon up damage as well as achievement, and by the middle of the 1970s it seemed to some of them that even if the story of growing human mastery of the environment was an epic, that epic might well turn out to be a tragic one.

SCEPTICISM

Suspicion of science had never wholly disappeared in Western societies. It had tended, nevertheless, to be confined to a few surviving primitive or reactionary enclaves as the majesty of what the scientific revolution of the seventeenth century implied gradually unrolled. History can provide much evidence of uneasiness about interference with Nature and attempts to control it, but until recently such uneasiness seemed to rest on non-rational grounds, such as the fear of provoking divine anger or nemesis. As time passed, it was steadily eroded by the palpable advantages and improvements which successful interference with Nature brought about, most obviously through the creation of new wealth expressed in all sorts of goods, from better medicine to better clothing and food. In the 1970s, though, it became clear that a new scepticism about science itself was abroad, even though only among a minority. Suspicion of what is one of the greatest tools of man-made change was marked, it is true, only in developed countries. There, a cynic might have said, the dividends on science had already been drawn. None the less, it manifested itself there first and in the 1980s there were signs that uneasiness was spreading as "Green" political parties sought to promote policies protective of the "environment". They were not able to achieve much, but they proliferated; the established political parties and perceptive politicians therefore toyed with "green" themes, too. Environmentalists, as the concerned came to be called, benefited from the modern communications which rapidly broadcast disturbing news even from the still uncommunicative USSR. In 1986, an accident occurred at a Ukrainian nuclear power station. Suddenly and horribly, human interdependence was made visible. Grass eaten by lambs in Wales, milk drunk by Poles and Yugoslavs, and air breathed by Swedes, were all contaminated. An unknown number of Russians, it appeared, were going to die over the years from the slow effects of radiation. The alarming event was brought home

Demonstrators march past a chemical works in Louisiana in the United States, in protest against the plant's toxic emissions.

An onlooker watches as the American space shuttle *Challenger* explodes above Cape Canaveral in Florida as it is launched on 28 January, 1986. The shuttle programme was suspended for nearly three years after the accident, which claimed the lives of all seven crew on board.

to millions by television not long after other millions had watched on their screens an American rocket blow up with the loss of all on board. Chernobyl and *Challenger* showed to huge numbers of people for the first time both the limitations and the possible dangers of an advanced technological civilization.

QUESTIONING THE BENEFITS OF SCIENTIFIC PROGRESS

The terrible Chernobyl and *Challenger* accidents reinforced and spread more widely

The Chernobyl nuclear power plant in the Ukraine is pictured five months after an explosion destroyed one of its reactors.

the new concern with the environment. It is a complex matter and became tangled with other matters. Some of the doubts which have recently arisen accept that our civilization has been good at creating material wealth, but note that by itself that does not necessarily make people happy. This is hardly a new idea. Its application to society as a whole instead of to individuals is, none the less, a new emphasis. It has been pointed out that improvement of social conditions may not remove all human dissatisfactions and may, indeed, actually irritate some of them more acutely. Pollution, the oppressive anonymity of crowded cities and the nervous stress and strain of modern work conditions, easily erase satisfactions provided by material gain. Even in the 1960s, there was a recognition that things had come to a pretty pass in one of the most beautiful cities in the world when the noise level in the Place de l'Opéra in Paris was found to be greater than that at the Niagara Falls, and the Seine was carrying more sewer water than its natural flow. Scale had become a problem in its own right. Some difficulties posed by modern cities may even have grown to the point at which they are insoluble. Still greater misgivings began to be felt by more people about the threat of overpopulation, increasing pressure on diminishing resources, and the possibility of intensified competition for them in a world politically unstable.

FINITE RESOURCES

It can at least be said that energy and material resources are now so wastefully and inequitably employed that a new version of the Malthusian peril is possible. We may well have by no means reached the end (or anything like it) of our capacity to produce food, and it is far more likely that other things than

The vanishing tropical rainforests

The systematic destruction of the tropical rainforests is symbolic of the havoc that human beings are currently wreaking on the environment. Tropical rainforests are among the most advanced ecological systems on earth, as well as being the most complex, the most diverse and also the most fragile. They take up just 6 per cent of the earth's surface, but contain 60 per cent of its biological species. It is estimated that around 170 of these species are made extinct in these forests every day. According to a report by UNESCO, 60 per cent of the world's tropical rainforests have already been felled and the destruction is continuing all the time, at the rate of an area the size of a football pitch every second.

Scenes of devastation such as this are increasingly common in the Amazon rainforests of Brazil.

food will run out first. There would at once be an impossible situation if the whole world sought to consume other goods than foods at the level of developed countries today. There is a limit to what any one human being can eat, but virtually no limit to the goods he or she can consume in terms of a better environment, medicine, social services and the like. Yet the supply of such goods depends ultimately on energy and material resources which are finite. The social and political changes which must follow from this fact have hardly begun to be grasped. The human race has to face the difficulty that to deal with such problems nothing like the knowledge or technique exists which is available, for example, to put someone on the moon.

GLOBAL CLIMATIC CHANGE

In the 1970s a new spectre began to be talked about, the possibility of man-made, irreversible climatic change. Nineteen-ninety had hardly ended before it was pointed out that it had been the hottest year since climatic records began to be kept. Was this, some asked, a sign of "global warming", the "greenhouse effect" produced by the release into the atmosphere of the immense quantities of carbon dioxide produced by a huge population burning fossil fuels as never before? Nor was this the only contribution to the phenomenon of accumulating gases in the atmosphere whose presence prevents the planet from dissipating heat; methane, nitrous oxides and chlorofluorocarbons all make a contribution. And if global warming is not enough to worry about, then acid rain, ozone depletion leading to "holes" in the ozone layer, and deforestation at unprecedented rates, all provided major grounds for new environmental concern.

It is easier to sense the scale of such problems, and so the danger, than to envisage feasible solutions, and while this remains so it is almost certain that uneasiness about interference with Nature will persist. To take only one problem: one estimate is that there is now some twenty-five per cent more carbon dioxide in the atmosphere than in pre-industrial times. It may be so (and as the world's output of the stuff is now said to be six thousand million tons a year, it is not for the layman to dispute the magnitudes). The consequences, if the trend proved to be established and no effective counter-measures were forthcoming, could be enormous, expressing themselves in climatic change (average surface temperature on the earth might rise by between 1 and 4 degrees Celsius over the next century), agricultural transformation, rising sea-levels (6 centimetres a year has been suggested as possible and plausible), and major migrations. It was clear by 1990 that if the superpowers could eventually come round to cooperate rather than compete, there would be plenty of common interests to cooperate about – if they could agree on what had to be done. Beginnings have been made in controlling chlorofluorocarbons; and in February 1991, the officials from newly created environment ministries met in Washington to begin to try to work out a treaty on global climatic change.

Human beings are beginning to realize that industrialization has come at a price: environmental damage. Here, chimney stacks at a steel mill in Bihar, India, pollute the air in a scene that is still duplicated on every continent. Pollution from industries and vehicles is thought to be partly responsible for global warming.

6 IDEAS, ATTITUDES AND AUTHORITY

I T SHOULD BY NOW hardly need reiteration that it is difficult for historians to say anything very confidently about what goes on in the minds of most people, and what effect it may have on the maelstrom of historical events. Yet there is evidence that changing or new ideas can have an impact on our collective life (for instance, in the recent political responses to environmental concern). Such impacts are expressed at a level implying a certain sophistication and refinement of mental processes; even now, only minorities worry about the ozone layer. But there are other impacts harder to assess. The "cake of custom", to use a Victorian's phrase, formed by deep-seated, sometimes almost unrecognized assumptions and attitudes, is another matter altogether. To talk about changes in ideas which may affect it is much harder. But

the effort has to be made. It is, for example, almost certainly true that, more than any other single fact, force, or idea, the abundance of commodities has shattered for millions a world of stable expectations. The effect of this is still spreading. Whatever has happened in developed countries, it is now most striking in poor countries, where cheap consumer goods – transistor radios, for example – can bring huge social changes in their train. Such goods confer status. They provide an incentive to work for higher wages to buy them (a spread of a cash economy is another aspect of the process). This often means leaving the villages in which so many still live and, in the process, the severing of ties with tradition and with ordered, stable communities.

A NEW SENSE OF OPTIMISM

The always-hastening onrush of a modernity rolling outwards from industrialized societies has other expressions and effects. Notably and paradoxically, the unprecedentedly dreadful tragedies and disasters of this century have left more people than ever before believing that human life and the condition of the world can be improved, perhaps indefinitely, and therefore that they should be. There is less willingness to recognize unavoidable, irredeemable tragedy as part of human destiny. The origins of such a new, optimistic, idea lie in Europe and until quite recently it was confined to cultures of European origins. For the majority of the human race, and in most parts of the globe, it is still unfamiliar,

P ictured is the Sunday market in a Peruvian village near Cuzco, once an Inca city. In spite of technological progress and the spread of consumer society, millions of people around the world still carry out economic transactions today in the way they have done for centuries in such markets.

barely a half-century old. Few could yet formulate it clearly or consciously, even if asked. Yet it already affects behaviour everywhere.

It has almost certainly been spread less by conscious preaching (though there has been plenty of that) than by material changes which have since 1900 affected more and more people. The fact that they happened at all was the most important thing about many of them. Their psychological impact began to break up the cake of custom by setting out for the first time to many societies the implicit proposition that change is possible, that things need not always be what they have been. Of course the gulf which separates the modern European factory-worker from the Indian or Chinese peasant is vast. In terms of consumption it is certainly wider than that between their ancestors a thousand years ago. Yet to have implanted the notion that change is not only desirable but possible, perhaps even inevitable, is the most important of all the triumphs of the culture, European in origin, which we usually call "Western".

THE MOMENTUM OF PROGRESS

Technical progress has almost always turned out to be a solvent of inherited ways. Sometimes this shows very directly and obviously; it is difficult, for instance, not to feel that radio and television imply a qualitative change in the history of culture greater even than the coming of print. Technical progress has also affected mentality less directly through the testimony it provides of the seemingly magical power of science to transform life by way of technology. In other ways, too, acquaintance with science and awareness of its importance is more widespread than ever before. There are more scientists about; more attention is given to

science in education; scientific information is more widely diffused and more readily comprehensible through the media. Most of this has only come about since 1918; a significant break in scale becomes observable about then. Paradoxically, this has perhaps led to some diminution of the wonder felt in earlier times at what science could do. Success has provided diminishing returns in awe. When more and more things prove possible, there is less which is very surprising about the latest marvel. There is even (unjustifiable) disappointment and irritation when some problems prove recalcitrant. Yet the master idea of our age and perhaps the most widespread, the notion that purposive change can be imposed upon Nature if sufficient resources are made available, has grown stronger. It is a European idea, and the science now carried on around the globe is all based on the European experimental tradition. It continues to throw up ideas and implications disruptive of traditional, theocentric views of life and so we have reached the high phase of the long process of dethroning the idea of the supernatural.

In recent years, the appearance of enormous commercial centres has radically changed shopping habits in the Western world. These sanitized "temples of consumption", as they have been called, attract people not only to shop, but also to be entertained, with the result that small local shops are gradually put out of business.

THE IMPACT OF FAITH IN SCIENCE

Both the brute facts of a new economic order created by technology and a new appreciation of the power of science and the expectations it arouses have in the end a tendency to undermine traditional authority. Even if clear ideas about what science and technology might do have hardly filtered through to most laymen in developed societies, and even if

much of humanity rests undisturbed in its traditional pieties, whether Christian, Hindu, Marxist or anything else, and whether diluted or not, well-being, science, technology and even mere improvement have made persistence in established ways harder. This has happened both at the levels of intellectual élites (who are, of course, disproportionately prominent in histories of thought and culture which stress documents they generate) and in shaping (even if sometimes in nonsensically distorted ways) the climates of opinion in which most people live. The second effect is perhaps more important in recent history than at earlier times because rising literacy and increasing rapidity of communication have pushed new ideas into mass culture more than ever before. But the impact of scientific ideas on élites is easier to trace. In the eighteenth century, Newtonian cosmology had been able to settle down into coexistence with Christian religion and other theocentric modes of thought without troubling the wide range of social and moral beliefs tied to them. As time passed, though, science has seemed harder and harder to reconcile with any fixed belief at all. It has appeared to stress relativism and the pressure of circumstance to the exclusion of any unchallengeable assumption or viewpoint.

PSYCHOLOGY

A VERY OBVIOUS INSTANCE of the tension between science and religion can be seen in some scientific attempts to investigate human behaviour, a topic particularly likely to raise questions about traditional attitudes. The most important of these were made by the practitioners of a new branch of study, psychology, which had evolved from a traditional interest in "mental philosophy". After 1900, psychology tended to take one of two

A Buddhist monk in Punakna in the Himalayan country of Bhutan listens to music through the headphones of a personal stereo for the first time. Ownership of Western consumer goods such as computers and telephones is limited to a tiny élite in Bhutan, where 90 per cent of the mainly Buddhist population is dependent on agriculture. King Jigme Singye Wangchuk, the head of state and of the government, is currently attempting to modernize his country while avoiding the erosion of its cultural traditions. As a result, there are no daily newspapers, and television is banned on the grounds that it would dilute traditional Bhutanese values.

The plot of Alfred Hitchcock's film *Spellbound* (1945) centred on psychoanalysis. The film included a dream sequence based on paintings that had been specially commissioned from the Surrealist artist Salvador Dali (1904–1989), who was heavily influenced by Freud's work.

paths. One was to be followed by, among others, Freud (the social impact of whose work has already been touched upon). Broadly speaking, it arose from clinical observation of mental disorder. It is, certainly, a clear example of something which a layman – though not all scientists – would call "science", which has had an important and widespread effect. Comparatively rapidly, Freud's work became both famous and notorious, and influential. In the first place, it undermined confidence in many traditional assumptions. His ideas (or what were thought to be his ideas) and those of other teachers were diffused through advanced societies in derivative forms, such as in new attitudes to sexuality, or to responsibility and therefore to punishment. Secondly, Freudian ideas stimulated a body of work which, whatever its exact status and method, was based on the belief that therapy could be pursued and relevant material assembled by interrogating subjects about their wishes, feelings and thoughts, and interpreting this data in accordance with an appropriate body of theory. This was the foundation of the activities which may conveniently be grouped under the name Freud applied to his own work, psychoanalysis, and was the inspiration of many artists, novelists, teachers and advertising specialists.

BEHAVIOURISM

The other notable early twentieth-century approach to psychology was more mechanistic and it had deeper roots in the past than psychoanalysis. Theoretically, it was quickly demolished by the philosophers. But this did not dispose of it; it went on to achieve much applause and apparent practical success. "Behaviourism" (as it has been termed, though the word is often used imprecisely) appeared to generate a body of experimental data certainly as impressive (if not more so) as the successes claimed by psychoanalysis. The outstanding name associated with it is still that of the Russian, I.P. Pavlov. In a series of celebrated experiments in the first decade of this century he established generalizations which, with modification, seemed to be applicable to human beings. His most important single discovery was the "conditioned reflex". Essentially this was the manipulation of one of a pair of variables in an experiment in order to produce a predicted piece of behaviour by a "conditioned stimulus". The classical experiment provided for a bell to be sounded before food was given to dogs. After a time, the sounding of the bell produced in the dog the salivation which had earlier been produced by the appearance of food. Refinements and developments of such procedures followed. They provided new insights into human psychology which were exploited in many ways (one of the most depressing features of our age, perhaps, is the use made of them by torturers, though this did not produce successes which conclusively demonstrated superiority to earlier practitioners).

The study of human behaviour

In around 1900, the Russian scientist Pavlov started a long study on association in animals. He developed a technique to associate one stimulant with another and to measure the reaction when each of the stimulants was present. One experiment involved associating the aural stimulant of a bell with the stimulant of food proffered. His experiments demonstrated the conditioned reflex, and he applied his findings to an interpretation of human and animal behaviour, which he saw as an interrelated set of such reflexes.

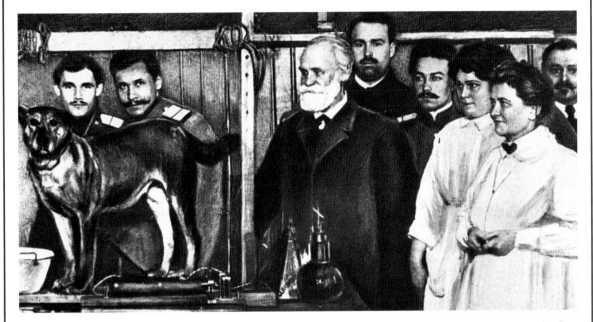

The Russian physiologist Ivan Pavlov (1849–1936), pictured with his team in 1904, demonstrates the conditioned reflex.

Some beneficent results were forthcoming, notably in the treatment of mental illness and the improvement of teaching techniques. But if an attempt is to be made to grasp so shapeless a subject, the diffused effect of behaviourism, though confined consciously to relatively few, seems curiously parallel to that of Freudianism, in that its bias lay towards the demolition of the sense of responsibility and individualism which was at the heart of European moral tradition. This, though, was a demolition also advanced by more empirical and experimental approaches to one aspect of the understanding of the mind, notably through the treatment of mental disorder by chemical, electrical and other physical interference.

RELIGION

IT IS DIFFICULT TO BELIEVE that behaviourist and psychological studies, like those of other sciences, have not contributed importantly to a decline of religious belief simply by making more people conscious that something hitherto mysterious and inexplicable was now seen by respected men and women to be susceptible to scientific (as opposed to magical or religious) management, in however elementary and halting a way. But this decline, often alleged to be characteristic of the contemporary era, needs very careful qualification. When people talk about the waning power of religion, they often mean

Some religious denominations are enjoying a growth in the size of their congregations, in spite of the general trend away from mass spirituality in the developed world. Russian Orthodoxy is one of the beneficiaries of the end of Communist rule in the former Soviet Union – as the number of worshippers at this service in a Ukrainian cathedral indicates.

only the formal and organized authority of Christian churches. What people believe and do is quite a different matter. The last English monarch to take the precaution of consulting an astrologer about an auspicious day for her coronation was Elizabeth I, nearly four and a half centuries ago. Yet in the 1980s the world was amused (and perhaps just a little alarmed) to hear that the wife of the president of the United States was in the habit of seeking astrological advice, while in 1947 the timing of the ceremony marking the achievement of Indian independence was only settled after appropriate consultation of astrologers. This is, perhaps, only superstition. But there are other important facts to be taken into account in considering the power of religion. India is now a republic which is non-confessional and secular in its constitution; to that extent it reflects the adoption of Western ideas. More generally, confessional states and established religion are now unusual anywhere, outside Muslim countries. This does not mean though, that the real power of religions over their adherents has everywhere declined even if it indicates the movement of ideas among directing élites, whether or not they are able to impose them successfully. The founders of Pakistan were secular-minded, westernized men, but in a struggle with the conservative ulema after independence they lost. Pakistan became an orthodox Islamic state, and not a secular democracy on Western lines which merely respected Islam as the religion of the majority of its people.

Western society, as an instigator of social unrest, is often viewed as an enemy in Islamic societies. However, such perceptions do not mean that there is never conflict among Islamic countries. Here, jubilant Iraqi soldiers are pictured in front of a bullet-riddled portrait of the Iranian leader Ayatollah Khomeini in 1988, during the Iran–Iraq war.

A small Muslim girl carries a sign vowing to kill Salman Rushdie. The Ayatollah Khomeini issued a fatwa (death warrant) against the author after the publication of his book *The Satanic Verses* (1988), which is considered blasphemous by radical Muslims.

THE INTERPLAY OF RELIGION AND SOCIETY

It may not be a paradox of our age that more people than ever before now give serious attention to what is said by religious authorities than have ever done so: there are more people alive, after all. Many people in England were startled in the 1980s when Iranian clergymen denounced an author as a traitor to Islam and pronounced a sentence of death upon him; it was a surprise to them to discover that, as it were, the Middle Ages were still in full swing in some parts of the world, without their having noticed it. They were even more startled when numbers of their Muslim fellow-citizens appeared to agree with the fatwa. Nevertheless, some believe that here as elsewhere Western society has indicated a path which other societies will follow, and that conventional Western liberalism will prevail. It may be so. Equally, it may not be. The interplay of religion and society is very complex and it is best to be cautious.

It is not obvious, for example, that even Islamic societies can avoid cultural corruption by the technology and materialism of the European tradition, though they appear to have been able to resist that tradition's ideological expression in atheistic communism. On the other hand, Islam is still an expanding and missionary faith and the notion of Islamic unity is not dead in Islamic lands. Recent events show only too well that it can still nerve believers to political action, too. The example should suggest others elsewhere. United with strong social forces, religion produced terrifying massacres in the Indian subcontinent both during the months of partition in 1947 and in the struggles which led to the breaking away of East Bengal from Pakistan and the establishment of the new state of Bangladesh in 1971. In Ulster, a minority of British citizens still mouth their hatreds and bitterly dispute the future of their country in the vocabulary of Europe's seventeenth-century religious wars. Though the hierarchies and leaders of different religions find it appropriate to exchange public courtesies and occasionally provide a gaping world with such bizarre spectacles as the hobnobbing of Tibetan Lamas with Anglican bishops, it cannot be said that religion has ceased to be a divisive force because doctrine has become more amorphous. Whether, on the other hand, that means that the supernatural content of religion is losing its hold and that it is important today merely as a badge of group membership, is debatable. What is less debatable is that within the world whose origins are Christian, the decline of sectarian strife has gone along with a general decline of Christian belief and, often, of a loss of nerve. Ecumenism, the movement within Christianity whose most conspicuous expression was the setting up of a World Council of Churches (which Rome did not join) in 1948, owes much to Christians' growing sense in developed countries that they are living in hostile environments. It also owes something to greater uncertainty about what Christianity is, and what it ought to claim.

ROMAN CATHOLICISM

The only unequivocally hopeful sign of unexhausted vigour in Christianity has been

the growth (largely by natural increase) of the Roman Catholic Church. Most Roman Catholics are now non-Europeans, a change dramatized by the first papal visits to South America and Asia in the 1960s. By 1980 forty per cent of the world's Catholics lived in South America, and a majority of the College of Cardinals came from non-European countries.

As for the papacy's historic position within the Roman Church, that appeared to be weakening in the 1960s, some symptoms being provided by an ecumenical council held at the Vatican in that decade. But 1978 (a year of three popes) brought to the throne of St Peter John Paul II, the first Polish pope, the first non-Italian for four and a half centuries, and the first whose investiture was attended by an Anglican archbishop of Canterbury. His pontificate soon showed a determination to exercise the historic possibilities of his office. It is hazardous to project trends in the history of an institution whose fortunes have so obviously fluctuated across the centuries

Religion is still used to justify social hatred and violence. In a Northern Ireland torn by sectarian conflict, Roman Catholics demonstrate in front of British soldiers in Belfast in 1972.

In December 1964 huge crowds of believers greeted Pope Paul VI (1897–1978) when he visited Bombay, India, during the 38th International Ecumenical Congress. Paul VI, who travelled more widely than any previous pope, worked hard during his reign to promote Christian unity.

(up with Hildebrandine reform, down with Schism and conciliarism; up with Trent, down with the Enlightenment; up with the first Vatican council ...) and safest simply to recognize that contraceptive practice – an issue sharpened by science and technology – may face it for the first time with a mortal threat to its unquestioned authority in the eyes of millions of Catholics.

THE STATE

ORGANIZED RELIGION and the notion of fixed, unchanging moral law often linked to it, have always provided some of the most impressive underpinnings of human achievements in social regulation. If they have both been much weakened in recent times, the state, the third great historic agent of social order, has kept its end up much better. It has probably never been so widely taken for granted as the normal form of political organization. There exist more states – that is, recognized and geographically defined political units claiming legislative sovereignty and a monopoly of the use of force within their own borders – than ever before. More people than ever before look to government as their best chance of securing well-being rather than as an inevitable enemy. In many countries politics has apparently replaced

In 1991, the tiny region of Chechnya in southwestern Russia declared itself independent from the Russian Federation. Russian troops were sent to capture the Chechen city of Grozny in December 1994, at a huge cost in life to both sides. Here Chechen soldiers wave their flag in front of Grozny's presidential palace after defeating the Russian army in a battle in June 1995.

religion (sometimes even appearing to eclipse market economics) as the focus of faith that can move mountains.

THE AGGRANDIZEMENT OF THE STATE

The success of the state has been marked (and is partly caused) by governments' growing powers. For the greater part of a century the state has been given more and more power to do what was asked of it. Great wars and peacetime tensions helped. Both required huge mobilization of resources and this led to unprecedented extensions of governmental power. To such forces have also been added demands that governments indirectly promote the welfare of their subjects and undertake the provision of services either unknown hitherto, or left in the past to individuals or such "natural" units as families and villages. There has also been the urge to

modernize. Few countries outside Europe achieved this without direction from above and even in Europe some countries have owed much of their modernization to government. The twentieth century's outstanding examples, though, are Russia and China, two great agrarian societies which sought modernization by using the power of the state to impose it. Finally, there is technology. Better communications, more powerful weapons, more comprehensive information systems have, by and large, advantaged those who could spend most on them: governments.

THE CONTINUING POWER OF NATIONALISM

At this point, a further explanatory factor, and one which is an important qualification, has to be introduced. The state has succeeded above all as the expression and instrument of nationalism. Where it has been in conflict

The explosion of nationalism in the former Yugoslavia shocked onlookers around the world in the last decade of the 20th century. Yugoslavia was created by the Versailles Peace Treaty in 1919. From 1945 it was ruled by Tito's Communist régime: on his death in 1980 the tensions between ethnic Serbs, Croats, Bosnians, Slovenes, Macedonians and Montenegrins came to the fore and civil war broke out. Here, residents of war-torn Sarajevo walk past a building destroyed by shelling in 1992.

with nationalism, the state has often been disadvantaged. This has been true even when, to all appearances, enormous power has been concentrated in the state apparatus. Shaped by the traditions of Communist centralization though they have been, both the USSR and Yugoslavia have now disintegrated into national units. Quebec may separate from Canada. If speculation was the purpose of this book, it would be possible to cite other instances of much more violent potential. In each instance, nationalism – whose bad name is tribalism – is the explanation. When it has found an expression in a state-form, on the other hand, nationalism has greatly reinforced the power of government and extended its real scope; so much so that politicians in many countries are hard at work fostering new nationalisms where they do not exist in order to bolster shaky state structures which have emerged from decolonization.

LIBERAL ASSUMPTIONS LOSE GROUND

The aggrandizement of the state – if we may so put it – long met with little effective resistance. Even in countries where governments have traditionally been distrusted and where institutions exist to check them, people tend to feel that they are much stronger and less resistible than even a few years ago. The strongest checks on the abuse of power remain those of habit and assumption; so long as electorates in liberal states can assume that governments will not quickly fall back on the use of force, they do not feel very alarmed. But the cause of liberal democracy worldwide does not always look very hopeful; there are now more dictators and more authoritarian political régimes in the world than in 1939 (though, since changes in

Greece, Portugal and Spain in the 1970s, and in Eastern European countries in the 1980s, few in Europe). Like the undermining of other liberal assumptions, this is a measure of the narrowing base of what was once thought the cause of the future, but seemed to turn out to be only that of a few advanced societies of the nineteenth century. This does not mean that the forms of liberal politics have not survived. They have, indeed, in one sense prospered, for the rhetoric of democracy and constitutionalism has never been more widely employed, and nationalism is stronger than ever. Yet the substantial freedoms once associated with these ideas are often non-existent or conspicuously in danger and the lack of connexion between nationalism and liberalism is more obvious than ever.

One reason for this is that they have been exported to contexts inimical to them. It is unhistorical to deplore what has followed; as Burke pointed out long ago, political principles take their colour from circumstances. Often in the last half-century it has been shown that representative institutions and democratic forms cannot work properly in societies lacking solid foundations in habits

In Europe, democracy has formally gained ground in the form of elections to a European parliament. These Spanish citizens are casting their votes in such an election, held in 1994.

coherent with them, or where there are powerful divisive influences. In such circumstances, the imposition of an authoritarian style of government has often been the best way of resisting social fragmentation once the discipline imposed by a colonial power is withdrawn. Only too obviously, this has not meant great freedom in most post-colonial countries. Whether greater happiness has followed may be more debatable, but is certainly not to be taken for granted.

The role played by the urge to modernize in strengthening the state – something prefigured long ago outside Europe in a Mehemet Ali or a Kemal – was an indication of new sources from which the state increasingly drew its moral authority. Instead of relying on personal loyalty to a dynasty or a supernatural sanction, it was to rest increasingly on the democratic argument that it was able to satisfy collective desires. Usually these were

for material improvement, but sometimes not. If one value more than any other legitimizes state authority today it is that of nationalism, still the motive force of much of world politics. Its tenacity is remarked on page after page of this book and it has been successful in mobilizing allegiance as no other force has been able to do. Against it, ideologies have not proved effective; the forces working the other way, and helping to make the whole world one political system, have been economics, communications and technology, rather than comparably powerful moral ideas or mythologies.

STATE POWER

Of course, the sheer technical prowess of the state has improved out of recognition since the days when even the great European

The undeniable influence of the mass media means that any attempt to seize power in a Western country is unlikely to be effective if the media cannot also be controlled. Here, anti-Yeltsin demonstrators attack the national television station during the failed coup of October 1993.

The growth of the welfare state

A product of the 20th-century concept of government whereby the state plays a key role in the protection of its citizens' social and financial security, the welfare state is a feature of the most advanced industrialized countries. The fundamental feature of this social care package is social insurance (such as National Insurance in Britain), usually financed by compulsory contributions. This revenue is used to provide unemployment and sickness benefit, old-age pensions, health-care, housing and, in some countries, anti-poverty schemes and taxation plans.

Most modern versions of the welfare state are based on the measures adopted in Britain in 1948 after the Second World War. These were suggested by Sir William Beveridge in his 1942 report *Social Insurance and Allied Services*, in which he advocated state protection for the individual "from the cradle to the grave". In spite of the inherent difficulties of creating such a national "safety net" – financing the services and accurately gauging adequate individual provision while maintaining an incentive to work – welfare states across Europe thrived until the 1980s. From that period governments began to reconsider or dismantle them: for example, in Britain pension provision, the bedrock of the system, was under review in the late 1990s.

A mother and her children arrive at a new council estate in Liverpool, England, in 1954. At that time the demand for houses in Liverpool was high – thousands of families were on the council waiting lists. On just two estates in the city's Kirkby district, 30 or 40 houses were built every week in the mid-1950s.

monarchies could not carry out a census or demolish the obstacles to a unified internal market. Even the growth of international terrorism has left the state with a virtual monopoly of the main instruments of physical control. Already a hundred years ago, the police and armed forces of governments unshaken by war or uncorrupted by sedition gave them almost certain assurance of survival. Improved technology has only increased this near-certainty. New repressive techniques and weapons, moreover, are now only a small part of the story of state power. State intervention in the economy, through its power as consumer, investor or planner, and the improvement of mass communications in a form which leaves access to them highly centralized are also political facts of great importance. They did not appear suddenly in 1945. The welfare state was a reality in Germany and Great Britain before 1914; Hitler and Roosevelt made great use of radio (though for very different ends); and attempts to regulate economic life are as old as government itself. These were, however, all only slight prefigurings of the Leviathan of our own age. When a British foreign secretary said in the late 1940s that he wished to see a state of affairs in which a man could set off for a foreign country with no need to worry about anything except buying a ticket, without passport, visa or other officially imposed documentation, he was virtually asking for

the return of conditions taken for granted eighty years earlier. They still do not exist today – though are now at least conceivable as practical goals in Europe.

RESTRAINTS ON STATE POWER

Since 1945 four new factors have come into play which may indicate the start of a turn in the tide which began to run in favour of the state in sixteenth-century Europe, and has so run ever since. The first is more effective international organization. The United Nations is made up of sovereign states. It has, none the less, shown its capacity to organize collective action against its individual members as the League of Nations and earlier, even less substantial associations and

The European Parliament in Strasbourg is pictured in session. Because of widespread hostility to the idea of a central European "government", the European Union places much emphasis on its democratic institutions and the forum for international debate that they provide.

Water cannons from a supply boat bombard the *Brent Spar* oil platform after a helicopter delivered supplies to Greenpeace activists on board the installation in the North Sea in 1995.

institutions never did. On a smaller, but still huge scale, the nations of Europe inch forward into an institutional framework which day by day encroaches upon their independent power to act as sovereign states. Nor are formal organizations, like the UN and the European Community, the whole story. Many non-economic problems today are tackled internationally and, given concerns over the environment, it is to be presumed that this tendency will continue.

The second force encroaching upon the state is the persistence of some supranational forces which from time to time eclipse by their magnitude the freedom of action of individual sovereign states. Islam is at times such a force; the modern state has never been so successful in the Middle East as elsewhere in assuring its authority. So, perhaps, is the racialist consciousness of pan-Africanism or what is called *négritude* an inhibition on some form of state action. A third curb (or

determinant – words are not easy to choose at so general a level) for the state has been the reintegration of the world economy. Institutionalized by (sometimes) international agreement or by the simple organic growth of large companies, and driven by rising expectations, this has often dashed the hopes of statesmen seeking to order the economies over which they are expected to preside. It is a factor which is closely linked, moreover, to the fourth emerging restraint on state power, the emergence of regional groupings of nations which require the observance of common disciplines. Some, like those of Eastern Europe, have proved evanescent. Others, among which Western Europe is the most obvious example, have slowly advanced their influence, even if the visions of some of their founders are as yet unrealized.

The effect of these forces will often be discernible in the background to the story told in the following volume. Perhaps they prefigure the end of the state's supremacy as the characteristic political institution of modern history. More probably, though, they may bring about some reduction in state power, while leaving forms largely intact (perhaps while power flowers and accumulates elsewhere instead). This is at least more probable than that radical forces will succeed in destroying state power. Such forces exist, and at times they draw strength and appear to prosper from new causes – ecology, feminism and a generalized anti-nuclear and "peace" movement have all patronized them. But in forty years of activity such causes have only been successful when they have been able to influence and shape state policy, changing laws, and setting up new institutions. The idea that major amelioration can be achieved by bypassing so dominant an institution still seems as unrealistic as it was in the days of the anarchistic and utopian movements of the nineteenth century.

Peace protesters have placed a bunch of carnations in the gun carried by this Soviet soldier in Vilnius, Lithuania, in 1991. The Baltic states' emergence from the Soviet Union, following their declaration of their independence, was achieved relatively peacefully.

Time chart (1897–1969)

1897
Zionist Congress

Planck formulates
the quantum theory

1898	1900	1902

1899–1902
The Boer War

Albert Einstein (1879–1955) issued
his special theory of relativity in
1905. In 1915 he formulated the
general theory of relativity, which
was published the following year.

Albert Einstein

1911–1912
The Chinese Revolution

1913
Second Balkan War

1910	1912	1914

The First World
War begins

In 1924 the Chinese Kuomintang officer
Chiang K'ai-shek (1887–1975) was sent
to the USSR for military training. After
the death of Sun Yat-sen in 1925,
Chiang became the KMT leader.

Chiang K'ai-shek

Fascist march on Rome:
Mussolini comes to power

1923–1930
Dictatorship of Primo
de Rivera in Spain

1922	1924	1926

Adolf Hitler's Nazi party rose to power
in Germany in 1933 and immediately
set about destroying the country's
democratic institutions. In 1935 Hitler
began German rearmament.

Hitler (left) with Mussolini

German delegates are pictured on their way
to sign the 1925 Treaty of Locarno, by which
Germany gave her consent to the Versailles
territorial settlement in the west. The issue
of revision in the east was left unresolved.

Signatories of the Treaty of Locarno

Nuclear fission is discovered

1934	1936	1938

1935
Italy invades
Ethiopia

1936–1939
The Spanish
Civil War

1945
End of the Second
World War

Churchill denounces
the "Iron Curtain"

1947
India gains independence
Creation of Pakistan

Gandhi is assassinated
Foundation of Israel

1946	1948	1950

Mahatma Gandhi and Jawarhal Nehru
were the key figures in the fight for
Indian independence. They are pic-
tured during a meeting of the Indian
Congress in 1946, the year in which
Britain offered to relinquish its rule.

Gandhi and Nehru

The Japanese occupation of China ended
in 1945. The Civil War between the
Nationalists and Communists raged
until 1949, when the People's Republic
of China was proclaimed under the
leadership of Mao Tse-tung (1893–1976).

Mao Tse-tung

First US satellite
is sent into orbit

1958	1960	1962

1961
Soviet astronaut Gagarin is
the first human in space

	1905 Revolution in Russia		Creation of the Muslim League		1907 First production line for Ford's Model T cars	
1904		1906			1908	

Thomas Edward Lawrence (1888–1935) is portrayed in 1918. This British agent, who became famous as Lawrence of Arabia, played a crucial role in the Arab rebellion against the Ottoman Empire during the First World War.

Lawrence of Arabia

	1917 The USA enters the First World War The Russian Revolution				
1916		1918		1920	
		End of the First World War	1919 Peace Treaty signed at Versailles	1920–1922 Greco-Turkish War	

Great Britain recognizes the government of Chiang K'ai-shek		Military coup in Argentina	1931 Japan invades Manchuria	Roosevelt is elected president of USA
1928		1930		1932
	1929 The Wall Street Crash			

Winston Churchill (1874–1965) personified the British determination to defeat Hitler even in the face of Germany's initially successful invasion of Russia in 1941.

Winston Churchill

1939 The Second World War begins				The Allied invasion of Normandy
1940		1942		1944
	1941 Japanese attack on Pearl Harbor	Nazi leaders agree to impose their "Final Solution" on Europe's Jews		

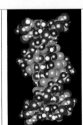

German troops parade through Paris in August 1940, two months after the French signed an armistice with the invaders. Italy joined the war on Germany's side and Great Britain was left without an ally on the continent.

German troops in Paris

			Uprising against Hungary's Communist régime	1957 Launch of Soviet satellite Sputnik I
1952		1954		1956

The double-helix model of the structure of DNA was established in 1953. This discovery made it possible to manipulate organisms' genes and growth processes.

Computer-generated image of a segment of a DNA molecule

In 1961 President Kennedy announced that the USA aimed to send a man to the moon by the end of the decade. On 21 July 1969 American astronaut Neil Armstrong, commander of the Apollo 11 space rocket, became the first human being to set foot on the moon.

The first moon landing

1964		1966		1968
	1965 Soviet astronaut Leonov makes the first "space walk"		1967 The first human heart transplant	

VOLUME 9 *Chapters and contents*

SERIES CONTENTS

Volume 6

THE MAKING OF THE EUROPEAN AGE

A New Kind of Society: Early Modern Europe
Authority and its Challengers
The New World of Great Powers
Europe's Assault on the World
World History's New Shape

Volume 7

THE AGE OF REVOLUTION

Ideas Old and New
Long-term Change
Political Change in an Age of Revolution
A New Europe
The Anglo-Saxon World

Volume 8

THE EUROPEAN EMPIRES

The European World Hegemony
European Imperialism and Imperial Rule
Asia's Response to a Europeanizing World
Strains in the System
The Era of the First World War

Volume 9

EMERGING POWERS

A New Asia in the Making
The Ottoman Heritage and the Western Islamic Lands
The Second World War
The Shaping of a New World
Population, Economy and the Management of Nature
Ideas, Attitudes and Authority

Volume 10

THE NEW GLOBAL ERA

The Politics of the New World
Inheritors of Empire
Crumbling Certainties
New Challenges to the Cold War World Order
The End of an Era
Epilogue: in the Light of History

INDEX

Page references to main text in roman, to box text in **bold** and to captions in *italic*.

ACKNOWLEDGMENTS

The publishers wish to thank the following
for their kind permission to reproduce the
illustrations in this book:

KEY

b bottom; **c** centre; **t** top; **l** left; **r** right
AGE: AGE Fotostock
AISA: Archivo Iconografico S.A., Barcelona
AKG: AKG, London
BLV: Bertelsmann Lexikon Verlag, Under
  Sublicence of Bertelsmann Picture Pool,
  Gütersloh / München 1997
CB: Corbis-Bettmann, Under Sublicence of
  Bertelsmann Picture Pool, Gütersloh / München
  1997
BAL: Bridgeman Art Library, London / New
  York
RMN: Réunion des Musées Nationaux, Paris
SPL: Science Photo Library, London
UPI: United Press International

Front cover: Corbis-Bettmann / National
  Archives, Washington D.C.
3 Zardoya / Magnum Photos / Koyo Kageyama
7 CB
8 AISA
9 Roger-Viollet / Harlingue
10 CB
11 CB
12 CB / UPI
13 CB
15 CB
16 Hulton Getty
17 CB
18 Popperfoto
19 Archives Ringart
21 CB / UPI
22 Hulton Getty
23 CB / UPI
24 Zardoya / Magnum Photos / Koyo Kageyama
25 CB / UPI
27 AGE
28 CB / UPI
29 CB / UPI
30 CB / UPI
32 AISA
33t Zardoya / Camera Press
33b AISA
34 AISA
35 AISA
36 CB / UPI
37 CB / UPI
38 Popperfoto
39 Zardoya
40 AGE
42 Roger-Viollet
43 Hulton Getty
44 CB
45 AGE

47 Hulton Getty
48 CB / UPI
49 CB
50 BAL / © VEGAP 1999
51 CB
52 CB
53 CB / UPI
54 CB / UPI
55 CB
56 CB
57 CB
58 CB / UPI
59 Zardoya / Magnum Photos / Robert Capa
60 CB
61 CB
62 CB / UPI
63 CB
64 Oronoz / Museo Reina Sofia, Madrid / ©
  VEGAP 1999 / © Succession Picasso, Paris
66t CB / UPI
66b CB
67 AGE
68 CB / UPI
70 CB / UPI
71 CB / UPI
72 CB / UPI
73 CB / UPI
74 CB / UPI
75 Zardoya / Len Sirman Press
76 Zardoya / Magnum Photos / Koyo Kageyama
78 CB
79 CB
80 CB / UPI
81 CB / UPI
83 Hulton Getty / Fred Ramage
84 CB / UPI
85 United Nations
86 Zardoya / Camera Press
87 Rex Features / United Nations
88 Hulton Getty
89 AKG
90 David King Collection
91 Hulton Getty
93 AGE
94 CB / UPI
95 Zardoya / Camera Press
96 Zardoya / Camera Press
97 David King Collection
98 Zardoya / Camera Press
99 CB / UPI
100 Popperfoto
101 CB / UPI
102 AGE
103 CB
104 CB / UPI
105 Zardoya / Camera Press
106 AGE
107 CB / UPI
108 Image Bank / Archive Photos
109 CB / UPI
110 Zardoya / Magnum Photos / Paul Fusco
112 CB / UPI
113 Magnum Photos / Robert Capa

114 SPL / NASA
115 AGE
116 CB / Reuters
117 Zardoya
118 Panos Pictures / Alain le Garsmeur
119 SPL / Steve Grand
120 CB / UPI
122 Zardoya / Magnum Photos / Hiroji Kubota
123 AISA
124 CB
126 CB / Reuters
128t The World Bank, Washington D.C.
128b International Monetary Fund, Washington
  D.C.
129 AGE
130t AISA
130b AISA
131 SPL / Simon Fraser
133 AGE
134 CB
135 CB
136 CB
137 AGE
138 Advertising Archives
139 SPL / Jerrican / Galia
140 AGE
141t CB
141b CB / UPI
142 CB
143 RMN / Blot / Lewandowski
144t Popperfoto
144b AGE / SPL / James King-Holmes
145t AGE / SPL / Jon Wilson
145b SPL / J.C. Revy
146 CB / UPI
147 CB / UPI
148 CB / UPI
149 CB / UPI / NASA
150 BLV / NASA
152 AGE / NASA
153 CB / Reuters
154 Panos Pictures / Sam Kittner
155 CB / UPI
156 CB / Reuters
157 Rex Features / Sipa-Press
159 Panos Pictures / Paul Smith
160 AGE
161 Zardoya / Magnum Photos / Martin Parr
162 AGE
163 Panos Pictures / Alain le Garsmeur
164 Selznick / United Artists (courtesy Kobal
  Collection)
165 CB
166 Network
167 CB / Reuters
168 CB / Reuters
169 BLV
170 Popperfoto
171 Magnum Photos / Paul Lowe
172 Popperfoto
173 AISA
174 Network / Anthony Suau
175 Hulton Getty

176 Photo European Parliament
177 CB / Agence France Presse
179 Magnum Photos / Abbas

MAPS AND DIAGRAMS
Maps copyright © 1998 Debate page 77
Maps and diagrams copyright © 1998
Helicon/Debate pages 26, 69, 111, 121,
125, 127, 132

TEXT CREDITS
The publishers wish to thank the following
for their kind permission to reproduce the
translations and copyright material in this
book. Every effort has been made to trace
copyright owners, but if anyone has been
omitted we apologize and will, if informed,
make corrections in any future edition.

p.60 an extract from *Mein Kampf* by Adolf
Hitler, translated by Ralph Manheim (Pimlico
1992). Reproduced by permission of Random
House UK Limited; p.131 an extract from *The
Asian–African Conference, Bandung, Indonesia,
April 1955* by George McTurnan Kahin (Cornell
University Press 1956). Reproduced by permis-
sion of the publisher, Cornell University Press;
p.146 an extract from *The Cosmic Connection:
An Extraterrestrial Perspective* by Carl Sagan,
produced by Jerome Agel. (For further informa-
tion: Jerome Agel, 2 Peter Cooper Road, New
York, New York 10010, USA).

THE OLD ONES

ROBERT COLES

THE OLD ONES

OF NEW MEXICO

Photographs by ALEX HARRIS

UNIVERSITY OF NEW MEXICO PRESS

Albuquerque

The chapter *Una Anciana* appeared originally in *The New Yorker*.

Composed by the University of New Mexico Printing Plant.
Printed and bound by North Central Publishing Co.
Designed by Dan Stouffer.

To the people who appear and speak in this book, and to others like them we have been privileged to meet and come to know.

ACKNOWLEDGMENTS

Portions of this book have appeared in *The New Yorker, The American Poetry Review*, and *Commonweal*. I wish to thank the editors of those periodicals for the space they judged worth giving to these somewhat obscure people, not always considered worth the interest and favorable regard of other Americans. I also wish to thank Elizabeth Heist and Carl Mora of the University of New Mexico Press. Alex Harris and I have been offered much by the state of New Mexico. The state's university press has not only given our work sanction, but helped it out considerably, because the editors have known themselves who it is and what it is we have wanted to describe or evoke, and so have been especially thoughtful critics.

CONTENTS

INTRODUCTION

One mother after another urged me to pay special attention to the old people. Here is what one of them told me in December of 1972: "You should talk with the children's grandparents. You should tell the Anglos about our old men and women. With us the grandfather and the grandmother are very important. I see on television how the Anglos treat their old people: to the garbage heap they go. For me my parents and my husband's parents are the most important people in the world—along with our priest, of course."

I came to live in New Mexico in 1972 so that I could get to know the children: children of Spanish background as well as the children of the Pueblo Indians who live in large numbers north of Albuquerque. I had begun my work with Spanish-speaking children in Florida, where Chicanos now make up about one-third of the so-called Eastern stream of migrant farmworkers, traveling from Florida to Maine and back, year in, year out. In the 1960s I spent much time with such people, and I have written about what I saw and heard in the second volume of *Children of Crisis: Migrants, Sharecroppers, Mountaineers*. Many of the Chicano children I met on the Eastern seaboard had been born in Texas; in search of a better life, their parents had left the Rio Grande Valley, where thousands of agricultural workers from Mexico live and work under extremely difficult and often oppressive circumstances. I began to visit the Rio Grande

Valley—Texas towns like Edinburg, Crystal City, McAllen—in 1970. I had by then largely finished the work I have described in three volumes of *Children of Crisis*, and had decided to work more closely and at greater length with Chicano families.

In Texas I heard about New Mexico; often I was told that if I wanted to see a "different" kind of Spanish-speaking person, I had best move next door, to that state. So I eventually did, taking up residence in Albuquerque and from there traveling widely in all directions, especially to the east of the city, through the Sandia mountains, and up north to the highland country well above Santa Fe. In those areas one finds settlements of families headed for many generations by small farmers or ranchers. The people are strong, proud, vigorous, independent. They are of "Spanish" descent, yet can be called "old-line" Americans: they have been here far longer than many other well-established "groups." They have clung tenaciously to their own traditions and values, not the least of which is their language; they have by and large learned English, especially the younger people have, but they have kept fluent in Spanish. Apart from the language, they live in towns which often seem right out of Spain in appearance, and they retain customs and habits that are clearly Spanish: preferences for particular foods, ways of speaking to one another, religious attitudes, a view of life, really. Still, one has to note that the colonization of New Mexico—and other areas which made up the northern frontier of what was known from the sixteenth century through the mid-nineteenth century as "New Spain"—was largely accomplished by settlers from central Mexico. The conquerors were Spanish officers and mestizo soldiers—people of mixed Spanish and Indian blood, and in their wake came mestizo settlers who were thoroughly Hispanicized culturally.

As a child psychiatrist I have been trying to find out how that Hispanic view of life is transmitted to children and shapes for them a distinctive kind of experience—a childhood obviously, in certain respects, like that of other children around the world, but a childhood also quite unique. I have written this book in the midst of that study, and, I repeat, at the behest of a number of people I have been getting to know, not only the mothers but the priests. One priest stated the connection between the children and the old people most emphatically: "If you want to know about the children, you must first speak with the old people; what they believe, the child soon believes. The parents are go-betweens, I often think: they are very close to *their* parents, and hand down beliefs from the very old to the very young."

I protested to him. Isn't that always the case, even among the Anglos he often talks about? And besides, the priest himself was one of several quite old village curates of Spanish descent I'd met; perhaps he was feathering his own generation's cap. But over the months I was more than persuaded. I came to see how extraordinarily important these elderly men and women are in the lives of their children and grandchildren; I also came to see that, old as they are, there is a remarkable strength and vitality to them as human beings. Others from the Anglo world might consider them aloof, old-fashioned, superstitious, all too set in their ways. They themselves look upon their situation quite differently; they hold to certain values and assumptions, and, God willing, they will not forsake them.

I hope in the future to indicate how childhood goes for New Mexico's Chicano children, who might also be referred to as American children of Spanish ancestry (and such descriptive words are treacherous, because different individuals or communities have their own definite preferences and prejudices as to what they ought be called). Here I hope to indicate something of what old age is like for people not always given the most attention or respect by the so-called dominant culture of this nation. I also hope to convey some of the strengths these aged men and women have managed to acquire over the many years of their lives. Over and over again in the medical and psychiatric literature and in books aimed at the general public one learns of the increasing sadness and even despair that come with old age: the body becomes more and more debilitated, and for that reason, as well as for those "socioeconomic" reasons we hear so much of, the elderly are described as having a thoroughly awful time of it. They not only feel weak and quite possibly in pain, they also feel ignored at best—and quite likely rebuffed or avoided like the plague.

Nor do I want to take issue with the observations of various psychological and sociological students of old age. There is no doubt that in this country old people are a threat of sorts: everyone wants to be young or look young—or at the very least, not be thought old and "out of it." The nation itself is young, as countries go, and its population is by no means old, relatively speaking. Moreover, the cult of youth is an established one in the United States—perhaps because so many people who have come here have felt the need to forsake their own cultural traditions. No matter what new attitudes replace those traditions, one thing has, alas, been evident: the immigrants must be succeeded by a generation of native-born Americans who are quite different—hence the development of an important split, one that has to do with language, customs, a whole sense of where loyalties belong and what a person ought to strive to obtain out of life.

In contrast, the families whose aged members I have been spending time with have not had to go through that kind of split—one that involves a difference of actual experience, followed by the onset of those ideological or philosophical rifts that often simply reflect various efforts at self-justification made by people who can no longer share certain assumptions about life. The old men and women this book aims to describe are not necessarily beyond the criticism of their children or grandchildren. Nor is it true that in New Mexico, if nowhere else in America, there is a thoroughly static society, a strict continuity of manners, convictions, articles of faith from one generation to the next. None of the old people I have worked with in New Mexico, or in any other part of the country, however contented or self-assured they seem, however honored by their families and friends and neighbors, have the idea that their children and grandchildren are extensions, pure and simple, of themselves in a generational progression that the Bible describes as "world without end." I have heard old men or women wish it could be that way: "I sometimes wonder why we can't be allowed to stay as we are; I have liked the life I have lived, and wanted the same kind of life for my sons and daughters, and for their sons and daughters. No such luck, though; the world presses down on us—even in this village it does, and I know we are removed up here in the mountains."

Such a wish is followed inevitably by the realization that there is just so much isolation a nation like this one allows even its more peripheral communities. And no doubt about it, these men and women, in their seventies or eighties, are Americans; they have lived through the Great Depression of the 1930s, have seen their sons and grandsons leave to fight in the wars this country has fought, one after the other, in recent decades, have heard on the radio what the rest of us have heard. If they are old Spanish-speaking inhabitants of one state, they are also Americans who in many ways resemble others of their age elsewhere, regardless of racial or ethnic background. On the other hand, I believe they themselves express those qualities of mind, heart, and spirit that distinguish them from some of the rest of us.

A word or two about "method"—the way this "research" has been done. I have been visiting certain families, talking with them, trying to find out how they live and what they believe in. I make weekly, sometimes twice-weekly, calls, but have no standard questions in mind, no methodology to implement. I simply talk with my hosts at their leisure; whatever comes up, I am grateful to hear about. The men and women have spoken to me in both Spanish and English, often in one language for a spell, then in the other. They have all been *able* to speak English, even if haltingly at times; but I have encouraged them to speak in Spanish, and they have encouraged me to try my Spanish, which I would have to describe as broken or at best passable. I do believe, however, that I can understand the language fairly well. And I have made every effort to translate the speech I have heard in such a way that its flavor and tone come across to the middle-class "Anglo" people who will read this book.

A word about the photographs: Alex Harris is a friend of mine and a photographer who has spent time with migrant farmers and sharecroppers of the rural South as well as in New Mexico. He is the first person I have worked with as I have gone out on my visits—in contrast, that is, to joining a text of mine to pictures taken quite independently by a photographer. We both came to New Mexico under the same generous grant from the Ford Foundation, and we have shared our thoughts and impressions from week to week as we went about the state, trying to respond to its rich and unusual social and cultural life. He has wandered far and wide, and though his photographs are meant to dovetail with this text, they also represent his own attempt to do justice to the people he has met, and, I might add, become a friend of—a visitor anticipated and welcomed, in spite of all the amusing and puzzling equipment he necessarily has to bring along. The state of New Mexico has long fascinated photographers; its land, its skies, its flora and fauna, its hills and canyons, deserts and grazing lands, all have drawn attentive witnesses, who have come forth with much for us to see in exhibitions and books. But ironically the state's men and women and children are not so well known—too often they are overlooked. They deserve a photographer's respectful and thoughtful notice, and I believe that in the kind of observations he has recorded, Mr. Harris is a pioneer.

The people he presents here are not the people whose words I present, but they might well have been, because they are very similar in appearance and life-history, and in their faith. I cannot emphasize strongly enough my gratitude to this young and dedicated photographer-colleague of mine. If I have learned a lot from listening to the people about to have their say on this book's pages, I have also learned so very much from looking at Alex Harris's photographs and talking with him about what he has seen and heard. This book is our joint effort to set down some of our observations—observations made almost accidentally: we

with my hosts at their leisure; whatever comes up, I am grateful to hear about. The men and women have spoken to me in both Spanish and English, often in one language for a spell, then in the other. They have all been *able* to speak English, even if haltingly at times; but I have encouraged them to speak in Spanish, and they have encouraged me to try my Spanish, which I would have to describe as broken or at best passable. I do believe, however, that I can understand the language fairly well. And I have made every effort to translate the speech I have heard in such a way that its flavor and tone come across to the middle-class "Anglo" people who will read this book.

A word about the photographs: Alex Harris is a friend of mine and a photographer who has spent time with migrant farmers and sharecroppers of the rural South as well as in New Mexico. He is the first person I have worked with as I have gone out on my visits—in contrast, that is, to joining a text of mine to pictures taken quite independently by a photographer. We both came to New Mexico under the same generous grant from the Ford Foundation, and we have shared our thoughts and impressions from week to week as we went about the state, trying to respond to its rich and unusual social and cultural life. He has wandered far and wide, and though his photographs are meant to dovetail with this text, they also represent his own attempt to do justice to the people he has met, and, I might add, become a friend of—a visitor anticipated and welcomed, in spite of all the amusing and puzzling equipment he necessarily has to bring along. The state of New Mexico has long fascinated photographers; its land, its skies, its flora and fauna, its hills and canyons, deserts and grazing lands, all have drawn attentive witnesses, who have come forth with much for us to see in exhibitions and books. But ironically the state's men and women and children are not so well known—too often they are overlooked. They deserve a photographer's respectful and thoughtful notice, and I believe that in the kind of observations he has recorded, Mr. Harris is a pioneer.

The people he presents here are not the people whose words I present, but they might well have been, because they are very similar in appearance and life-history, and in their faith. I cannot emphasize strongly enough my gratitude to this young and dedicated photographer-colleague of mine. If I have learned a lot from listening to the people about to have their say on this book's pages, I have also learned so very much from looking at Alex Harris's photographs and talking with him about what he has seen and heard. This book is our joint effort to set down some of our observations—observations made almost accidentally: we set out to come to children and were directed by them and their parents to grandparents—a rather interesting turn of events to happen these days. This book is also a statement of our own, as well as one about others; we have grown to admire and respect the people whose lives and fate we make a particular effort to portray in the following pages, and if some of our affection comes across, some of our gratitude, too, as well as a number of "facts" or "impressions" or "ideas," then it will have been an effort well worth making.

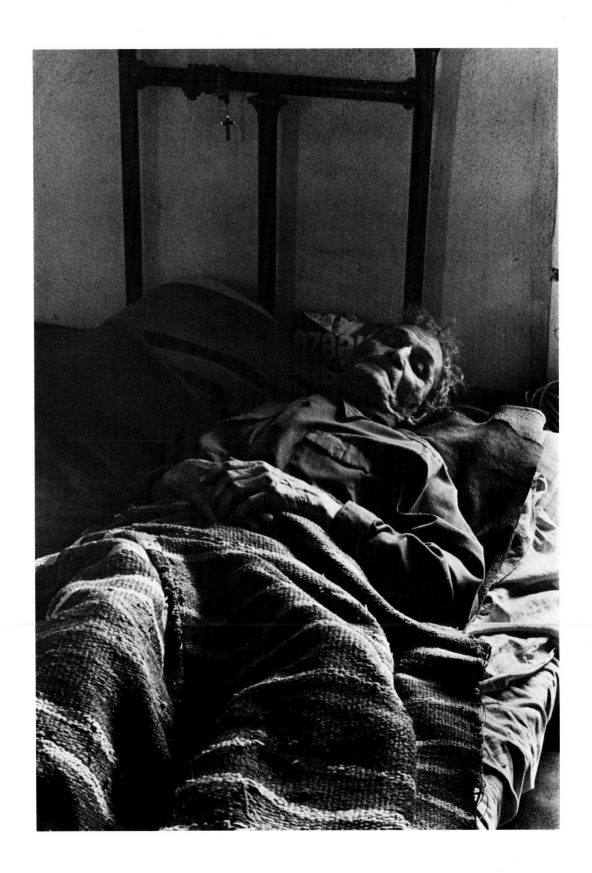

1

TWO LANGUAGES, ONE SOUL

The Spanish-speaking people of the Southwest continue to be considered one of this nation's "problems," and for understandable reasons. In large measure they are poor, and their lot has by no means improved universally in recent years, for all the steps taken in the 1960s to make life easier for our so-called minorities. In the Rio Grande Valley of Texas even the vote cannot be taken for granted by many Mexican Americans, as they are called there. In the barrios of Los Angeles the "brown berets"—one more term—struggle on behalf of people plagued by joblessness and a host of discriminatory practices. "Chicano power!" one hears—yet another phrase; and looking at the power others have, it is not easy to disagree with the exhortation. In New Mexico there are distinct differences; unlike Texas or California, the state has long been responsive to its Spanish-speaking people. In fact, along with the Indians, they made up its "first families," and to this day, despite Anglo political and economic dominance, Spanish surnames are to be found everywhere: among holders of high political office, in the business world and the professions, and among storekeepers, small landowners, and blue-collar workers. Such a state of affairs has to be contrasted with conditions in Texas, where thousands of "Mexicanos" (as "gringos" sometimes call them with barely concealed disdain) are either migrant farmworkers or go jobless, or in California, where César Chávez continues his not altogether successful struggle, and where "Latinos" (one hears that word used, too) share with blacks all the misery of the urban ghetto, most especially the sense that there is no one very important to call upon for help.

Still, even in New Mexico there is no reason to rejoice at the position the state's Spanish-speaking people occupy—especially when one compares it with the social and economic condition of Anglos. In many towns and villages those who speak Spanish are desperately poor; they lack work, or, if they do have jobs, they are menial ones, the only kind available. In the schools their children are often enough treated badly; reprimanded for using Spanish words, told that they are not suited for school, and made to feel that they will soon enough be living the same circumscribed lives their parents have known. Many who want better for the poor and struggle on their behalf—whether for the Anglo poor, black poor, Spanish-speaking poor—know how particularly destructive that kind of educational experience can be for young children, whose whole sense of "expectation" (What do I dare see ahead for myself, aim at, hope for?) is so crucially determined by the atmosphere in the elementary school.

Efforts to improve the condition of the Spanish-speaking poor of New Mexico have been predominantly educational. No one in the state has difficulty in voting, and the economy is unfortunately not advanced enough for those on the bottom to have any great success in demanding a larger share of the available wealth. Businesses are very much being courted, not with quite the desperation one sees in Alabama or Mississippi, but with a certain grim determination. And labor unions are not the power they are in Michigan or Pennsylvania. But the schools have traditionally been the hope for the future all over this country; and they lend themselves more easily to change than a newly arrived factory or a firmly entrenched political hierarchy. So, one hears about "culturally disadvantaged" children and "culturally deprived" children; and among those both more knowledgeable and less given to condescension, "bilingual" education. Such terms are meant to convey the difficulties Spanish-speaking people have as outsiders of sorts. "America is Anglo," one hears Indian and Chicano children say in various parts of the Southwest, and that is that.

At least those children are granted a degree of hope by those of us who spend our time making judgments about the fate or destiny of one or another racial or ethnic group: they are young; changes are taking place; their lives will be less shame-ridden, more fulfilled. There are "job opportunity" programs. There are also various "enrichment" programs in the schools. Spanish is now increasingly allowed in those schools—to be spoken, even to be used by teachers.

In the words of one Chicana social worker I have talked with: "We are determined to move ahead, even if there is great resistance from the power structure. No longer will Chicanos in New Mexico grow up feeling like second-class citizens. No longer will they feel misunderstood or scorned. In the old days they received the worst kind of schooling. They were made to feel stupid and awkward. They were made to feel they have nothing worthwhile to say or contribute. The Anglo teachers, the Anglo-run school system looked down on Chicanos. We were given no credit for our own values, for our culture and traditions. And the contempt showed on the people; they felt ashamed, inferior. They never learned to speak English the way the teachers did. They never learned to express themselves in school and they dropped out soon, usually well before high school was over. We hope to change that. We can't do anything about what has already happened. The old people are the way they are—it is too late for them to change. But it will be different for the young. They will have pride in themselves, and they will not only think well of themselves, but speak well. They won't have memories of Anglo teachers laughing at their Spanish, or punishing them for using it. They will speak Spanish with joy."

As she said, "the old people are the way they are." But exactly how is their "way" to be characterized? That is to say, how badly have they been scarred by the awful conditions described so forcefully by this particular political activist, among others? No doubt she is right—down to the last detail of her remarks; in recent years I have seen enough first-hand to more than confirm the basis for her sense of outrage. Still, I have to think of the people I have come to know in New Mexico—the old, thoroughly poor, certainly rather uneducated people, who have lived the hard, tough, sometimes terribly sad lives that the Chicana just quoted describes, and yet don't quite feel as she does about themselves. Nor do they speak as if they have been systematically brutalized, robbed of all their "self-esteem," as social scientists put it. In their seventies or eighties, with long memories of hardships faced and perhaps only partially (if at all) surmounted, "deprived" of education, made to feel hopelessly inarticulate, and obviously out of "the American mainstream," they are nevertheless men and women who seem to have held on stubbornly to a most peculiar notion: that they are eminently valuable and important human beings, utterly worth the respect, even admiration, not to mention the love, of their children and grandchildren.

Moreover, they are men and women who, for all the education they lack, all the wrongheaded or just plain mean teachers they once ran up against, all the cultural bias and social discrimination they may have sensed or experienced outright, still manage not only to feel fairly assured about themselves as human beings, put here by the Lord for His own purposes, but also to say rather a lot about what is on their mind—and in such a way that they make themselves unmistakably clear. In fact, I have found myself at times overwhelmed by the power of their speech, the force that their language possesses, the dramatic expressions they call upon, the strong and subtle imagery available to them, the sense of irony and ambiguity they repeatedly and almost as a matter of course demonstrate. Perhaps my surprise and admiration indicate my own previous blind spots, my own ignorance and even prejudice. If so, I have been more than brought up short again and again.

Here are the words of an elderly woman who has had virtually no schooling and speaks a mixture of Spanish (which I have translated) and terse but forceful English. She lives in a small, isolated mountain community well to the north of Santa Fe and enjoys talking with her visitor: "Sometimes I have a moment to think. I look back and wonder where all the time has gone to—so many years; I cannot say I like to be reminded how many. My sister is three years older, eighty this May. She is glad to talk of her age. I don't like to mention mine. Maybe I have not her faith in God. She makes her way every day to church. I go only on Sundays. Enough is enough; besides, I don't like the priest. He points his finger too much. He likes to accuse us—each week it is a different sin he charges us with. My mother used to read me Christ's words when I was a girl—from the old Spanish Bible her grandmother gave to her on her deathbed. I learned that Christ was a kind man; He tried to think well of people, even the lowest of the low, even those at the very bottom who are in a swamp and don't know how to get out, let alone find for themselves some high, dry land.

"But this priest of ours gives no one the benefit of the doubt. I have no right to find fault with him; I know that. Who am I to do so? I am simply an old lady, and I had better watch out: the Lord no doubt punishes those who disagree with His priests. But our old priest who died last year was so much finer, so much better to hear on a warm Sunday morning. Every once in a while he would even lead us outside to the courtyard and talk with us there, give us a second sermon. I felt so much better for listening to him. He was not in love with the sound of his own voice, as this new priest is. He did not stop and listen to the echo of his words. He did not brush away dust from his coat, or worry if the wind went through his hair. He was not always looking for a paper towel to wipe his shoes.

My husband says he will buy this priest a dozen handkerchiefs and tell him they are to be used for his shoes only. Here when we get rain we are grateful, and it is not too high a price to pay, a little mud to walk through. Better mud that sticks than dust that blows away.

"Well, I should not go on so long about a vain man. We all like to catch ourselves in the mirror and find ourselves good to look at. Here I am, speaking ill of him, yet I won't let my family celebrate my birthdays any more; and when I look at myself in the mirror a feeling of sadness comes over me. I pull at my skin and try to erase the lines, but no luck. I think back: all those years when my husband and I were young, and never worried about our health, our strength, our appearance. I don't say we always do now; but there are times when we look like ghosts of ourselves. I will see my husband noticing how weak and tired I have become, how hunched over. I pretend not to see, but once the eyes have caught something, one cannot shake the picture off. And I look at him, too; he will straighten up when he feels my glance strike him, and I quickly move away. Too late, though; he has been told by me, without a word spoken, that he is old, and I am old, and that is our fate, to live through these last years.

"But it is not only pity we feel for ourselves. A few drops of rain and I feel grateful; the air is so fresh afterwards. I love to sit in the sun. We have the sun so often here, a regular visitor, a friend one can expect to see often and trust. I like to make tea for my husband and me. At midday we take our tea outside and sit on our bench, our backs against the wall of the house. Neither of us wants pillows; I tell my daughters and sons that they are soft—those beach chairs of theirs. Imagine beach chairs here in New Mexico, so far from any ocean! The bench feels strong to us, not uncomfortable. The tea warms us inside, the sun on the outside. I joke with my husband; I say we are part of the house: the adobe gets baked, and so do we. For the most part we say nothing, though. It is enough to sit and be part of God's world. We hear the birds talking to each other, and are grateful they come as close to us as they do; all the more reason to keep our tongues still and hold ourselves in one place. We listen to cars going by and wonder who is rushing off. A car to us is a mystery. The young understand a car. They cannot imagine themselves not driving. They have not the interest we had in horses. Who is to compare one lifetime with another, but a horse is alive and one loves a horse and is loved by a horse. Cars come and go so fast. One year they command all eyes. The next year they are a cause for shame. The third year they must be thrown away without the slightest regret. I may exaggerate, but not much!

"My moods are like the church bell on Sunday: way up, then down, then up again—and often just as fast. I make noises, too; my husband says he can hear me smiling and hear me turning sour. When I am sour I am really sour—sweet milk turned bad. Nothing pleases me. I am more selfish than my sister. She bends with the wind. I push my heels into the ground and won't budge. I know enough to frown at myself, but not enough to change. There was a time when I tried hard. I would talk to myself as if I was the priest. I would promise myself that tomorrow I would be different. I suppose only men and women can fool themselves that way; an animal knows better. Animals are themselves. We are always trying to be better—and often we end up even worse than we were to start with.

"But now, during the last moments of life, I think I have learned a little wisdom. I can go for days without an upset. I think I dislike our priest because he reminds me of myself. I have his long forefinger, and I can clench my fist like him and pound the table and pour vinegar on people with my remarks. It is no good to be like that. A man is lucky; it is in his nature to fight or preach. A woman should be peaceful. My mother used to say all begins the day we are born: some are born on a clear, warm day; some when it is cloudy and stormy. So, it is a consolation to find myself easy to live with these days. And I have found an answer to the few moods I still get. When I have come back from giving the horses each a cube or two of sugar, I give myself the same. I am an old horse who needs something sweet to give her more faith in life!

"The other day I thought I was going to say good-bye to this world. I was hanging up some clothes to dry. I love to do that, then stand back and watch and listen to the wind go through the socks or the pants or the dress, and see the sun warm them and make them smell fresh. I had dropped a few clothespins, and was picking them up, when suddenly I could not catch my breath, and a sharp pain seized me over my chest. I tried hard to stand up, but I couldn't. I wanted to scream but I knew there was no one nearby to hear. My husband had gone to the store. I sat down on the ground and waited. It was strong, the pain; and there was no one to tell about it. I felt as if someone had lassoed me and was pulling the rope tighter and tighter. Well here you are, an old cow, being taken in by the good Lord; that is what I thought.

"I looked at myself, sitting on the ground. For a second I was my old self again—worrying about how I must have appeared there, worrying about my dress, how dirty it would get to be. This is no place for an old lady, I thought—only for one of my little grandchildren, who love to play out here, build their castles of dirt, wetted down with water I give to them. Then more pain; I thought I had about a minute of life left. I said my prayers. I said goodbye to the house. I pictured my husband in my mind: fifty-seven years of marriage. Such a good man! I said to myself that I might not see him ever again; surely God would take him into Heaven, but as for me, I have no right to expect that outcome. Then I looked up to the sky and waited.

"My eye caught sight of a cloud. It was darker than the rest. It was alone. It was coming my way. The hand of God, I was sure of it! So that is how one dies. All my life, in the spare moments a person has, I wondered how I would go. Now I knew. Now I was ready. I thought I would soon be taken up to the cloud and across the sky I would go, and that would be that. But the cloud kept moving, and soon it was no longer above me, but beyond me; and I was still on my own land, so dear to me, so familiar after all these years. I can't be dead, I thought to myself, if I am here and the cloud is way over there, and getting further each second. Maybe the next cloud—but by then I had decided God had other things to do. Perhaps my name had come up, but He had decided to call others before me, and get around to me later. Who can ever know His reasons? Then I spotted my neighbor walking down the road, and I said to myself that I would shout for him. I did, and he heard. But you know, by the time he came I had sprung myself free. Yes, that is right, the pain was all gone.

"He helped me up, and he was ready to go find my husband and bring him back. No, I told him, no; I was all right, and I did not want to risk frightening my husband. He is excitable. He might get some kind of attack himself. I went inside and put myself down on our bed and waited. For an hour—it was that long, I am sure—my eyes stared at the ceiling, held on to it for dear life. I thought of what my life had been like: a simple life, not a very important one, maybe an unnecessary one. I am sure there are better people, men and women all over the world, who have done more for their neighbors and yet not lived as long as I have. I felt ashamed for a few minutes: all the complaints I'd made to myself and to my family, when the truth has been that my fate has been to live a long and healthy life, to have a good and loyal husband, and to bring two sons and three daughters into this world. I thought of the five children we had lost, three before they had a chance to take a breath. I wondered where in the universe they were.

In the evening sometimes, when I go to close loose doors that otherwise complain loudly all night, I am likely to look at the stars and feel my long-gone infants near at hand. They are far off, I know; but in my mind they have become those stars—very small, but shining there bravely, no matter how cold it is so far up. If the stars have courage, we ought to have courage; that is what I was thinking, as I so often have in the past—and just then he was there, my husband, calling my name and soon looking into my eyes with his.

"I'm all right, I told him. He didn't know what had happened; our neighbor had sealed his lips, as I told him to do. But my husband knows me, so he knew I looked unusually tired; and he couldn't be easily tricked by me. The more I told him I'd just worked too hard, that is all, the more he knew I was holding something back. Finally, I pulled my ace card. I pretended to be upset by his questions and by all the attention he was giving me. I accused him: why do you make me want to cry, why do you wish me ill, with those terrible thoughts of yours? I am not ill! If you cannot let me rest without thinking I am, then God have mercy on you for having such an imagination! God have mercy! With the second plea to our Lord, he was beaten and silent. He left me alone. I was about to beg him to come back, beg his forgiveness. But I did not want him to bear the burden of knowing; he would not rest easy by day or by night. This way he can say to himself: she has always been cranky, and she will always be cranky, so thank God her black moods come only now and then—a spell followed by the bright sun again.

"I will say what I think happened: I came near going, then there was a change of heart up there in Heaven, so I have a few more days, or weeks, or months, or years—who knows? As for a doctor, I have never seen one, so why start now? Here we are so far away from a hospital. We have no money. Anglos don't like us, anyway: we are the poor ones, the lost ones. My son tells me the Anglos look down on us—old people without education and up in the hills, trying to scrape what we can from the land, and helped only by our animals. No matter; our son is proud of us. He is proud to stay here with us. He says that if he went to the city he would beg for work and be told no, no, no: eventually he might be permitted to sweep someone's floor. Better to hold on to one's land. Better to fight it out with the weather and the animals.

"Again I say it: doctors are for others. My mother and my aunt delivered my children. I once went to see a nurse; she worked for the school and she told me about my children—the diseases they get. Thank you, I said. Imagine: she thought

I knew nothing about bringing up children, or about the obstacles God puts in their way to test them and make them stronger for having gone through a fever, a rash, some pain. No, I will see no nurse and no doctor. They are as far from here as the stars. Oh, that is wrong; they are much farther. The stars I know and recognize and even call by name. They are my names, of course; I don't know what others call the stars. Is it wrong to do that? Perhaps I should ask the priest. Perhaps the stars are God's to name, not ours to treat like pets—by addressing them familiarly. But it is too late; my sins have been recorded, and I will soon enough pay for each and every one of them."

True, I have pulled together remarks made over a stretch of months. And again, I have translated her Spanish into plain, understandable English, or at least I hope I have done so. I have even "cleaned up" her English to an extent; that is, I have eliminated some of the repetitive words or phrases she uses—as we all do when we talk informally to visitors in our homes. On the other hand, I have made every effort to keep faithful to the spirit, and mostly to the letter, of her remarks. I have found that her Spanish is as bare, unaffected, and strong as her English. I have found that in both languages she struggles not only to convey meaning, but to enliven her words with her heart's burden or satisfactions. I have found that she struggles not only with her mind but with her body, her whole being, to express herself. Nor is she unique, some peculiar or specially gifted person whose manner of expression is thoroughly idiosyncratic. She certainly can be saddled with negatives, however compelling her way of speaking. She is uneducated. She is superstitious. She has never attended any bilingual classes. She is poor. Maybe some doctor would find her at times forgetful, a little "senile." She and others like her are rural people; they belong to a social and economic "system" that we all know is "out of date," because the future of America is to be found in cities like Albuquerque and their suburbs. Or so we are told.

Nor is she saintly. She can be morose, and at times quite cranky and reticent. Once she asked me, "What is the point of trying to talk to those who are deaf?" She had in mind some Anglo county officials who refused to give food stamps to a needy cousin of hers. She had in mind an Anglo teacher or two, and yes, a Spanish-speaking teacher or two; they had said rude things to her grandchildren and to their parents, her children. So, she becomes bitter and tense, and after a while she explodes. She admits it is not in her nature to hold in her beliefs, her feelings. She must have her say. And when she does her hands move, her body sways a bit, and sometimes, when she is especially worked up, there is a lurch forward from the chair, so that suddenly she is standing—giving a sermon, almost like the priests she has listened to all these years. A hand goes out, then is withdrawn. The head goes up, then is lowered. A step is taken forward, then back she goes—and soon she is seated again, ready to sew and continue the conversation on a less intense level. When she searches for a word, be it in Spanish or English, she drops her needle and thread, drops a fork or spoon, drops anything she may have in her hands. She needs those old, arthritic fingers of hers. They flex and unflex; it is as if before her is a sandpile of words, and she must push and probe her way through it until she has found what she is looking for. Then the fingers can stop, the hands can relax and go back to other business, or simply be allowed a rest on her lap.

The more time I spend with this woman and her husband and their friends and neighbors and relatives, the more confused I become by much of what I read about them and their so-called cultural disadvantage. I have no inclination to turn such people into utterly flawless human beings, to create yet another highly romanticized group that can be used as a bludgeon against the rest of the country. They can be mean and narrow at times; the woman I have been quoting says things about hippies, and even, at times, about Anglos, that I disagree with or find exaggerated, unfair, distorted. As for her own disposition, she is clearly aware of her personal limitations. Still, she and her kind are at best pitied by many who have described their "plight." If there are grounds for pity (poverty, substantial unemployment, a degree of prejudice even in New Mexico, never mind Texas or California), there are also grounds for respect and admiration—maybe even envy. Some of us who have gone through all those schools and colleges and graduate schools, who have plenty of work and who live comfortable upper-middle-class lives, might want to stop and think about how *we* talk.

Occasionally I come home from a day spent with Chicano families or Indian families and pick up a psychiatric journal, or for that matter, the daily newspaper. Or I happen to go to a professional meeting and hear papers presented, or, afterwards, people talking in lobbies or corridors or restaurants—all those words, all those ideas, spoken by men and women who have no doubt about their importance, the value of their achievements, and certainly not about their ability to "communicate." No one is proposing that jargon-spewing scholars of one sort or another overcome their "cultural disadvantage." Few are examining closely the rhetoric of various business and professional people, or that of their elected leaders—the phony, deceiving, dull, dreary, ponderous, smug, deadly words and phrases such people use and use and use. Relatively few are looking at the way such people are taught in elementary school and high school and beyond. Who is to be pitied, the old lady who can't recognize a possible coronary seizure and instead sees the hand of God approaching her, or some of us who jabber with our clichés and don't have the slightest idea how to use a metaphor or an image in our speech?

True, we have no "illusions"; we are educated, and pain in the chest is for us pain in the chest. Nor do we get carried away with ourselves; we are as sober as can be—so sober the whole world trembles at what we as the owners of this nation can do and have done amid our sobriety, our controlled speech and controlled actions. No hysteria for us. No gesticulations. No demonstration of exuberance, passion, heartiness, excitability. We are cool, calculating; we keep under wraps whatever spirit we have left, if any. And no doubt about it, the grandchildren mentioned so often by this particular old lady are not going to be like her: they are learning in school all sorts of valuable information—but also how to curb their imaginations, restrain their lively interest in harnessing language to the mind's rush of ideas, the heart's movements.

Their grandmother, soon to die, she knows, has said it far more precisely than I can—if with unintended irony: "My grandchildren will not struggle as I do to make myself clear. They are being fed words, Anglo words, by their teachers. They are learning the Spanish language; I only speak it, I don't know how to pick it apart! My oldest granddaughter showed me a book; it was about the Spanish language. I told her she does not need it; she can speak Spanish quite well. No, she said, she has to learn more, and the same with English. Who am I to disagree? Children have so much to learn. The better they can speak, the better it is for them. My grandchildren will speak better Spanish than I; and they will be good at English, too. There is change; there is progress. I am grateful. When I wonder whether there is any hope for my people, I look at my children's children and I say to myself: yes, there is hope. My husband says he hears the little ones chattering away: back and forth they go, from Spanish to English and then to Spanish again. I tell him that we haven't done so bad ourselves; we can make ourselves understood in both languages. But he says—and he is right—that it is not the struggle for them that it has been for us. There is enough struggle for any of us in this world; so, the less the better.

"I only worry that the more people have, the less grateful they feel to God. I know, because a while back, when we had an even harder time than now, we prayed to Him more often. Now our stomachs are full, our children give us money—not a lot, because they don't have much themselves, but some; and the result is that we ignore Him, or we only thank Him on Sundays, when we are in church. I have always felt that He listens more to our daily prayers at home, rather than those we offer in church, when it is a mere habit being practiced. But I am speaking out of turn; I have no right to speak for Him! He knows which prayers mean the most to Him. I have no right to feel sorry for my grandchildren, either. There are moments when I wish they put more of themselves into their fine English and their fine Spanish, but misery likes company, I guess. My husband and I reach out, cry out, for our words, and we are so surprised at the little ones: what we can never take for granted, they have in such large supply. No wonder they have other things to think about than how to get their message across to people! No Anglo is going to make them feel speechless. I can't say I've felt speechless with Anglos, either; but I am sure that they have looked down on me, or not understood my English. As for my Spanish, it has served me well. The Anglos don't understand it, and a Spanish gentleman, one of great learning, would no doubt feel sorry for me, the way I use his language. But I repeat, it has served me well, the way I talk; that is as much as I can say, no more.

"Well, I do have another thought to offer. My daughter told me the other day that all our lives we have been split: we are Spanish, but we are Americans; we have our Spanish language, but in this country the Anglos are kings, and everyone has to speak their English or pay the penalties. I could not disagree. I took my daughter to me and told her she was right to listen to those teachers. I only worry that she and her children will take the message too seriously—will feel ashamed of their own parents, their own people's history. After all, even if there has been trouble, there has been God's grace: He has helped us; He has healed us; He has enabled us to try to be worthwhile and decent people. We have two languages, I know. We are in the middle; we don't know where to go, who to turn to. Or is it that we turn in one direction, then another? But God has given each of us a soul, and it is the soul that really counts. I do not have a Spanish soul, or a soul that is part Anglo. The soul is the place where each of us, no matter what language we speak, no matter our color, meets the Creator. We live the best we know how to live, and our actions are words to God, and He makes His judgment. Through our soul we speak to Him and He to us. Oh, I am not very clear today! This is the end of my life, the month of December for me; and I fear my talk shows it! I only want to say that even though there are two languages to speak, there is only one soul. But maybe the time has come for me to stop speaking in any language. The soul finally tires of the body; it is a prison, and the soul wants to leave. Words struggle to leave us, but once spoken they are dead. The soul leaves and lives forever. I believe it does. I hope it does.''

She makes that last distinction between faith and hope rather innocently. Not for her a dramatic division: I want something to be, but I'm not sure my wish will be realized; and so there is my religious conviction as opposed to my intuitive sense that one cannot be certain by any means. As for those words she mentions, they do indeed struggle for expression. She knows all the pain of the translator. She knows she has one range of expression given her by the Spanish language and another that is set by the English she uses. She moves back and forth, calls upon words and phrases and expressions and proverbs and sayings she has gathered together over the decades and made into her own particular way of both thinking and speaking. Who can (who wants to?) titrate the mixture, resort to percentages or long analytic statements about which idiom makes for what degree of her "pattern" of speech? In each home I visit, the language differs; it all depends on so much—a particular person's manner of getting on with people, a person's responsiveness to sounds (in contrast, say, to visual images), a person's experiences as a worker, a host of accidents and incidents and encounters that may have caused one person to be more talkative, more expansive, more sensitive to the requirements of "bilingual" life than others turn out to be. (A kind Anglo boss, for instance, who took pains once to offer some help with pronunciation, or with the mysteries of a given phrase of construction; or a priest who is especially devoted to the life of a parishioner, including his or her interest in self-expression; or a teacher who was encouraging rather than intimidating.)

Beyond all those "variables" there is the daily rhythm of a given kind of living—close to the land, in touch with nature, very much part of a community's collective experience. We who have become locked up in city apartments or small suburban lots may find the language of an old "illiterate" grand-mother—from a settlement in north central New Mexico too small even to qualify as a village—unusually vivid or figurative. The fact is that such a woman has her heritage, her surroundings, her everyday experience, even as we have ours—hence the difference in language. But the power is ours, and also the numbers—we are the vast majority. Moreover, historically America is a "melting pot"; there is, there has been all along, the expectation that those who come here, or for that matter (the gall!) were here before anyone else, respond to the nation's "manifest destiny"—and such a destiny has its cultural as well as its brute military or political components. Meanwhile that woman and thousands like her, old and tired, proud and energetic, do what we all try to do: look at the world, listen to its sounds, figure out its outlines, its structure, its signficance. Then comes that attempt at coherence which is language—and with it the connections that words provide: one person to another, the two of them to a neighborhood, and beyond.

There is no point holding up anyone's struggle with language as a standard by which others must measure themselves. I have probably not emphasized strongly enough the silences I have heard, the almost desperate search for words which quite frequently turns out to be unsuccessful. I am myself a writer, hence wordy. And my work makes me utterly dependent on the words of others—or at least when I write up that work I have to come forth with those words. The point is not to deny her wish—at least for her grandchildren, if not herself—to speak better, more fluent, English, maybe even a "higher" form of Spanish, too. The point is simply to emphasize the particularity and complexity of her life; and, not least, its integrity.

Against considerable odds she and her husband have carved out a "moment" for themselves on this earth. They happen to be alert, vigorous, stubborn people. They don't let things go; their ears prick up, their eyes dart, they love to smell food as well as taste it, and they enjoy touching people, objects, animals. They possess adequate if not superior intelligence. That being the case, for all their cultural and educational "deficits," for all the "handicaps" they have had to face, for all the difficulties of a "bilingual" life, they nevertheless prove themselves altogether adequate to the demands of their day-to-day existence. They make themselves known. They affirm themselves. They speak out of their minds and hearts. They reveal once again that a lean and willing soul can find its own carefully chosen if hesitantly uttered words, even as others, grown fat and sassy spiritually, can pour forth statements and remarks but worry little about what they sound like. After all, there is so much to lay claim upon through words, there are so many people to keep up with and impress and win over or argue down—rather than, as is the case with the woman I have quoted, simply reach and arouse and stir.

2

UNA ANCIANA

He is eighty-three years old. Once he was measured as exactly six feet tall, but that was a half a century ago. He is sure that he has lost at least an inch or two. Sometimes, when his wife has grown impatient with his slouch, and told him to straighten up, he does her suggestion one better and tilts himself backward. Now are you happy? he seems to be asking her, and she smiles indulgently. His wife is also eighty-three. She always defers to her husband. She will not speak until he has had his say. She insists that he be introduced first to strangers. As the two of them approach a door, she makes a quick motion toward it, holds it patiently, and sometimes, if he is distracted by a conversation and slow to move through, one of her hands reaches for his elbow, while the other points: Go now, is the unstated message, so that I can follow.

They were born within a mile and within two months of one another in Cordova, New Mexico, in the north central part of the state. They are old Americans not only by virtue of age but by ancestry. For many generations their ancestors have lived in territory that is now part of the United States. Before the Declaration of Independence was written there were people not so far away from Cordova named Garcia living as they do, off the land. They are not, however, model citizens of their country. They have never voted, and no doubt the men who framed the Declaration of Independence would not be impressed by the boredom or indifference these New Mexicans demonstrate when the subject of politics comes up. They don't even make an effort to keep abreast of the news, though they do have a television set in their small adobe house. When Walter Cronkite or John Chancellor appears, neither of the Garcias listens very hard. For that matter, no programs really engage their undivided attention—and at first one is tempted to think them partially deaf. But the issue is taste, not the effects of age. Mrs. Garcia does like to watch some afternoon serials, but without the sound. She takes an interest in how the people dress and what the furniture in the homes looks like. The actors and actresses are company of sorts when Mr. Garcia is outside tending the crops or looking after the horses and cows. Nor is language the problem; they both prefer to speak Spanish, but they can make themselves understood quite well in English. They have had to, as Mrs. Garcia explains, with no effort to conceal her longstanding sense of resignation: "You bend with the wind. And Anglo people are a strong wind. They want their own way; they can be like a tornado, out to pass over everyone as they go somewhere. I don't mean to talk out of turn. There are Anglos who don't fit my words. But we are outsiders in a land that is ours. We are part of an Anglo country and that will not change. I had to teach the facts of life to my four sons, and in doing so I learned my own lesson well."

She stops and looks at the pictures of her sons that stand on top of the television set. Holding those pictures is an important function of the set, which was given her and her husband by their oldest son. Like his father he is named Domingo, but unlike his father he attended, though he did not finish, high school, in Española, on good days a ride of twenty or so minutes from the Garcias' home. Mrs. Garcia loves to talk about him: "I am a mother. You will forgive me if I am proud; sometimes I know I have been boastful, and I tell the confessor my sin. Domingo was a smart child. He walked quickly. He talked very well from the start. He did good work in school. We would take a walk, and he would point something out to me; often I had never noticed it before. Before he'd entered school he told me he wanted to become a priest. I asked him why. He said because he'd like to know all the secrets of God. It was my fault, of course. He would ask me questions (those endless why's all children ask—I later learned, after I had my second and third and fourth sons) and I would be puzzled, and not know what to answer. So, I would say the same thing my mother used to say to us: that is one of God's secrets. She died when she was ninety, and well before that my little Domingo had asked her when she would die. I lowered my head in shame, as I was taught to do when I was a girl, as I brought up my children to do, as thank God, my grandchildren now do. But my mother smiled and said, 'That is one of God's secrets.' After that, I think, I started to copy her words with my boy Domingo—though memory becomes moldy after a while and falls into pieces, like the cheese I make.

"I am taking you through side streets. I am sorry. Maybe we never know our own confusion; maybe it takes another to help us see what we have come to. I wanted to tell you about Domingo's teachers. They were Anglos. Today some of our own people teach in the schools, but not that many. Domingo was called brilliant by his teachers. They called me in. They said he was the only child in his class who was bright, and who belonged, really belonged in school. They made me listen to their trials with the other children they taught. I was young then, and obedient. I listened. Maybe now I would ask them please to excuse me, but I have to go home: the bread to make, you know, before supper. But my husband says no, even this very year we still would stay and nod our heads. Can you dare turn away from your child's teacher, just to satisfy your own anger? Our young people, our college students, say yes; but they live far away, under different conditions, not these here.

"The teachers never mentioned college to me. They weren't *that* hopeful about Domingo. I don't think they even thought about a person like us going to college. He just might be worthy of high school, I was told. She had never before said that to one of our children, I was told. He is an exceptional boy, I was told. How did it come about, I was asked. Well, of course, I smiled and said I didn't know. She asked about Domingo's father: was he smarter than the others? I said no, none of us are 'smart,' just trying to get by from day to day, and it's a struggle. That was a bad time, 1930 and the years right after it. Weeks would go by and we would see no money. (We still see little.) And I had already lost four children: the last two had been born in good health, but they died of pneumonia, one at age two, one at age three. You can put yourself in my shoes, I hope. Then, if you will just carry yourself back in time and imagine how hard it was for us, and how little we knew, you will see that I had no way of answering that teacher. On the way home I asked myself, *is* young Domingo 'smart'? Is his father 'smart'? I was afraid to ask his father that evening. He was so tired, so fearful we'd lose even the land under us. He said he'd die and kill us, the child and me, before we went to a city and became lost. When I heard him speaking like that, I forgot the teacher and her question. I served him my bread, and he felt better. Reassured, that is the word."

She stops and serves bread. She pours coffee. It is best black, she says in a matter of fact way, but the visitor will not be judged for his weak stomach or poor taste. She again apologizes for her failure to tell a brief, pointed, coherent story. Her mother was "sunny," was "very sunny" until the end, but she worries about "clouds" over her own thinking. The two Domingos in her life scoff at the idea, though. After the coffee she wants to go on. She likens herself to a weathered old tree that stands just outside, within sight. It is autumn and the tree is bare. She likens the coffee to a God-given miracle: suddenly one feels as if spring has come, one is budding and ready to go through another round of things. But she is definitely short of breath, coffee or no coffee, and needs no one to point it out. "Tomorrow then."

In the morning she is far stronger and quicker to speak out than later in the day. "Every day is like a lifetime," she says—immediately disavowing ownership of the thought. Her husband has said that for years, and to be honest, she has upon occasion taken issue with him. Some days start out bad, and only in the afternoon does she feel in reasonably good spirits. But she does get up at five every morning, and most often she is at her best when the first light appears. By the time her visitor arrives, early in the morning by his standards, she has done enough to feel a little tired and somewhat nostalgic: "Each day for me is a gift. My mother taught us to take nothing for granted. We would complain, or beg, as children do before they fall asleep, and she would remind us that if we are *really* lucky we will have a gift presented to us in the morning: a whole new day to spend and try to do something with. I suppose we should ask for more than that, but it's too late for me to do so.

"I prefer to sit here on my chair with my eyes on the mountains. I prefer to think about how the animals are doing; many of them have put themselves to sleep until spring. God has given them senses, and they use them. Things are not so clear for us—so many pushes and pulls, so many voices; I know what Babel means. I go in town shopping and there is so much argument: everyone has an opinion on something. The only time people lower their heads these days is on Sunday morning, for an hour, and even then they are turning around and paying attention to others. What is she wearing? How is he doing with his business? Do we any longer care what the Lord wants us to know and do?

"I am sorry. I am like a sheep who disobeys and has to be given a prod. I don't lose my thoughts when they're crossing my mind; it's when they have to come out as words that I find trouble. We should be careful with our thoughts, as we are with the water. When I'm up and making breakfast I watch for changes in the light. Long before the sun appears it has forewarned us. Nearer and nearer it comes, but not so gradually that you don't notice. It's like one electric light going on after another. First there is dark. Then the dark lifts ever so little. Still, it might be a full moon and midnight. Then, like Domingo's knife with chickens, the night is cut up; it becomes a shadow of what it was, and Domingo will sometimes stop for a minute and say: 'Dolores, she is gone, but do not worry, she will be back.' He has memories like mine: his mother lived to be eighty-seven, and all her life she spoke like mine: 'Domingo, be glad,' she would tell him. Why should he be glad? His mother knew: 'God has chosen you for a trial here, so acquit yourself well every day, and never mind about yesterday or tomorrow.' We both forget her words, though. As the sun comes out of hiding and there is no longer any question that those clouds will go away, we thank dear God for his generosity, but we think back sometimes. We can't seem to help ourselves. We hold on and try to keep in mind the chores that await us, but we are tempted, and soon we will be slipping. There is a pole in our fire station. Once the men are on it, there is no stopping. Like them with a crash we land on those sad moments. We feel sorry for ourselves. We wish life had treated us more kindly. The firemen have a job to do, and I wonder what would happen to us if we didn't have ours to do. We might never come back to this year of 1972. We would be the captives of bad memories. But no worry; we are part of this world here; the sun gets stronger and burns our consciences; the animals make themselves known; on a rainy day the noise of the water coming down the side of the house calls to me—why am I not moving, too?"

She moves rather quickly, so quickly that she seems almost ashamed when someone takes notice, even if silently. Back in her seat she folds her arms, then unfolds them, putting her hands on her lap, her left hand over her right hand. Intermittently she breaks her position to reach for her coffee and her bread: "Domingo and I have been having this same breakfast for over fifty years. We are soon to be married fifty-five years, God willing. We were married a month after the Great War ended; it was a week before Christmas, 1918. The priest said he hoped our children would always have enough food and never fight in a war. I haven't had a great variety of food to give my family, but they have not minded. I used to serve the children eggs in the morning, but Domingo and I have stayed with hot bread and coffee. My fingers would die if they didn't have the dough to work over. I will never give up my oven for a new one. It has been here forty years, and is an old friend. I would stop baking bread if it gave out. My sons once offered to buy me an electric range, they called it, and I broke down. It was a terrible thing to do. The boys felt bad. My husband said I should be more considerate. I meant no harm, though. I didn't deliberately say to myself: Dolores Garcia, you have been hurt, so now go and cry. The tears came and I was helpless before them. Later my husband said they all agreed I was in the right; the stove has been so good to us, and there is nothing wrong—the bread is as tasty as ever, I believe. It is a sickness, you know: being always dissatisfied with what you have, and eager for a change."

She stops here and looks lovingly around the room. She is attached to every piece of furniture. Her husband made them: a round table, eight chairs, with four more in their bedroom, the beds there, the bureau there. She begins to tell how good Domingo is at carving wood: "That is what I would like to say about Domingo: he plants, builds, and harvests, he tries to keep us alive and comfortable with his hands. We sit on what he has made, eat what he has grown, sleep on what he has put together. We have never had a spring on our bed, but I have to admit, we bought our mattress. Buying, that is the sickness. I have gone to the city and watched people. They are hungry, but nothing satisfies their hunger. They come to stores like flies to sticky paper: they are caught. I often wonder who is better off. The fly dies. The people have to pay to get out of the store, but soon they are back again, the same look in their eyes. I don't ask people to live on farms and make chairs and tables; but when I see them buying things they don't need, or even want—except to make a purchase, to get something—then I say there is a sickness.

"I talked to the priest about this. He said yes, he knows. But then he shrugged his shoulders. I knew what he was thinking: the Devil is everywhere, and not until Judgment Day will we be free of him. I watch my son Domingo and his son Domingo; they both have plans: next year we buy this, and the year after, that. Such plans are sad to hear. I try to tell them, but they do not listen. Those are the moments when I feel suddenly old, the only time I do. I turn to the priest. He says I am sinning: my pride makes me think I can disagree with the way the whole country works. I reply, 'No, father, just what I hear my own son and grandson saying.' Hasn't a mother got the right to tell her own flesh and blood that they are becoming slaves—that is it, slaves of habits and desires that have nothing to do with living a good life?"

She sighs and stops talking. She breaks her bread up into small pieces and eats them one by one. She stirs her coffee with a stick her husband made especially for that purpose: it is about six inches long, smoothed out and painted green. He jokes with her: one day she will decide to add milk to her coffee, because her stomach will demand it, and she will comply. Then she will really need the stick. But she has never used milk. Eventually she puts the stick down and resumes: "I am not a priest. I read the Bible, go to church, make my confession, and know I will soon need to come back to tell more. But a good life is a life that is obedient to God's rules, and a life that is your own, not someone else's. God and God alone owns us; it is not right that others own us. There are many kinds of slavery. My children would come home from school and tell me that they were glad they were not colored, because colored people once were slaves. 'Watch out,' I'd say. Their father would agree: you can become a slave without even knowing it. You can be white and have money, but not own your soul. I remember years ago I took the children to town; they were young and they wanted to see Santa Claus. He would come once and only once—and it turned out we missed him. Next year, I told the boys. They pouted. They beseeched me. They wanted me to take them somewhere, anywhere—so long as they could catch sight of Santa Claus. I held my ground. They would not stop. I said no is no. They said please. Finally I had to go after them. I talked as if I was giving a sermon in church. Maybe I ought not have spent so much of their time and mine, but I had to tell them, once and for all, that we have our land, and we feed ourselves and live the best lives we know how to, and we must never feel empty and worthless because of a Santa, or because a salesman has beckoned us, and we have said No, I haven't the money.

"Later I wondered whether I'd done the right thing. I told my husband that Santa Claus is different.Children love him, and why not try very hard to take them to see him? He thought for a while. When he thinks he takes up his pipe and uses it more than he usually does. With each puff I say to myself: there goes one of his thoughts—and I wonder when he'll share them with me. Soon he does, though. It never fails: he puts his pipe down, and then I know I'm to get ready, and pay attention. I sit down and soon I hear. He always starts with: 'My wife, let me tell you what I think.' Soon I know what he thinks, because he's not one to hide behind pretty phrases. As for Santa Claus, Domingo told me what he thought of him: very little. I will never forget his words. He said that Santa Claus has been captured by the storekeepers. He said that they have him locked up, and he will never be free until we stop turning Christmas into a carnival, a time when people become drunk on their greed and take to stores in order to indulge themselves. Of course, the priest lectures us in the same way. And I know we all can be greedy. I eat too much of my bread, more than I need. I shouldn't. Sometimes I punish myself: the oven is empty for a day or two—once for a week, after a holiday. That time Domingo couldn't stand it any longer. 'I am starving' he told me—even though I made him cereal and eggs instead. But bread for him is life, and I never stopped so long again. I had made a mistake. A nun said to me, Punishment for a sin can *be* a sin. If you are proud of yourself for doing penance, you are defeated before you start."

She stops to open the window and summon her husband. Maybe *he* should say exactly what he told his boys a long time ago about Santa Claus. But no, it is hopeless; he will not come in until he has finished his work. He is like a clock, so-and-so-many minutes to do one thing, then another. The cows know the difference between him and anyone else. He is quick. They get fast relief. When one of her sons tries to help, or she, or a grandchild, it is no good. The animals are restless, make a lot of noise, and Domingo pleads: leave him his few jobs, then when he goes, sell the animals. As for Santa Claus, forgotten for a moment, the gist of Domingo's speech is given by his wife: "My children, a saint is in chains, locked up somewhere, while all these stores have their impostors. Will you contribute to a saint's suffering? Santa Claus was meant to bring good news: the Lord's birthday is in the morning, so let us all celebrate by showing each other how much love we feel. Instead we say, I want, I want, I want. We say, More, more, more. We say Get this, then the next thing, and then the next. We lose our heads. We lose our souls. And somwhere that saint must be in hiding, may be in jail for all we know. If not, he is suffering. I tell you this not to make you feel bad. It is no one's fault. We are all to blame. Only let us stop. If we stop, others will not, I know. But that will be their sorrow, not ours to share with them."

She is not ready to guarantee every word as his. He is a man of few words, and she readily admits that she tends to carry on. Then, as if to confess something that is not a sin, and so not meant for a priest, yet bothers her, she goes further, admits to talking out loud when no one is around. She is sure her husband doesn't do so, and she envies him his quiet self-assurance, his somewhat impassive temperament: "He is silent not because he has nothing to say. He is silent because he understands the world, and because he knows enough to say to himself: what will words and more words do to make the world any better? I have wished for years that I could be like him, but God makes each of us different. When our son Domingo went to school they began teaching him English. We had learned English ourselves, enough to speak. But we didn't speak it, only Spanish. When Domingo started learning English we decided to speak it more and more at home. The same with the other boys. Often I would rehearse my English by myself. I would learn words and expressions from the priest and from the mayor of the town. He was a cousin, and always doing business with Anglos. I learned to talk to myself in English—to my husband in Spanish, but to myself in English! Once my husband overheard me, and he thought I was delirious. He asked if I had a fever. I said no, none at all. He said I sounded as if I did. I said I was learning to speak English. He said he could speak English—but not to himself. Then he laughed and said, 'Dolores, you have spoken Spanish to yourself, too. I have heard you.' Since then I have been more careful, and I don't believe my husband knows that I still have the habit. I don't talk to teach myself English, though. I talk because my mind fills up with words, and then they spill out. Sometimes I talk with someone I imagine nearby. Sometimes I talk to myself. Sometimes it is in Spanish, sometimes in English."

After all the talk of talk, she has nothing more to say. She has to clean the house. She has to start a soup. She always has soup. As one pot begins to empty, she starts another going. It contains bones and vegetables. Soup, that is all it is called. Then she has to sew. There are clothes to mend, clothes to make. Her eyes aren't what they used to be, but with glasses she can see well enough. And finally, the radio. She prefers radio to television. She listens to music. She listens to the weather forecast and either nods or scoffs. Her sons hear the weather and actually believe what they hear. She knows better. She decides early in the morning what the weather will be like and only wants to know how good those weathermen are, with their gadgets and their reports from God knows what far-off cities. She feels sorry for them: they have a lot to learn. She hopes that one day they will go outside and look at the sky, rather than take their readings. It is one more bit of foolishness we have to live with now: "Years ago there were not these weather reports all the time. We would go out and size up the morning. We could tell. We felt the moisture before it turned to rain. If we had any questions we prayed, then more often than not we had an answer. I don't believe it was God's, either. The priest long ago warned us not to ask Him for favors, and not to expect His Answers for the small favors we want. He is up there; we are down here. Once we are born, it is up to us. We pray to show our faith. If we have faith, we can do what is necessary. Not everything was good in the old days; we used to ask God's help all the time and be disappointed. My mother would pray that her bread came out good. I would pray for rain. I think we have stopped that, Domingo and me."

Now it is time to rest. Several times each day she and her husband do so. It is up to her to call him and she does it in such a way that he knows why. In a matter-of-fact way she speaks his name, and slowly he comes in. It is ten o'clock when they rest first. They lie down for five or ten minutes only, but that does miracles for them. They get up refreshed not only in body but in mind, and, evidently, soul: "I pray. I thank God for the time he has given me here, and ask Him to take me when He is ready, and I tell Him I will have no regrets. I think of all I have seen in this long life: the people, the changes. Even up here, in this small village, the world makes its presence felt. I remember when the skies had no planes in them, houses no wires sticking up, trying to catch television programs. I never wanted a refrigerator. I never needed one. But I have one. It is mostly empty. I have one weakness: ice cream. I make it, just as I make butter. I used to make small amounts and Domingo and I would finish what was there. Now I can make and store up butter or ice cream and give presents of them to my sons and their children. No wonder they bought us the refrigerator! As I lie on our bed and stare at the ceiling I think how wonderful it is: eighty-three, and still able to make ice cream. We need a long rest afterwards, but between the two of us we can do a good job. The man at the store has offered to sell any extra we have; he says he can get a good price. I laugh. I tell him he's going to turn me into a thief. It would be dishonest to sell food you make in your home for profit at a store. That's the way I feel. My husband gets angry: What do you mean 'dishonest?' he will say. I answer back: my idea of what is dishonest is not his. So we cannot go on about this. It is in my heart where the feeling is, not in my head. 'Oh, you are a woman!' he says, and he starts laughing. Later he will tell me that he was picking weeds, or taking care of our flowers, and he thought to himself: She is right, because to make food is part of our life as a family, and to start selling that is to say that we have nothing that is *ours*. It is what he always comes back to: better to have less money and feel we own ourselves, than more and feel at the mercy of so many strangers."

The two of them show a burst of energy after they get up. As they have rested, said their prayers, reminisced, they have given thought to what they will do next, and so, when they are ready, they set out decisively. It is almost as if they know they have limited time, know that soon they will again have to interrupt their working rhythm for lunch and another rest afterwards. "I am a new person several times a day," she points out, then adds right away, "But I can suddenly get quite tired." She feels "weakness" and "a loss of breath" come on, her way of describing the effects of a cardiovascular difficulty common to people in their eighties. Yet she sees no doctor, hasn't seen one in decades: "There are no doctors near here. I would have to go to Espanola. I would, if there was a need. I have pains all over; it is arthritis, I know. One can't expect joints to hold up forever. I do not believe in aspirin. I do not believe in medicines. I have to pant like our dog when I move too fast for too long. I have to stop and catch up. It is the lungs and the heart, I know. My son wants me to go get a checkup. My ankles swell at the end of the day, but the next morning they are down again. The body has its seasons. I am in the last one; winter is never without pain and breakdowns. I don't want to spend my last years waiting on myself and worrying about myself. I have already lived over twice as long as our Savior. How greedy ought one be for life? God has his purposes. I wake up and feel those aches and I notice how wrinkled my skin is, and I wonder what I'm still doing alive. I believe it is wrong, to ask a question like that. One lives. One dies. To ask questions with no good answers to them is to waste time that belongs to others. I am here to care for my husband, to care for this house, to be here when my sons and my grandchildren come. The young have to see what is ahead. They have to know that there is youth and middle age and old age. My grandson Domingo asked me a while ago what it is like to be one hundred. He is ten. I told him to be one hundred is to live ten of his lifetimes. He seemed puzzled, so I knew I had been thoughtless. I took him around. I put my hand besides his and we compared skins. I said it is good to be young and it is good to be old. He didn't need any more explanations. He said when you're young you have a lot of years before you, but when you're old you have your children and your grandchildren and you love them and you're proud of them. I took him around again and hugged him tightly, and in a second he was out there with his father and his grandfather looking at the cows."

She doesn't spend too much time with the cows, but the chickens are hers to feed and look after. She cleans up their fenced-in enclosure, and delights in their eggs. She and her husband have one hard-boiled egg each for lunch every day. She gives her sons eggs regularly; a nephew and niece also get some. She feeds the chickens leftovers, and some of her fresh bread as well. She is convinced that they lay better eggs because of her bread. One day for the sake of a visitor she borrowed a store-bought egg and compared it with one of hers: each was dropped in hot water for poaching, and hers did indeed stay much more intact and turn out tastier. "Animals today are turned into machines," she remarked after the experiment. She shook her head. She tried not to be gloomy, but she was worried: "No one my age has the right to demand that the world stand still. So much was wrong in the past that is better now. I didn't want this refrigerator, but it is good to have, now that I'm used to it. My grandchildren have had narrow misses with death, but doctors have saved them. I still mourn the babies I lost. Even if I'd been rich back then I might have lost them. Now there are medicines to kill the bad germs. But to see chickens or cows being kept in one place and stuffed with food that isn't really food—Domingo says they are fed chemicals—so they will grow fat all of a sudden, and have their eggs or become fit for slaughter: that is unnatural. I ask myself: Did God form the beasts of the field, and the fowl of the air so that they should be treated this way by man? I asked the priest once, and he scratched his head and said he would have to think about it. The next time I saw him I looked at him hard and he remembered my question. 'Mrs. Garcia, you don't make it easy for me,' he said. I smiled and said I didn't want to cause any trouble, but I can't help thinking about some of these things. He answered. 'I don't know what to say.' Then I decided I'd best not trouble him any more. He once told me that a priest only knows what Christ promised us; how He will bring about His promises—that's not for man to know. I thought afterwards I ought to confess to him my boldness—the sin of pride. Who am I to decide they have no right to run those chicken farms? But God forgive me, I still believe it is wrong: I still believe animals ought not to be turned into machines."

She arranges the eggs she brings in very carefully; she takes them out of her basket and puts them in a bowl. Some are brown, some white. She likes to fix them up like flowers; they give a freckled appearance from afar. When she uses some, she rearranges those that are left. She handles them not only with care but with pride and affection. Sometimes as she talks and does her work with the eggs she will hold a warm one in her hand: "I feel comforted by a fresh egg. It is sad to feel it get colder, but that is life. My grandaughter loves to help me collect eggs. The other day she asked me if the eggs inside a woman are the same kind as those that come out of a chicken. I was taken aback. I told her I didn't think so. Then I wondered what else to say. My husband said later there isn't anything more to say. The priest agreed. I felt I'd failed the little girl, though: I changed subjects on her before she even knew what had happened. A few minutes later I could tell her mind was back with the eggs, and she wanted to ask me more questions. But I wouldn't let her. I didn't tell her no, at least not directly. I just kept up my line of chatter. The poor girl, she was overcome by her grandmother's words—and by her own shyness! This time I didn't go to the priest later and ask him what I should have said. I have never talked to him about such matters. When one is young they are too personal; and besides, what is there to ask, and what is there to say? Also, a priest is entitled to respect: they are not living a worldly life, and there is much they don't know. I think our new priest is like a youth, even if he is fifty; I mean, he has never tasted of life. That is what a priest is about, of course; his passions go up toward the altar, and then to Heaven. So, I sat and thought about how to talk with my granddaughter the next time. I hope I can do her some justice. Time will tell. One never knows what to say except when the moment is at hand. I do rehearse conversations sometimes, though, I have to admit."

She stops abruptly, as if this is one conversation she doesn't want to pursue. Anyway, she has been dusting and sweeping the floor as she talks and now she is finished. Next come the plants, a dozen or so of them; they need to be watered and moved in or out of the sun. She hovers over them for a minute, doing nothing, simply looking. She dusts them, too. She prunes one: "I've been waiting for a week or so to do this. I thought to myself: that plant won't like it, losing so much. I dread cutting my toenails and fingernails. I am shaky with scisssors. But I go after the plants with a surer touch. They are so helpless, yet they are so good to look at. They seem to live forever. Parts die, but new parts grow. I have had them so long—I don't remember the number of years. I know each one's needs, and I try to take care of them the same time each day. Maybe it is unnecessary nonsense, the amount of attention I give. I know that is what Domingo would say. Only once did he put his belief into words, and then I reminded him that he has his habits, too. No one can keep him from starting in one corner of his garden and working his way to the other, and with such care. I asked him years ago why not change around every once in a while and begin on the furthest side, and go faster. 'I couldn't do it,' he said, and I told him I understood. Habits are not crutches; habits are roads we have paved for ourselves. When we are old, and if we have done a good job, the roads last and make the remaining time useful: we get where we want to go, and without the delays we used to have when we were young. How many plants died on me when I was first learning! How often I forgot to water them, or watered them too much because I wanted to do right. Or I would expose them to the sun and forget that, like us, they need the shade, too. I was treating them as if they needed a dose of this, a trial of that. But they have been removed from God's forests, from Nature it is; and they need consideration. When we were young my husband also used to forget chores; he'd be busy doing one thing, and he'd overlook the other. But slowly we built up our habits, and now I guess we are protected from another kind of forgetfulness: the head tires easily when you are our age, and without the habits of the years you can find yourself at a loss to answer the question: what next?"

She turns to lunch. She stirs the soup. She warms up the bread. She reaches for the eggs. She sets a simple, careful table, a large spoon and a knife for herself, her husband, and their guest. Each gets a napkin from a set given her half a century ago by her mother, and used on Sundays, holidays, special occasions. She is apologetic: "I fear we often look at these napkins but don't use them. No wonder they survive so well! They remind us to behave ourselves, because it is no ordinary day; and so, we eat more carefully, and don't have to use them. They are usually in the same condition when I put them away as when I took them out. My grandmother made them, gave them to my mother, and now I have them. My three daughters died as infants; I will give the napkins to my eldest son's wife. I tried to do so when they were married, but she said no. I insisted, and only got more refusals. If she had been my daughter, she would have accepted. But I was not hurt. It takes time to move over from one family and be part of another. She would accept the napkins now, but they would become frightened if suddenly I offered them. Is she sick? Does she know something we don't know? What have we done to neglect her, that she offers us what she loves to put on her own table? So, I will have them until the end, when all possessions obtain new masters."

She has to go outside. It is cold and windy, but sunny. There is some fresh milk there in a pail—from cows which, she hastens to add, present no danger of sickness to a visitor who up until that moment had taken for granted the word *pasteurized* that appears on every milk bottle or carton. And she has herself and her husband as proof—a touch of reassurance which she obviously enjoys being able to offer: "My sons' wives sometimes hesitate, too. I can see what they think on their faces. They deny it, but I know: Is it safe to drink milk right from the cow? They are from the city, and they have no way of understanding that many cows are quite healthy; their owners know when they are sick. Anyway, Domingo and I survived without store milk, and we are not young, and not so sick we can't work or eat—or drink milk."

She wraps herself in a sweater she has made and upon opening the door quickly turns back for a moment: "Oh, the wind." But she persists, and is gone. When she is back, she resumes where she has left off: "The wind can be a friend or an enemy. A severe wind reminds us of our failures: something we forgot to fasten down. A gentle wind is company. I have to admit, I can spend a long time listening to the wind go through trees, watching it sweep across the grass. Domingo will come in and say, 'Oh, Dolores, come out and watch the wind go through the grass.' I hurry out. I often wonder if the ground feels it—like hair being combed and brushed. I walk with our dog and he gets scents from far off, carried by the wind. I tell him not to be tricked. Better to let things quiet down, then take another scent. He is over ten, and should not run long distances. He doesn't know his own limits. But who does, exactly? It takes a lifetime to get used to your body, and by the time you do, then it is almost time to say good-bye and go elsewhere. I often wonder whether the wind carries our soul skyward. It is another of my foolish ideas, and I put it to the priest long ago—not this one, but the one who came before him. He was annoyed with me. 'Mrs. Garcia,' he said, 'you have an active imagination.' I apologized. He reminded me that God's ways are not ours. I wanted to tell him that the wind comes mysteriously from above and might be one of many good, strong arms our Lord has. But I knew to keep quiet was best. He was a very stern priest, and outspoken. He would not have hesitated to dress me down severely and warn me publicly that I would pay for that kind of talk in Hell. Once he cuffed my husband because Domingo told him he'd heard that much of our weekly collection was going to Africa or Asia, to places way off, and meanwhile so many people hereabouts are without work and go hungry.

"It was in the bad years, in the 1930s. We were poor, but at least we had our land. Others had nothing. And the priest was fat. He was waited on, and he dined on the best; we were told that by the woman who cooked for him. Mind you, she did not serve him. He had to have someone special to do that. And he paid them a pittance. They had children they were supporting; and, alas, husbands too. In a good mood he would promise them an eternity in Heaven. On bad days he would threaten them with Purgatory and no escape—so, of course, they would leave his kitchen in tears, clutching their rosary beads all the way home. My husband heard of this, and was enraged. He said terrible things. I pleaded with him to stop. We were so poor, and the bank threatened to take away our small farm. Some people had thought of marching on the bank. The bank officials heard of the plan and never made a move against us. By then I had lost four children. I will not repeat what Domingo said about the priest—or the Church. The worse his language, the harder I prayed. I kneeled by my bed and prayed one evening after he had carried on a full hour, it seemed; it must have really been a few minutes, I now know, but I thought he would never stop. Then a heavy wind came, later that evening, and I was sure: God was approaching us to exact his punishment. And why not, after Domingo's outburst? He was tidying up outside. He had calmed down. I had heard him say a Hail Mary, but I pretended to be lost in my own work. He didn't want me to know that he had taken back the words he had spoken; he is proud. I decided to pray for him, but I was sure something bad would happen. Nothing did, though; the wind came, then left. A week afterwards I told Domingo of my fears. He laughed and said we are too intelligent, both of us, even without education, to be superstitious. I agreed. But a month later he came in one day for lunch and he told me he had to confess something to me. I said, Not to me, to the priest. No, he had very little to tell that priest, only the briefest of admissions once a month. I said nothing. He said that he'd been afraid too, that evening after he'd lost his temper. When the wind came, and he was outside, and the horses started whinnying and the dog ran back and forth, he did not know what to do or why the animals were upset; so he had gotten down on his knees and asked God's forgiveness. He'd even asked Him to take us both, with the house: through a tornado, perhaps. But soon it became very still, and I think each of us must have been holding our breaths, without knowing we were doing so together, like so much else we do! I fear that when he goes, I will, or when I go, he will. But I have no right to such thoughts: it is not up to me or to Domingo, but to our Lord and Savior. We are sinners, though, and we can't help being selfish. There will be no future for either of us alone. I only hope we are not tested by being separated for too long by death!"

When her husband comes in, without being called, she says that it is now noon. They go by the sun. They have a clock in their bedroom, but they rarely use it. They forget to wind it, except when their son is coming and they want to show him that they like his present: "Domingo gave us the clock, and I treasure it. I look at it and think of him. We only have two sons. It is nice to be reminded of them. I don't mean to sound as if I pity myself. Our son Domingo works at Los Alamos. He says it is maintenance he does; he looks after all those scientists. They leave their laboratories in a mess, and someone has to pick up after them, or everything would stop cold one day. He gets a good wage, and jobs are few around here, so he is lucky to be there. He could have stayed with us, worked on the land. But all we have is our animals and the crops—no money. I put up many jars for the winter, but jars of food are not enough to attract young people, and I see their view. There are a hundred like Domingo who would like his job. Before they brought in the laboratories at Los Alamos, there was nothing anywhere near here. Domingo would be in Albuquerque, I believe, if it hadn't been for Los Alamos. My younger son is down there. I've never even been to Santa Fe. He drives up here on weekends. His life is difficult, living in the city. I don't ask him much; I wouldn't understand. His wife longs to come back here. He does, too. But how can they? No work. Domingo was interviewed several times for his job. He took a test, I believe. He did well. The teachers who predicted good for him, they were right. It's too bad he didn't finish high school; the war came, the one against Japan and Hitler.

"Then came the next war. My second son, Francisco, went to Korea. He was there for many months. I remember well the Saturday morning that I got news of him. I remember the day he came home. I was sitting in this very chair. I had to mend some of my husband's clothes. I was almost through, and as it does, my mind was already preparing for the next step in the day: a visit outside to pick some tomatoes. Suddenly the door opened, with no warning. Who could it be—the front door, hardly ever used, rather than the side one right here? My boy Domingo—he lived with us then, and worked as a handyman in the school where they had always thought so well of him. He had his suit on. 'Domingo,' I said, 'why the suit?' He did not answer. For a second I wondered how he had slipped in and put it on without my knowing. We will do anything not to see what is right before us. I believe I might have wondered and wondered about such petty questions—but after Domingo came his father, also with a suit on. I got up and shouted, 'It is not Sunday!' I said it over and over again. 'It is not, it is not!' Then I started crying. They never told me. I never asked. I just knew. My husband asked me if I wanted to change my dress. I said no. I am a plain woman, and my son was a plain man—no pretenses. He did not die in his Sunday clothes. They turned around and I followed them. We walked down that road, two miles. I saw nothing. I heard nothing. I was alone, even though they were with me, one on each side. Once I must have looked near collapse. I felt their hands and was surprised to see them standing there. Then I dropped my beads. I picked them up, but I didn't say the Rosary. I just kept holding onto the beads. They had brought the body to the basement of the school building, a United States flag around it. Later, after the funeral, they wanted to give me that flag; I said no, it could stay at the school. Let the children see what war means. That is something they should learn—as much as how to read and write and count. It is no good when flags are used that way."

She has gone too far to suit her sense of propriety. She insists upon her ignorance. Who is she to talk about wars? They come about through events she has no knowledge of. She has a place in God's scheme of things; best to stay in it. But something makes her restless, no matter how she tries to put aside her doubts and misgivings. She stands up, walks toward her plants, and examines them, one by one. They are all right. She goes back to her chair. Then she is up offering coffee, serving a delicious chocolate marble cake she has made—from a packaged mix, a concession on her part to her daughter-in-law's urging. Once again seated, she interrupts a conversation about the "new road"—the road in front of her house which now for the first time is paved—to put into words what she can't stop thinking about: "There was another time. Two years ago, before that road was fixed up to be so strong it can ignore the weather, I had walked down to talk with my neighbor. She had suffered badly from pneumonia, but was on the mend. As I came toward the house I saw them again. You know, this time I thought my mind had left me. I wiped my eyes, but they wouldn't go away. I called to them, but they didn't answer, so I was sure they weren't there. It was late afternoon, a time when shadows begin to appear, and one can be fooled, anyway. So I wiped my eyes again, and when they remained, I looked around, hoping to see them in back of me, too. Then I would know; my eyes, my head—something for a doctor to heal, or a warning from God that it won't be long. Well, soon they were upon me; it was only when I *felt* them that I believed they were there and I was there. I remember thinking that perhaps I'd fallen asleep at my neighbor's, or maybe I'd taken a nap at my own house and now was waking up. In a second one can have such thoughts. In another second one can know everything without hearing a word. I said, 'How did it happen?' My husband couldn't talk. I held on to him and wanted him to tell me, but he was speechless. My son tried to tell me, but he couldn't finish his story. He used the word 'car,' and that was enough for me. Later they tried to give me the details, and I begged them to stop. Those suits on a day in the middle of the week! There have been days since when I have wanted to burn those suits or tear them to shreds. There have been days when I have lost all faith. I dared not go to confession; I could not let a priest hear what was on my mind. I cringed before God, knowing He hears everything, even what is not spoken but crosses the mind, a rabbit of an idea, suddenly upon you, quickly chased away, but back again in an unsuspecting moment, when all is quiet."

With that she stopped talking and looks out the window. What ought a visitor do—sit still and wait or find an excuse to leave immediately? Suddenly, though, she is talking again, a bit more softly and slowly and reflectively, but with no apparent distress. And she seems to want to talk: "The mountains, our mountains—I look at them when I need an anchor. They are here. They never leave us. Birds come, stay a while, leave. The moon is here, then gone. Even the sun hides from us for days on end. Leaves don't last, nor flowers. We have had a number of dogs, and I remember them in my prayers. But those mountains are *here*. They are nearer God than us; sometimes I imagine Him up there, on top of one or another mountain, standing over us, getting an idea how we're doing. It is wrong to think like that, I know. But a poor old woman like me can be allowed her foolishness. Who is without a foolish hope? Who doesn't make up dreams to fit his wishes? Sometimes I walk up toward the mountains. I can't go as far now as before. I don't tell my husband I'm going; he would worry that I'd lose my breath completely and no one would be around. But I pace myself, and, as I say, I have to be content with approaching those hills.

"The other day I walked toward them and there was a meeting on the side of the road. I stopped and listened. I never went any further. They were our young men, and some people from the city. *Chicanos*, they spoke of Chicanos. We are Chicanos; nothing else will do, they said. I came home and told my husband. Yes, he said, we are Chicanos. We are so many things, he said. 'Mexican American,' 'Mexicano,' they'd call my boys at school, those Anglo teachers. I would say nothing. They thought then it was their right to call us what they pleased. Spanish, we are Spanish. Many of us may have some Indian blood, too. But I will tell you: I am a woman and a mother and Domingo a man and a father, and both of us belong to this country and no other, and we owe allegiance to the state of New Mexico. Should we give ourselves one name or another, or should we get each day's job done? I can't believe Christ wants us to be Anglo against Chicano, or Chicano against Anglo; but the world is full of bitterness, and when will there be an end to it, *when?* I wondered while I walked home. It is a bad thing to say, but I was glad to come upon that meeting; it took my mind off myself and my memories. I saw that others want to know why there is so much injustice in the world. For a few days after my son was killed in the accident I wondered again whether God cared. I know He is there, watching over us; but I would wake up in the night and my forehead would be wet and I would be shaking. I had dreamed that God had fallen asleep, and so we all were going to suffer: the Devil would win his fight. I thought of those days, now gone, while I listened to the young people shouting 'Chicano!' They mentioned all the bad, nothing good; Domingo says that is how it goes when people have been hurt, and I nodded, because I remembered how I once felt."

One morning, in the midst of a conversation, she scolds herself for talking too much. She falls silent. She glances up at the picture of Christ at the Last Supper. Her face loses its tension. She slumps a bit, but not under the weight of pain or even age. She feels relaxed. There are a few dishes to wash. There is a curtain that needs mending. There is not only bread to make, but pies. Her grandchildren love her pies, and she loves seeing them eaten. "Children eat so fast," she says with a sigh of envy. She begins talking again. She resumes her activity. She has to pick at her food now. "When one is over eighty the body needs less," she observes—but immediately afterwards she looks a little shy, a little apprehensive: "I have no business talking like a doctor. Once the priest told me I talk like him. I told him: I have raised children; it is necessary at times to give them sermons, and hear their confessions. He smiled. If I had another life I would learn to be a nurse. In my day, few of our people could aim so high—not a woman like me, anyway. It is different today. My sons say their children will finish high school and my Domingo in Los Alamos says *his* Domingo does so well in school he may go on to a college. I laugh with my husband: a Domingo Garcia in a college. Maybe the boy will be a doctor. Who knows? He likes to take care of his dog. He has a gentle side to him. He is popular with the girls, so I don't think he's headed for the priesthood. He tells me he'd like to be a scientist, like the men his father looks after in the laboratories. I worry that he would make those bombs, though. I wouldn't want that on his conscience. My son told me they do other things there in the laboratories, not just make bombs. I said, 'Thank God!'

"Of course all of that is for the future. I don't know if I will be around to see my grandchildren have children of their own. One cannot take anything for granted. The priest laughed at Domingo and me last Sunday, and said, 'You two will outlast me; you will be coming here when you are both over one hundred.' I said, 'Thank you father, but that is a long way off, to be a hundred, and much can happen.' 'Have faith,' he said, and he is right: one must."

She pauses for a few seconds, as if to think about her own admonition. Then she is back on her train of through: "Sometimes after church Domingo and I walk through the cemetery. It is a lovely place, small and familiar. We pay our respects to our parents, to our aunts and uncles, to our children. A family is a river; some of it has passed on and more is to come, and nothing is still, because we all move along, day by day, toward our destination. We both feel joy in our hearts when we kneel on the grass before the stones and say a prayer. At the edge of the cemetery near the gate is a statue of the Virgin Mary, larger than all the other stones. She is kneeling and on her shoulder is the Cross. She is carrying it—the burden of her Son's death. She is sad, but she has not given up. We know that she has never lost faith. It is a lesson to keep in mind. We always leave a little heavy at the sight of our Lord's mother under such a heavy obligation. But my husband never fails to hold my arm, and each Sunday his words are the same: 'Dolores, the Virgin will be an example to us this week.' It is as if each Sunday he is taking his vows—and me, too, because I say back to him, 'Yes, Domingo, she will be an example to us.' Now, mind you, an hour later one of us, or both of us, will have stumbled. I become cranky. Domingo has a temper. I hush him, and he explodes. He is inconsiderate, and I sulk. That is the way with two people who have lived together so long: the good and the bad are always there, and they have become part of one life, lived together."

She hears his footsteps coming and quickens her activity a bit. She will not be rushed, but he needs his coffee and so does she. Often she doesn't so much need it as need to drink it because he is drinking it. He lifts his cup, she follows; he puts his down, and soon enough hers is also on the table. Always they get through at the same time. This particular morning Domingo is more expansive and concerned than usual—a foal has just been born. "Well, enough. I must go check on the mother and her infant." He is up and near the door when he turns around to say goodbye: "These days one never knows when the end will come. I know our time is soon up. But when I look at that mother horse and her child in the barn, or at my children and their children, I feel lucky to have been permitted for a while to be part of all this life here on earth." His hand is on the door, and he seems a little embarrassed to have spoken so. But he has to go on: "I am talking like my wife now! After all these years she sometimes falls into my silences and I carry on as she does. She is not just an old woman, you know. She wears old age like a bunch of fresh-cut flowers. She is old, advanced in years, *vieja*, but in Spanish we have another word for her, a word which tells you that she has grown with all those years. I think that is something one ought hope for and pray for and work for all during life: to grow, to become not only older but a bigger person. She is old, all right, *vieja*, but I will dare say this in front of her: she is *una anciana;* with that I declare my respect and have to hurry back to the barn."

3

LA NECESIDAD

It is a miracle, she believes, that he still requires frequent haircuts at seventy-nine. Her own father was bald by forty, and her sons have tended toward baldness in early middle age. But in another year, she points out, he will be "twenty years short of a hundred," and yet his hair is as thick and bushy as it was years ago—and mostly black, too. Perhaps he is lucky in his ancestry, or perhaps it has to do with the care she has given him all these years. As for him, he mentions the alternatives, but inclines to the latter explanation: "There is a picture of my grandfather; it was taken in Albuquerque a long time ago, perhaps when this century was beginning its life. I must have been six or seven. I remember my father pointing to his father and saying 'My boy, there is someone for both of us to look up to. He will die a strong man, however old he is when God calls him. And look at his hair: as full and black as it was a long time ago.' I asked why people get white hair or lose their hair, and my father shrugged his shoulders: that is up to God.

"I do not mean to speak out of turn, but I believe my wife has been the one responsible for my condition. She has taken such good care of me; she keeps her eye on me as though she were my patron saint. She is more than a good woman whom I married and have loved all these years. She is like a watchdog. She would not mind the comparison. She senses something bad approaching well before it gets near, and she knows how to take a stand: Manuel, I don't like this, or

Manuel, let us beware—that is what I hear from her. So, then I know; and I do as she suggests.

"As for my hair, she has cut it every month or so for over half a century. The storekeeper tells me that hair runs in the family: father to son. I tell him no! Look at my sons! He scratches his head; he can't answer me. But I can explain things to him: the boys went into the army, and when they came back they did not want their mother to cut their hair. And that was that! They began losing their hair."

He puts his right hand through his hair. He suddenly feels shy and tries to change the subject: there is a wind coming up, and it will go through the canyon fast. But his mind is still on his hair. Embarrassed by his own pride, he tries again to call upon the weather: Why are New Mexico's winters these days so wet and cold? It has always been cold up in the Sandia mountains, east of Albuquerque; he knows that. But lately there have been extremes—more snow, lower temperatures, noisier and more forceful winds. As he mentions all that he edges closer to the mirror, the one mirror in his house; it hangs on the living room wall rather than in a bedroom or bathroom. For a second he tries to stop himself, but it is no use: better to let oneself go, submit to the pull upon him, and then make a public acknowledgement of what happened: "Mirrors have magnets in them; I've never seen one, but you know a magnet by its feel. Sometimes I will walk into this room, and the next thing I know, I am looking at myself. I don't know why. Maybe it is because I am soon to go, and one wants to say good-bye to an old friend. My mother used to say to us 'Be your own friend; be friendly to others, but don't forget yourself.'

"She did not mean for us to be greedy. She just wanted us to take care of ourselves. Respect your appearance; she would always give us that advice. I suppose that is why I have not fallen to pieces, even at my age. I am old, but I can still recognize myself—the man I used to be, and soon no longer will be! But I should not speak so much about myself. I should not take such pleasure in my health and my good head of hair. My wife always says that to me: What a good head of hair! And then I am once again overcome by her words: I move toward the mirror to take a look at myself and smile. That is not why we were put here, to pay so much attention to ourselves."

Now he is no longer intent on catching a glimpse of his mostly black hair, nicely combed back. He has been satisfied, and is genuinely anxious to get on with other matters: "I had word from my son today. He called our neighbors. He wants to know why I will never agree to a phone. I try to tell him that I have lived all my life without one, so why begin now? Besides, it costs money. I am not starving, but I am not surrounded by piles of money. We have all we can do to keep our heads high—and only when you own no one anything can you walk into church and feel you can look to the right or the left, and catch anyone's eye, and not be moved to lower your own eyes right away. I think it bothers my son more to ask a favor—that I be called over to talk with him—than it bothers me to come and speak.

"He is proud. He wants me to be my own master, he tells me. I tell him he is wasting his time: I am too near the end to start learning new tricks. It's not only the money; I think if I was rich I'd feel the same way about the telephone. I have been in homes and heard those phones ring. The church bells are more to my liking. They call you to prayer, but they are polite and not in such a hurry. The phone is like a knife; it lunges at you, then it lunges again: no mercy, no consideration, only determined to make you bow to its wishes. My son laughs; I am at his home and the phone rings, and his wife is out and he is unable to answer, and I know I must be of help, so I say 'I surrender,' and go to pick it up. Later we will be eating and for no reason at all he will look at me and begin to smile. What is on his mind, we all wonder. Finally he tells us: 'Father has one enemy that he cannot banish, but neither will he himself be conquered—the phone. He surrenders when it commands him, but he has his fortress, his own house, and it will never be conquered. It is a stand off.'' So, we all laugh.

"When you are old, people chalk up everything to your age. You are not entitled to have an opinion without someone saying 'It is because he passed three score and ten that he thinks like that.' My wife will tell our children how stubborn I am; I have had my ideas all my life. But the children, for all the love they have for us, will not listen. They are willing to ignore their own memories. When I try to remind them myself, I receive a smile and a nod: 'Yes, father, anything you say.' I want to stand up and shout, but an old man doesn't shout in his children's home, nor in his own. I would lose my temper years ago; my sons have heard me carry on. But once they left this house to live elsewhere and begin their own families, they returned as guests of mine. As for their mother, she has had a long vacation from my angry outbursts. When one gets older there is not the energy for them."

Perhaps he has given the wrong impression. He worries that he has portrayed himself a spent volcano. He looks for a way of correcting himself. Finally he abandons any need he may have felt for being casual, and instead speaks bluntly: "I no longer have children to discipline. When the boys were younger I would have to teach them how to behave. Their mother would go so far with them; then I had to step in. Six boys, and no girls; I was a father of sons! It would be the same with daughters, though: a father is the one to hand down the laws to children. Of course, there is always disobedience, and I never wanted to crush my young ones. They will never learn if they don't have a chance to go wrong; my wife and I both would say that, especially when we were tempted to go after one of the boys too much. But there is a line one draws, and it is just as well to make it clear; beyond this point—well, there will have to be punishment. I would not use my hands; I have never thought of hitting anyone. I would call them to me, and hold both their hands and look at them. They would lower their eyes, a signal to me that they knew they had done wrong. Then I would tell them what they had to do.

"So, I wasn't harsh. And I always had my father's example to call upon. I am now what he was: a grandfather. In this community a grandfather is respected; he has spent a lot of time bringing up children, making sure they learn to respect their parents, their teachers, their church. He is not put out to pasture when he gets old. He is asked to give advice. I believe my sons really want us to have a phone because it will make it easier for them to ask me questions. Now they have to leave their homes and come here, or wait until I go visit them. If we had a phone, they would just pick it up. But it is better we talk when we can see each other's faces. I tell my oldest son all the time: a voice without a face is like the wind, it comes and is soon gone. I will never forget my father's eyes. I will never forget his large hands, and how they would move toward me when he wanted me to know how serious he was. I remember he would be stern with me, then reach out and hold my upper arm and shake it a little; then I knew I was forgiven and was still loved.

"The other day my third son came to me and we talked about his children. He said they get very noisy sometimes, and their mother's nerves become worn thin. He said he wished I was there all the time, because when I enter the house, the children become like angels; they stop their mischief and look at me as if I was the priest and ready to say benediction—or give a strict sermon. I reminded my son of the mischief he used to cause. I was sitting in this, my chair, and he was over there on the sofa, and I suddenly lowered my voice and told him to come over. He was a little surprised, but he came immediately. Maybe at first he thought I was sick. But when I held his arms as I used to, he knew what I meant: when a father wants to, he can command silence. I used to walk into a room, and the boys would be going after each other, and at first they would not be sure what I was up to, so they would continue. (I never wanted my children to quake in their boots at the very sight of me!) Then I would make myself clear; I would clench my fist and pound the table or if there was no table in the room, I would hit the wall, just once. That was all I needed to do.

"Now it is for me to remind my sons what I used to do, and give them the courage to follow in my footsteps, just as I always turned to my father when I was in doubt about how to be a good example for my children. When he was alive he would show me. He would remind me of his stick. It was in the corner, and when he would be tired of putting up with our foolishness and mistakes, he'd walk over and grab the stick. He never used it. He never even came near us with it. We knew what he wanted. We became different. We stopped our noise and tears and went about our business. Now, I have to admit: I could never use a stick like that. I tried, but I found myself shaking. I had nothing to say, but my throat would catch. I told my wife that a stick was not for me. I talked with my father, and he said he had thrown the stick out after we were all grown, and it was up to me how I taught my children. He said that his father never used a stick; he would stamp his feet hard on the floor. That was all he had to do. I asked my father why he did not do the same. He said he tried, but his feet just wouldn't oblige. All of a sudden they became heavy and he found them more disobedient than us! So, one day he took mother's broom instead. Afterward, he decided he would find a stick for himself: 'It would have been wrong to depend upon your mother's broom,' he told me when I was already a father myself. 'That was for her to use—on the house, not the children!'

"So, you see, we each have to be ourselves. My father had helped me. I came home and thought to myself: why not be like my grandfather? The next day I stamped my feet when two of the boys needed to be told to stop fighting. But it was no good; they missed my point. I pounded on the table, and they heard. From that day on it was my way of being their father. One of my sons does the very same thing. Another takes off his belt and puts it on the table, but he doesn't have to use it. We took a long walk, and he told me his boy was getting fresh. I said that it was better to move quickly against the Devil, and he laughed. He said he wasn't going to pound on the table; and I laughed. I said I could understand.

He asked me if I wanted to try pounding the table with my grandchildren. I said they never show me how bad they can be; that is one of the joys of being a grandfather. Well, we walked further, and my son said he would do *something*, and I knew then he would find the answer. When I found out what the answer was I had to laugh: my great-uncle, my grandfather's older brother, was a great one for the strap. My father said his uncle could take off his strap so fast no one could see him do it; they only heard the snap. Then it was there, on the table. Maybe my son heard me tell the story years ago. We don't forget certain things we hear."

He fusses with his own belt as he talks, then catches himself doing so and gives his visitor a knowing smile. Snow has begun to fall, and he looks at it intently. The weather becomes an occasion for a speech of sorts—about the state of New Mexico, about the region in the state he and his family have considered their home for so long, about the difference between his kind of life and the life Anglo tourists or middle-class suburban people live. He begins, characteristically, with an apology or two. Who is he to speak with any authority? He is scarcely able to read and write. He is merely a working man who at this stage of his life has to be careful not to work very hard. For that reason he sometimes judges himself lazy—and a lazy man, an idle man, ought not impose his views on anyone else. Nevertheless, those views are there, inside him, and every once in a while they well up: "I have to clench my fist and hold it up to my own eyes! I have to remind myself to hold my tongue. But my sons and my grandchildren look to me for my opinion before they say what is on their own minds. It was like that when I was young. My grandfather and his older brother (the man of the strap!) would come visit us, and everything stopped, while mother and father tried to get them comfortably settled in chairs, with coffee at their side. Then we would all gather around, the children, and listen to what they had to say. My grandfather was a great one for stories, and now I find myself telling the same ones to my own grandchildren. Some of them are about animals, or about the mountains, and what you must do if you are to climb them and not get hurt. Some of them are about events: a trip to Albuquerque, or a time when it was so cold we all nearly froze to death.

"My great-uncle was very proud of our blood; he would argue with my grandfather right in front of us, and we would sit and watch them and forget everything else—and that does not happen often with young children! My grandfather would insist that we are American, even if we speak Spanish and come originally from Spain. My great-uncle would say that nations have empires, even when they lose the land that went to make up the empire: so long as the people are scattered all over, there is an empire. 'We are the Spanish empire,' he would say. My grandfather would then tell us children that his big brother has always been like that—a man of his own strange ideas. One time the uncle would laugh at the words of his brother, the next time he would become angry; we never knew what to expect. But they never argued for too long in front of us. They would tell each other that they would settle their differences later on. I must have been impressed; because I never have let my children see me disagree with their mother; and I notice that my sons keep quiet in front of their children, and have their fights with their wives in privacy."

Perhaps his presence is an element in his children's restraint. He wonders about that aloud, then dismisses the possibility. The issue is one of respect—how to obtain it from children, how to enable them, as they grow up and start families, to feel able to ask for it from their own children. Maybe, too, the issue is one those in a world other than his would call "cultural." Not that he, too, isn't aware of that aspect of things. He simply has his own way of getting at the subject: "We are Spanish, despite what my grandfather would say. I mean, we are citizens of this country, the United States of America; but Spain is where we all began, and Spain is here, even in this poor settlement, so unimportant that few people know us. In Albuquerque most people have never heard of our towns, even though we are only twenty or so miles east of the city. And the people of Albuquerque, so many of them, who come to these mountains to do their skiing, have no idea that some of us remember when no one wanted to slide down the sides of hills, just enjoy looking at them. Anglos cannot sit still and enjoy life. They are always on the move. Such restless people!

"I am sure that my sons will never turn into Anglo parents; they will always want to be the leaders for their children, knowing that a follower who has been well taught can become a good leader himself. When I was younger, I worked under Anglos for a while; I was a janitor, and so I came to know how they live. That was the time when money was scarce, and when I even thought of moving into Albuquerque with my family. We had our land, and we had a few chickens, but you can't live off a vegetable garden and some eggs, not with many children to raise and no work. I was lucky to get rides back and forth from here to the city, and sometimes I would sleep in the cellar—that is right, on the hard cement floor. It was stores and offices I cared for, but I would overhear them talk, those fortunate people who owned them. And believe me, they would carry their fights to work: 'I had a fight with the old lady, I told her off, I'm going to tell her off'—on and on they would go. Then they would send me out to their houses, to work on their grass or their trees, and I would hear them: such bad names they threw back and forth, and all within earshot of the children.

"Once a man told me I was lucky, because I spoke Spanish. At first I didn't quite know what he meant, but he explained himself: if he and his wife spoke Spanish they could argue in Spanish, and then the children wouldn't hear every awful word. I didn't say anything—I did not want to lose my job—but I was unfit for work the rest of the day. I worried about his poor children—they were poor in a way my children weren't. (Excuse my boasting; it is bad to do, but one gets tempted and gives in.) The Anglos are always fighting at work: dog eat dog. They like to lord it over others—us, the Indians, anyone who gets in their way. And there that boss of mine was ready to take our Spanish tongue and use it to try and fool his own children! Who would be fooled? I wonder. Children don't have to understand words to know that their parents are fighting. When parents have no respect for each other, the children will pretty soon find out. I wanted to shake my fist at him and tell him that I speak English well enough to use it in a fight with my wife, but I will never do so, nor she. We might have kept a few secrets from the younger children, who hadn't started school, and so didn't know much English, but we would soon have been found out: 'Those tricky two,' the children would think to themselves, 'calling each other names in a different tongue, then telling us to be honest and conceal nothing.'

"When I came home and told my wife what the Anglo had said, she shrugged her shoulders. Later she told me I was making too much of it. (She saw I was in low spirits at supper, and had nothing to say to anyone.) She brought me my coffee and gave me a candy she'd made, and said I was playing their game by exciting myself over a few words spoken by a man who had just squabbled with his wife. 'Pity them,' my wife said. Why? I wanted to know. 'Because they have such big appetites, and still they are unhappy.' I looked confused for a second or two, and I was going to get an explanation from my wife, but by the grace of God my own head made sense of what she was saying. I realized that for the Anglo the Spanish tongue was like land: get it, get anything that there is to get, and then there will be happiness. Of course, he was an unhappy man, and I ought to have realized it then and there, and not made *myself* unhappy all day, worrying because I had heard an insult to my people's language, and not been able to reply like a man. To think that a man would want to use Spanish like a knife or a gun—something to fight with!"

Upon occasion he has talked about what it is to be a man—or a woman. He is not given to long pronouncements on the subject. For a while, in fact,—until he has met a visitor over and over again and feels ready to relax with him—he will insist that there is nothing at all to say about the subject. He will smile, then adroitly shift to another topic. Or to silence: in which case a point has been made even more emphatically. But once he did mention some differences between himself and his wife, and after that the ice seemed broken for good; he would again and again quite naturally point out that he is like this, his wife like that—and both of them true to their kind. The first moment was brief but pointed; he had dropped his pipe and tried to clean up the tobacco but without full success: "I have not my wife's patience. I will die an upset, excited man. She will die quietly. Even if, God forbid, she is in pain, she will accept the Lord's decision to test her before taking her in His hands. I will be annoyed and bitter: why is He doing this to me? Why won't He let me go quietly and without suffering? I will be trying to tame my desire to fight. How dare anyone, man or woman, fight the Lord! My wife will have no such desire to fight."

Then he looked down at the tobacco he hadn't managed to pick up or brush aside with his foot, and drew the conclusion he believed appropriate: "You see, I am really fighting with that tobacco. I want to grab it; I want to kick it and push it in a corner. And it is all my fault; the poor tobacco has no will of its own. Now, my wife would not behave this way. She would be kind toward the poor tobacco—on the floor there when it should be in my pipe. She would lean over and pick up everything without saying a word, and there would be no problem. I have watched her all these years, picking up after each one of us, and wondered whether she doesn't feel put upon. We have even had our talks about that: no, she says, anymore than I used to feel it unfair to have to go out and listen to the insults of Anglos, and clean up after them, and take care of their garbage—while she sat home and listened to the radio, the music she loves so. She would send us all off and feel like a queen, alone and with music to hear all day."

Another time that radio and its music set him going again about women and men and how they age differently. He steered himself toward the points he wanted to make with a certain easy elegance: "Music touches the soul. I cannot imagine Church without music. Soon I will die, and I will admit that I wonder what will meet me in the beyond: the fires of Hell or the peace of Heaven. When

I think of Heaven I think of music—there must be good music up there. There have been times when I see my wife up there listening to music; meanwhile I am denied admission: my sins. Heaven cannot be only for women, nor Hell for men, I know, but it is a temptation to believe that is how God wills things.

"We are both old, so I guess we both think more of death. 'Do you think of death?' my sons will ask me. They mean no harm. They worry about us, and know we have little time left. I tell them no, not too much. But how much is too much? I don't know. I swear, until I was seventy I never thought of death at all. Then all the celebration: my seventieth birthday. And soon we were married fifty years. I turned to my wife one day and asked her—I hesitated a good long time before I dared speak—whether she worried about dying. No, she said. But she must have known what was on my mind, because she said she had been thinking a lot about death, lately—asking herself what it would be like after the heart stops and one is no longer among the living. I asked her when she'd first had her thoughts of that kind, and she said many years ago—perhaps when she was carrying our first son, and even before that, too. I was dumbfounded. I thought she was joking. No, she wasn't, though. We had a long talk. I had never before that day realized what it is to be a man, what it is to be a woman. There are some joys to old age, but none greater than realizing that finally you are learning about the really important things. Perhaps God reveals some of His mysteries to us at the very end, before He receives us into His Kingdom—or tells us no, we do not merit it."

He is not anxious to repeat what he and his wife talked about. Certainly he is not urged to do so. No one who has met him, tall and straight for all his years, sure of himself as he talks or walks or does his chores, can imagine him being successfully urged to do anything he hasn't of his own accord decided to embark upon. He likes to drink coffee, and usually his wife keeps a pot full on the stove. But sometimes she goes to church in the morning to sit with other women and sew, and on those days he more or less fends for himself: "I went to make coffee, and saw we had run out. She will bring some home, I am sure. She thinks I drink too much of it: maybe she forgets to make me some on purpose! Women have to remember everything, it seems: Is the coffee soon to be gone, or the flour, or the sugar? They know when the end is near, when a new supply is needed.

"Men go on, fighting against the odds; it is a hard world, and each man has to carve out his small place. Women are close to the seasons; they keep their eye on the sun and they know when life is starting and when it is stopping. They bring life into the world and they care for life. They make food—and without it we die. They are always worrying that the dog has not yet come home, or a bird has fallen from a nest and needs care, or the cake didn't turn out well, or one of the children seems frail and catches too many colds. Meanwhile the men are fighting with each other to be first, or going off to a job, even if they don't like it, so that they can have money to bring home.

"I don't mean to be unfair to may own kind! I went to the doctor last month—a cold that wouldn't leave, and perhaps it was pneumonia, we began to think—and he is a man quite like my wife. Everything she had asked me, he did! I told my wife she has been my doctor for over fifty-five years! And she said yes, a woman is always watching her children and her husband: How are they breathing and how are they eating and how do they look and what do they need to look even better and feel even better? Until then I'd never realized what crosses my own wife's mind so often—and imagine, over fifty-five years together! So, we talked some more, and she told me that years ago, while I slept she would listen to me breathing, and listen to the children as they moved about in their beds, and think about each one of us: what we like to eat, and what we would be doing that might be special the next day. Or she would be thinking of someone's birthday, or whose clothes needed mending. I have always gone to sleep right away and the next thing it is morning, and my wife is shaking me and I look up and she is dressed and I can smell the coffee, good and strong. Now that I am near eighty I have at last found out what has been happening all those nights: she has slept, too, but her sleep has been different than mine, much lighter. She had too much on her mind to let herself forget everything, the way I did.

"Now that I think back, I remember that she would doze a bit in the afternoon; she would tell me when I came home that a nap of fifteen minutes after lunch and before the children came home from school was as good as a night's sleep for her. I can never sleep in the day, even now, when I have more time. After we lost a child—he would have been another son—my wife told me she wasn't sleeping well; for a month or more it lasted, though I can't say I knew much about what it was like for her at night. She did tell me once that she wasn't feeling well, and the pain had kept her up. Only now do I know that it was her sadness; she would sit and wonder what kind of boy we might have had. I had told her we already had three, and best to be grateful for them, rather than feel sorry for too long that we have lost one. But for a mother each child is precious; and she carried the boy, not me! I don't think a man can put himself in a woman's shoes; but I think a woman is always putting herself in everyone else's shoes—her children's, her husband's, her neighbor's. It is only these recent days, when we both know that soon we are to go, that we share our lives with each other in words. To be old is to be given time to remember; and if you are blessed with good health, as we are, there is also energy to share memories with one another, and with the children and grandchildren."

He stops at the mention of his grandchildren. He has memorized the total number of them (twenty-four) but he has trouble remembering which son has how many children. And he is not all that good at keeping their names in mind. Again, there is the contrast with his wife, who knows exactly how old each child is, not to mention his or her name. How does she do it, keep so much in her head? What is the matter with his own thinking? He asks those questions of himself, and sometimes of his wife, too. She laughs and tells him he is making too much out of nothing. He has worked hard all his life and given her and her children a good life. She had been home bringing up the children, thinking about them day and night; no wonder the names of the grandchildren, however many, stay with her. Nor does she let the matter drop there. For the grandchildren he is the one whose every word is heeded, and she is glad that kind of respect, even awe, still obtains in the family. "My wife says it will be a sad day when children don't hold up their fathers and grandfathers as the ones who have the last word. I tell her that it is a different age, the one we now live in. Women are the equal of men. But not in our family; not among our people here in this part of New Mexico. My sons have wives who think as my wife does, and they are not old. My sons say that their children tell them, whenever there is an argument about something, that I should be called in for advice. I say to my sons, 'You must be tired of hearing that; you must get hot under the collar.' No, they tell me they have a lot to look forward to—they will also be grandfathers one day.

"Well, I have to be honest with them; I tell them that when I was first married, my grandfather was still alive, and I remember my father bowing to his every wish and word. But I go on to say that I think there should be some changes; because a man gets old is no reason to go along with his vices. If one is of good spirit, and has lived to sort out what makes sense from what doesn't, then all very well that others pay attention. If one has had bad judgment, then long years of being a fool don't deserve to be overlooked. My sons will hear none of that, however. I only hope they are wise when they tell me that they have made their decision: I am worth their complete respect!

"Of course the grandchildren take their grandmother and me on faith. I worry that sometimes I may say something that misleads them and they will not know it. My wife asks me if I ever had such second thoughts when our own children were young. No, of course not; there was no time then for anything but work and more work. Now with age we have the luxury of many hours to think about what we have done and what we are doing, and God willing, what we will do in the time left. But I have to admit that I'm not overcome by any doubts I may have. When I go to see my sons and grandchildren I am the only person I know how to be: myself. They come to me and tell me what has happened since I last saw them, and ask me questions; and they say, please, let us have another of your stories.

"My stories: they are memories that I have accumulated, memories of a long life, and now I have use for them. The children listen so eagerly, and often I find that my son or my daughter-in-law will put aside whatever they are doing and sit with the children. It is a temptation: I carry on like a talkative priest. But later I say to myself: we are all here for God's purposes, and through me younger people can learn about what it was like in the past, and they can find out about their family. No one should want to look only to the future. If there are some people who don't care about the past, they are lost souls.

"My sons and I are more on the same footing, you could say. No longer do they keep their tongues while I use mine. I ask them what they believe, and they tell me. We usually agree, but I am glad that sometimes we don't. Then I know they will turn into their own selves: not a grandfather who is exactly like me, just as I am different from my grandfather. Mind you, not so very different; on most things I am like he was.

"I never talk about the world's problems with my wife—she has no interest in such matters; but my oldest son, especially, wants to talk about our people, and what is happening to the country, and so I join him. This is when I do more listening than is usual for an old, bossy man like me, so used to being begged for words and more words. My son has moved to Albuquerque, and even though he is living outside the city, and has his chickens and a horse and a pony, I think the city has gone to his head a bit. He works in a supermarket, and has done well for himself. He is no manager, but neither does he wash and sweep the floors, like he used to do. They have him checking out customers, and I will tell you, it is almost impossible for me to understand how he does the work: all those numbers to read and register on the machine, and all the change to make, for one customer after another. I am glad I encouraged him to stay in school; and the army helped, too: he went to school while in the service and came out sure of himself with numbers and able to take a car apart and put it together so fast you think he's a magician, watching him.

"Maybe it is the world he saw when in the army, or the people he sees all day long—maybe that is why he has such strong ideas about what is good and bad here in this state or in other parts of the country. I never did read newspapers. He does, every day. He watches television in the evenings; we love our radio. We have a television set—the gift of our second son, who works as a repair man. You can imagine how much he sees of television! I ask him whether it isn't too much, repairing the sets by day, and looking at them by night, but he says no, he is happy. Sometimes we put on the set when the children come; the grandchildren like to watch. They ask me what my favorite program is, and I tell them that I have none. They think that means I like all of them equally; it really means I know none of them.

"*Chicano*, that is the word. My sons tell me they hear it all the time, and my oldest son wants me to think of myself as a Chicano. For a while I resisted him. I said I have no interest in these words—the politicians come up with them, then throw them aside for new ones. But the boy is stubborn. He is not a boy; he is a man. And he has won me over. We are Spanish people. We are Americans. We live here up in the mountains. To tell you the truth, we belong to no town, just a few houses here on the road. But the fact is that Anglos are the rich ones; they control the county, with their money and influence. Our own people have always had a good say about what happens in this state. We have sent men to big positions: senator, as high as that. Only a handful of us are rich, though; most of us are poor. With the Anglos it's a little different. They don't have too many rich, either. The rich are always few, compared to the poor—no matter the country or the people you are talking about. But the Anglos have more people than we do who have good jobs and live well. The Anglos are favored in the schools; their language is the one that is used, and our children have to go along. My son says mostly its Anglo managers and Chicano workers.

"I used to tell him to be glad there *is* work, but no more. One cannot go by the past. One loves the past, but one has bad memories as well as good. I don't tell my grandchildren how poor we were. We still are, but at least there is enough for food, and we live very simple lives. We ask for nothing but a little to eat and wood for our fireplace and some dollars to put in the tray on Sunday. I have one suit, and it is so old I can't remember when I bought it. But I only wear it on Sundays, so it has lasted. My son would want me to have more; he thinks all our people deserve more. Who would disagree? I remember that my father would take off his hat when talking to certain Anglos, but not with our own people. That is not right, to be afraid of people.

"Mostly we have our lives up here, away from Anglos; but in the city they are everywhere, and you have to make peace with them. My younger sons, the last two, are also in Albuquerque, but they don't have much to do with Anglos, not as much as the oldest one. Maybe that is why they don't get as angry as he does. They say live and let live; the oldest one says that is fine, but you have to struggle for your rights, or else you'll be pushed aside and treated like a child. I said to him I only wish Anglos treated more of us like children; then they would be nice to us, and let us grow up and have our own lives, like children have when they get bigger. But no, too often the rich people treat the poor like dogs: 'Stay around and do my bidding and don't dare be an equal with me, because you are not, and only the scraps go to you.'

"It is all too much for me to figure out. I will say this: my sons have more to fall back on than I've ever had. They work hard, but they get more money than I ever dreamed of making. Their children are getting good educations; they look up to me, but when I hear them talking, I think to myself that it is me who should be catching *their* every word. They listen to their father, too. They tell me that I should be proud because I am a Chicano who is old and has survived all the pains of this life. I tell them that I never thought of life as painful; I lived and enjoyed myself. There was sickness and suffering, too. I remember times when we never could be sure there would be food the next day. But one doesn't give up. If it will help my grandchildren to live better lives, I will call myself a Chicano and offer what strength I have left to *la causa.* I told my son as much, and he said he only wanted my approval. I embraced him for saying that."

With that he held out his arms, as if his son were there, waiting. His sons are his life, are him extended in time; in his own way he says that over and over again. If one of them thinks of himself as a Chicano, then part of him is indeed a Chicano. If another son says no, then he also has reservations about political slogans. His oldest grandson has a picture of César Chávez on his wall, and is very much a young Chicano. His oldest grandaughter is quite bright and wants to go to college. She, too, has a picture of Chávez looking down at her. She is a Chicana, and reminds her grandfather of that fact rather often: "I take her around and hug her, then I whisper to her that I am with her, and am a Chicano. She smiles."

When he is not talking about his grandchildren he is thinking of them; through them he can imagine the future. His life, he says in a sort of summary, has been "a hard one," but not so hard lately. His father and grandfather had it harder. Slowly the country has become richer, and some of the wealth—not much, but some—has filtered down. Once he smiled and became rather didactic: "I am on the bottom, and so naturally it takes time for a poor man like me to receive much of anything. I have worked all my life, and I have no regrets. I only hope that my grandchildren realize their dreams. Necessity has been my master. I have had no time to stop and ask questions. I have had no time to argue. Perhaps if I had been more like my oldest son, and if all of us my age had been like him, then we could have gained some concessions from the rich people who run businesses and run the government and decide the fate of the poor. But we did not know to fight for ourselves then. Besides, we are proud; we will not feel sorry for ourselves. Never do I want to go to someone with my hat in my hand or on my knees—never, never. I have kept quiet in the past when I wanted to shout at Anglos; but I have never lost my pride in myself in my dealings with them.

"A long time ago I asked the priest what will happen to us—so little work was to be had then, and I feared for the future of my children, and for my people all over. He said he could understand my fears. He said some priests might tell me to turn the other cheek and wait for the next world, but he wished there was some way that all of us who are living so close to hunger might find the jobs we seek, and get good wages for the hard work we're ready to do. I told him not to worry. I said we'd manage. He had started out feeling sorry for me, but I pitied him by the time we had talked a while. He seemed to regret he was a priest. He was ready, he told me, to take off his collar and become a fighter on our behalf. I said no, we would fight for ourselves, and not be beaten. I think I was only pretending when I said that; I had no reason to be hopeful then.

"But we never quite lost all hope, even during the worst of times. My grandfather used to say to me when I was but a boy that our people have been living on this land here in New Mexico for a long, long, time—many generations, back and back and back in time. Only the Indians were here before us. The Anglos came much later. So, we will not leave, and we will somehow keep ourselves alive. Necessity demands it. When the belly sends messages that it hurts, the man works harder to get food. He plants, he harvests. He keeps after

52

his chickens. He gets a job, even if the pay is very little. There are times when I want to tell my sons how lucky they are that necessity has let up on their generation. They have time to enjoy life, and to ask all the questions they now come up with: Why are things the way they are, why don't we have more to say in what happens to our people?"

He stops and thinks; then he wonders out loud what the answers to such questions are. He shakes his head. He puts his right hand through his hair. Suddenly he feels to blame—though for what he is not sure. His hair: perhaps it is not yet white at his age because he did not worry enough in the past about some of the issues that preoccupy his oldest son. Perhaps he ignored what was right in front of him—so much injustice, so much exploitation—in order to go his own way from day to day.

But no, he will not criticize himself unfairly. He stands up straight and holds both of his hands out as he talks: "A man does not become eighty in order to spend his last precious hours having regrets and calling himself bad names. We all stand on the shoulders of others. My grandfather used to hold me on his shoulders and tell me to put my arms around his head as if it were a steering wheel. Then he would carry me, and I would point the direction. When we got to our destination, he would put me down and say he was ready to take me back when I wished. Then he would help me climb a tree or carve some wood. I remember looking at that knife of his and wishing that someday I might have one like it. And the day came: he died and my father was given the knife and he came to me and said I was the oldest boy, and so I could have it—but for a while I had to share it with him. Now it is my first grandson's. Now I carry him on my shoulders. Each of us is given so far we can go—so much time, so much energy. We do our best, then stop and say good-bye. When I am on my deathbed, I will think of my wife and my children and my grandchildren, and I will say good-bye to them all, and I will picture the young ones, my sons and my grandsons and grandaughters, walking further up the road, and then one day the sons will have to say goodbye to *their* children, and so it goes."

He stops and returns to his seat. Some coffee he had been holding has now grown cold. He empties it and gets himself some more. It is chilly outside, an early February morning. But he loves to face down weather, however severe. So long as he is able, he will do chores, walk, greet neighbors, wave at children, give horses sugar, scold chickens for being lazy and threaten them with an hour or two in the oven. If one is to enjoy the radio's music, take a good rest in the afternoon, one must venture forth in the morning. That is how he believes he should spend his remaining days, and that is also how a life should be spent: a good deal of work, followed by a well-earned rest.

He tells his children what his philosophy is and they nod enthusiastically: "I say to them that they must prepare for the future; they must know how to be on time for appointments, and ready to give all the energy they have to the work they do. My grandson says he will go to the university and work hard there. I tell him that will be wonderful. Then he tells me that no matter what he learns there, he will still look up to me. I say that is also wonderful—and I pick him up and show him I still have some strength left in my arms. Then I put him down and tell him I had a teacher all my life, even though I had so little schooling: necessity is a demanding teacher. Yes, the boy agrees. Then I boast; it is bad to do, but I can't control myself. *Enseña más la necesidad, que un año de universidad.* How would an Anglo say it? Necessity teaches more than one year of university study? Yes, that is what I say. My wife tells me I should be ashamed of myself, bragging like that, but I want the children to know that their grandfather has a useful life. And they are not bothered by what I say. They clap their hands and say hurrah! And I clap back at them."

4

THE AGE OF A REPUTATION

Even people who work the land buy food at stores if they have any money at all. In the countryside of the South, in Appalachia, and in the semidesert country of New Mexico the store that rural people frequent is at once a source of needed supplies and a location where people meet and exchange news and gossip—a center of community life, really, and often the place one gets mail, emergency phone calls, messages of various kinds from relatives in the far-off city. A visitor who comes to a particular community or settlement in a large but for the most part thinly populated state like New Mexico in hopes of understanding how certain families live does well to make the acquaintance of the man and woman (usually it is both) who run the market or grocery store (the names seem interchangeable). One such store is called just that: "The Store." Most of the customers who go to that particular store are Spanish-speaking, as are the owners; but Indians and Anglos also come by. The owner is Señor Gallegos; for a long time he was called Mike, but as he grew older and older, he became Señor Gallegos to everybody, and his oldest son, who works with him, became Mike. Señora Gallegos, who for years has stood behind the counter alongside her husband, has never been anything but Señora Gallegos to her customers.

For a time, when she was bearing and rearing children, Señora Gallegos had a limited number of hours to spend in the store. The family has always lived in a house that connects to the store, and the children, even as infants, often played there. But their mother was strict and attentive: there were just so many liberties they were allowed, and she made sure *she* had a liberty—the right to gather herself and the children up and leave at moments when the store threatened to turn into a noisy nursery. As the children—four girls, three boys—grew up, their mother spent longer and longer uninterrupted stretches of time waiting on customers, and now she has more say than her husband about what happens in the store. "I am a year his senior," she explains, "but God has seen fit to keep me looking younger than him." Then she speaks of a certain irony in her life and his: "We are both over eighty, but I will not say by how much. I have never wanted to talk about age. It is a subject that brings up memories. Even after all these years I can still remember my mother asking me why I wanted to marry a man who was younger than I. And my husband, what he didn't hear from his mother—and his father, too! We both were made to think we were sinful. Imagine! When people have their ideas, they don't like anyone to disagree. The man should be older than the woman, that is what my parents and my husband's parents believed. They even went to the priest. What to do about this scandal?

"The old priest understood how they felt, but he told them that they were being foolish. I think he used that very word—my mother told me so, much later. He said it is foolish to let a year's time become a judgment on two people who love each other. With that, we were able to get married, and there was no trouble afterward. I can still remember, though, how people felt before we were married: I was a stained woman who was capturing a *boy;* and my husband, he was a nice child, innocent as could be, who was allowing himself to be tricked. It was an awful time, and for a while I wanted to say no, and never get married. I talked to the priest about becoming a nun, but he was so very helpful and wise: one doesn't turn to God because one has had trouble with one's friends and neighbors—that is what he told me, and I shall never forget his eyes, full of affection and understanding. Then I stiffened my back and decided to go ahead, and so did my husband; and here we are, sixty years later!

"For some strange reason I have always felt younger and been taken as younger than my husband. For a while I began to believe that it was God's way of punishing all the people who told stories about us and winked and showed those smiles that were meant to say: we know about those two! The priest told me to stop having such an idea about God; He has other things to do than help me get revenge on some idle, gossipy people who have no charity or kindness in their hearts. So, it is simply fate: my husband's to grow weak in his old age, and begin to lose his memory; and as for me, I still have a lot of my black hair, my teeth haven't fallen out, and I am sure that my head is still in good condition. After all, I can keep track of all the price changes these days, and that requires plenty of fast thinking. Last week my husband had one of his spells; he can be all right for a while, but then he goes back in time, and suddenly a customer is being told that she can have a loaf of bread for a dime, and the milk is that, too—or maybe fifteen cents. I have to humor him; I have to be gentle. I will tell him to stop trying to be funny, or stop having a daydream, and usually he will smile, and be grateful to me for helping him without causing any shame. And the customer will sigh and say, 'One day in the future it will be nice to have such prices'—something like that.

"My older sister—she is nearing ninety—tells me that I have been rewarded for being a good wife and mother: God has given me health and kept me young. I do not like her to talk like that. My husband has been a fine person all these years. I cannot imagine a life without him. If he has not been allowed to stay in the best of health lately, it is no reflection on his goodness. The wicked can often prosper; the finest of people can suffer terribly. I remind my sister of our Lord's life—so short; then she tells me to stop, and that way she has admitted her error.

"My sister is an inspiration to me; I don't mean to speak ill of her. She lost her husband many years ago; he had pneumonia and died. He was forty-five, I think. There were no doctors near here; there still aren't any. We couldn't get one to come and see him. The priest told me there was little a doctor could do; there was a crisis, and either one lived or died. Today they have good medicines; he would have lived—though we still cannot get a doctor to come visit, if someone suddenly becomes seriously ill. We would have to drive the person to Española. Since her husband's death, all these years ago, my sister has brought up a family, and helped us in the store. It was her idea to start cutting the hair of children; mostly in the town it is done at home by parents, but some fathers say no, and some mothers are not very good with the scissors—the children cry or fuss, and the mothers get nervous. My sister had been helping several of our cousins to cut their children's hair; she had always been so fast and in control of herself when she clipped—and in control of the boys and girls, too. When her husband died, they wanted to pay her. She said no. They pleaded. She said no.

"One day a mother came to her, not a relative, and asked for her help. The mother was afraid she'd hurt her children. As for her husband, he had epilepsy, and she was afraid he'd get a fit while holding the scissors over the heads of their children—and then, oh then! My sister reassured her; her trouble seemed to be her imagination—her 'fear,' my sister called it. My sister told her to bring the children to the store, and we brought a chair in and put it over in the corner there, an empty space, and put a table beside it, with a bowl—and soon the children had their haircuts. In the time it takes to blink the whole village knew, and the same thought came to everyone: my sister is wonderful with children who need to have their hair cut, and it is a polite way to be of help to her—the children to raise, and a husband taken away so early in life. And so she became a barber! The young priest here laughs; he says that all over America women are unhappy with their lives, and want more respect; and he says they should take their example from my sister who has performed the work of men for long years, and for doing so never paraded herself as someone special.

"For a time, before she became too old—her hands started shaking—she cut the hair of grown men, too. They would bring their children, and then they would begin teasing her, and saying, 'If you can work on them, why not on us?' So, she said yes, she would work on them, if they promised not to be vain and complain about the result. That is how my sister became a barber—when she wasn't being a mother and one of the people who runs this store. I believe on my deathbed I will think of her talking to our cousin one day long ago. He is probably the worst customer she has ever had; he cares about his appearance much too much. She has always tried to obey his instructions, but he has always wanted himself to be the most handsome man ever put here on New Mexico's land, and because he must realize that there are hundreds of miles between his wishes for himself and the way he looks to our eyes, he has to have someone to accuse: it is you or you or you who ruin my looks. Either his wife is scolded for keeping him fat, or someone like my poor sister is scolded.

"Well, the day I remember was rainy; we don't have much rain here. He had his haircut and he stood there looking at the weather outside. He had no hat, and he would look awful by the time he got home. I offered him my husband's hat, but he realized then what a peacock he was being. No, he would just go; but could he at least look at himself in a mirror, so that he would have the satisfaction of knowing what a good job my sister, his beloved cousin, had done? I winked at my sister and went to get a mirror. He looked. His face fell. Oh, how sad; too much had been removed. A pity! My sister stared right at him and replied, 'Dearest cousin, do not worry. A barber's mistakes grow out. A doctor's, the patient carries to the grave; and a priest's can lead one to Hell.' He sat up and took her around and said she was a wise woman. I will say so! And she still is, even at ninety.

"The other day I asked her how she can be in such good spirits; she has bad arthritis, and her digestion is not of the best. 'My sister,' she said, 'my life is not mine; it belongs to God. I am afraid to die. I do not want to die. I cannot persuade myself to like being old. I am no magician who can make a trance for herself, and end up welcoming what is a fearful moment: the last breath. But I have been given ten years short of a century already, and I don't seem to be leaving yet, for all my aches and pains. I am rich with years, a millionaire! I have been part of my own generation, then I watched my children's generation grow up, then my grandchildren's, and now my great-grandchildren's. Two of my great-grandchildren are becoming full-grown women now; they come visit me, and will remember me. Now, I ask you, how much more can a woman expect? My great-granddaughter told her teacher I was a barber fifty years ago, and the teacher wanted to send my name to Santa Fe, and they would honor me as a pioneer among women. Well, imagine that! I said no. I have been honored already—all this life I've been given is an honor God has chosen to offer. It is a big achievement, if I say so myself, to have accumulated all these years. And as I look back and think, I decide that I wouldn't have done things any different, not for the most part, anyway.'

"I am taking liberties with what she said, but I can remember her words, because my head tries hard to hold on to almost every one of them. I told my husband her message, and he nodded. I thought: It will not stay with him; he only keeps the old memories. But yesterday he said she is a wise woman, my sister—for two days he had been thinking of her speech to me. 'Do you think we should be proud, too, even if we have a few more years until we're her age?' he asked me. I didn't answer him. He didn't need an answer. I hugged him—oh, I was ashamed for a second, because my son walked in, and so did a customer. 'So, that's how you two mind the store for me,' our son said. And the customer, she was a young woman carrying her first child, and she said she had something to dream about now: if only she and her husband could live so long and still feel love for each other. I told her not to worry. God can be generous, even if there are disappointments and sadness in this life, too."

She may be stronger than her husband, but she still defers to him. She will make a remark about God and His loving-kindness, then look to Señor Gallegos for confirmation. Sometimes she will even ask "Yes?" of him. Usually he quickly gives what is requested of him, but once in a while he demurs. He does so by not saying anything for what strikes a visitor as rather a long time. Meanwhile his wife has quite clearly understood what he is up to. She moves toward him and begins to explain herself further. Her voice becomes not so much plaintive as appeasing, and also, reassuring: perhaps I have been a bit brusque, a bit inconsiderate in the way I throw off these remarks—and you, so busy working, for all the frailty of your years!

He does work. He opens up the store every morning at seven. He has already been up two, maybe three hours. He needs little sleep these days. His thoughts are pulled back at four or five in the morning to his childhood and youth; and, to a degree, he doesn't mind; he even enjoys recalling old experiences, visualizing faces long since gone. But eventually he is grateful for the requirement of work. If left to his mind's inclination he might never return to the year 1973. So, up he is, and soon at the stove making oatmeal—for sixty years his breakfast, regardless of the weather, the season—and drinking his black coffee. He has his ailments, but his stomach is in excellent shape. He takes coffee. He loves chili, the hotter the better—sometimes even for breakfast. When he himself feels his mind getting especially foggy or drawn to the past, he leaves the store and takes some chili, followed by bread without butter. The chili livens up his thinking, he is sure. And he does indeed seem more agile, more alert on his return. Who is his visitor, aware of what is peddled to millions of aging Americans in the name of aids for "fitness" or a youthful appearance, to come up with a note or two in his diary about Señor Gallegos's "superstitions"?

By dawn "the Señor," as his wife sometimes calls him in front of a visitor, has opened the store, put the daily five dollars of change in the various compartments of the cash register, crossed off the previous day on the calendar, and prepared himself for the first customer. That is the expression he uses: "prepare myself." One wonders why. Without being asked, he satisfies his guest's curiosity: "There are so many things to sell, and the prices do not stay the same. I like to keep the store clean. I like the first customer to come in and feel he is entering a home—spotless. I make a big pot of coffee; for years I have offered morning coffee. I like it myself. I like others to have it. For a while they wanted to pay, but I wouldn't hear of it. They will buy doughnuts, though. I have the radio going. I could put on television, but that is for later. The people who come by early do not want to look; they would rather listen. We don't talk much. In the early morning people are quiet. It is later in the day that children come in with their mothers or alone, and then it livens up. At seven the sun is up, but we are all still shaking off sleep—even me, and I've been up a couple of hours by then.

"The people near here like to come by every day. Some mothers send their husbands to the store each morning before breakfast. No wonder I have to be ready for them; they expect me to know by heart what they will be asking for. And why not? After all these years I'd be of no use if I couldn't predict what my customers want and need. Still, with age one has to think a little harder. So, about six-thirty I am picturing the men, and looking at the shelves to see that I have what they'll come for. Usually they don't even have to talk much when they enter. I look at them and go for the milk or some cereal or some cans—and of course, I have the doughnuts near the coffee. They put the money for the doughnuts in the glass jar; that is separate. The rest I ring up.

"We charge more than the big markets in the city. We must. We don't get to buy at the low prices a chain of stores can make the wholesale people set. Maybe one day there will be no stores like ours left. I apologize all the time to my customers. I tell them that if they would only drive twenty miles, they could do better. I know that some storekeepers like me have a fine time bleeding their customers—the people who can't travel or are in a hurry for something. But it is not in me to run that kind of business. I am too old to do a dance because I squeezed an extra nickel here, and a quarter there, out of some neighbors of mine. I would have nightmares, thinking of what they wished me: a long stretch in Hell. And I would belong there!

"The older I become, the more I think of others. Have I been a good husband and a good father? Will my friends think well of me when the casket with me in it moves down the street toward the cemetery? What will my cousins and my nephews and nieces and my neighbors and customers think when they stand there and see me put to rest: 'He is a scoundrel who took away from the poor and cheated people by touching the scale with his hand and raised prices far beyond what was fair?' or 'He did the best he could, and tried to be honest, and had a smile on his face most of the time?' I cannot say for sure; maybe I have been more thoughtless and rude than I will ever know. When God gives you the extra time he has given me, it may be because he expects you to examine yourself very closely, and think about what you have done wrong. I know that when I was younger I worried about money: I wanted there to be some for our old age. Back then I thought: If we live to be sixty-five, or seventy, we will be lucky, and we will no doubt be weak and so our son will have to run the store all by himself. But we lived longer, and here I am, still opening the store, so that my son can have a decent sleep, and see his children off to school.

"I didn't grow rich; nor will my son. He would like to make more money, I know. He resembles me; he is torn between the desire to make money for his wife and children, and a great loyalty to our customers. How can you take more than is due you—especially when you know you are lucky to have the store and live comfortably as you do, and many of your customers aren't at all in the same shoes? I have no answers; I wish everyone in the world had enough to eat, good clothes, and a roof that doesn't leak over their heads. I tell our priest all the time that it is no joy, taking money from people who don't have much, and who work so hard for the little they do have. He slaps me on the back and tells me that it is not me or Señora Gallegos or our son who are the enemies of the poor. He tells me about other stores he knows of, from his past work: the owners are politicians, and they push the people around and take every cent they can get. I feel good, hearing him speak well of me, but I still worry: God must know that I have had my moments of greed.

"There have been people I have not liked, and they have pushed me hard: Why do you charge such high prices? Why do you try to bleed us? I have tried to answer: it is trying and lonely running a store like this one, and if I give everything away, I will have to beg myself, rather than run the store. But I can hold firm; no one will knock me down, not when I think I am in the right. Sometimes I feel ready to fight; and sometimes I have said to myself, 'Take all you can get, because they are mean ones, and they will only respect a man who is as mean as they are.' And you know, that is true: there are people on this earth who have contempt for a man who tries to be generous; he is seen as a fool, or up to some clever trick. That is God's way—to put many different kinds of people here, and let us all prove ourselves before him."

He stops and adjusts his suspenders. It is as if he is worried: how does *he* look before God? How has *he* managed to "prove" himself, all these years? He feels his face: old as he is, he still has to shave, and every other day is not enough. He takes out his handkerchief, unfolds it, then folds it up again—a habit of his that his wife for a long time tried to break, then came to appreciate: his way of arranging and rearranging, and certainly of no harm to anyone. He moves toward the shelves, spots a can of peaches out of place, puts it back with the others, does the same with some cans of soup, and soon is standing near the cash register, his fingers playing on the keys. His daughter plays the piano; she bought a small one for her children, and has learned to play it herself. His piano is that cash register; it is a wonder, he observes, that the keys are still there; all the use over all those years.

Sometimes he sees people looking at the tray; he knows they wish they had the money inside—not that they would ever make a try to take anything. They are simply good friends who are human enough to know envy or lust. Besides, they are likely to be needy. Their eyes wander toward the tray only briefly, and he has learned never to let them catch him catching them. He can see them beginning to take note of the money, and then at all costs he finds some excuse to look away from them. He has taught his son to do likewise. He has also taught his son to be tough with wholesalers, easy with those who require something and don't have ready cash. There are no "charge accounts," but he does write down sums on slips of paper—and "the next time" the customer will pay, or "the time after that." He has never refused a customer anything. He would first close up the store. He may not be the most generous man in the world, but to turn away someone in need of food is simply wrong by his standards. As for his "people," those who come to his store and salute him warmly or with casual friendliness, he has no idea what they think of him, what they *really* think of him, what they say behind his back, never mind to his face, when he knows they will be polite.

He would like to think, though, that he will be missed when he goes, and that under difficult circumstances, as a storekeeper who attends to people who are not very prosperous, he has done his work reasonably well: "I have wanted to be of some help to others, even if it is true that I make a living out of doing so. A man has to make a living. In this country people are not encouraged to work for one another—to share and live as brothers and sisters, the way our Lord Jesus Christ would no doubt wish. My grandfather told me, 'Everyone for himself in America, but don't be *too* American!' I will not speak like that to my own grandchildren. I am confused myself how much to share with others, how much to keep for myself. Why confuse little boys and girls? There will be plenty of time for them to look around and figure out the answer to the important question: How do I make a good living in this country, and still keep some respect for myself and feel I am a Christian? I wish I could give them the answer in words; but I think you get the answer through living—it takes a lifetime to find out, and maybe after all those years you still don't really know how to conduct yourself in every situation.

"Well, I hope I have achieved a good reputation. A reputation takes time to establish. A reputation has an age, just as a person does. I hope my wife and I have earned some trust from our neighbors. My father would say to me, and I say to my son, *"Cobra buena fama y acuéstate a dormir, cóbrala mala y arranca a huir.'* That is our way of saying: If you have built a good reputation up for yourself, you can feel comfortable, but if you haven't, and people think ill of you, you had better leave. This I can say: we have stayed, Señora Gallegos and I."

5

THE OLD CHURCH,
THE SPANISH CHURCH,
THE AMERICAN CHURCH

In every town up in the hills of northern New Mexico or hidden among the mountains east of Albuquerque, the Catholic church is the tallest, most noticeable building to be seen. Some of the churches are nondescript, some are surprisingly flimsy: wood covered with shingles, or else brick put together without any real thought of beauty, or even, it seems, permanence; signs announcing the times of mass hung loose or crooked; no effort at landscaping, hence muddy, rutted roads in winter, or dry, dusty ones in summer—and a lonely, stark quality which a few trees might have diminished. Other churches are quite different; they are made of adobe or a mixture of adobe and cement, and are sturdy, fitting well into the town's setting, which is often evocative of the center of Spanish cities: the narrow streets, the plaza, the protective walls, and at the center of it all, His building, with the invariable announcement in Spanish (and sometimes but not always in English) that He will be worshipped at such-and-such times, and with the bell that doesn't hesitate to call on His behalf, and is immediately heeded. These are the churches that are likely to have nicely cared for grass—not to be taken for granted in semiarid country. Frequently there is also a small garden—a few cactus plants, some rocks arranged in a pleasing way. And there are usually trees, often quite massive, the best of the region's cottonwoods, for instance—and one is likely to look at them, admire them, wonder whether they haven't been put there especially to guard the church.

In the mountain communities everyone goes to church on Sundays, but there is no traffic jam as a result. The roads, so empty at times that they seem a pure indulgence on the state's part, suddenly are full of men, women, and children walking in the middle: what better use for asphalt than to help keep special clothes looking good before and after mass? As for anyone who happens to be driving toward the church, let him dare use his horn or try to nudge people with his noisy, racing motor or his tires coming rudely close. For that matter, a distant plane can receive a look meant not to kill, but merely to register the pain, confusion, and sorrow one world feels for another: how can it be that on a Sunday like this, which God has chosen to grace with His sun and with a cloudless sky, they are up there in that machine, rather than somewhere on this earth, praying?

Of course, such a question often goes unasked, merely kept in the back of the mind—a thought of sorts about the twentieth century, with its increasingly hard-to-fathom but inescapable contrasts. Time was when Santa Fe and Albuquerque were there, all right, but of no particular consequence or immediacy in the lives of various villagers for whom thirty or fifty miles might well have been three or five hundred miles. Time was when everything outside a given town's land was a limitless and not especially inviting beyond. Now there are planes, and increasingly noisy and aggressive automobile drivers, who, it seems, will no longer rest content with the usual tourist spots, but have to poke and pry their way into every corner of every county—even up dirt roads, so they can get what they call a "view." What to do but pray for them on Sundays? One may not really feel so inclined, but that is the point of prayer, to ask the hard things of God, not simply to beg in a self-centered manner for any little possession the mind may have come up with as desirable. "As the good priest says"; "as the father told us"; "as we heard in church"—the phrases vary, but they all are meant to indicate how carefully a person has listened to, and made his own, ideas handed down by another: him who helps us, leads us, urges us on to God.

"I am an instrument of the Lord's," one priest says, but not boastfully. Not coyly either; he is being matter-of-fact. "I try to do what I hope is likely to serve God's will best," he elaborates. Not that he *knows;* one can only try, and one can only hope, and one can only make a judgment about a likelihood. Then he quite consciously skirts egotism: "I have no right to set myself apart from other priests.

We all fail every day, certainly those who presume to speak on behalf of our Lord. But a long time ago I think I did learn one lesson: be firm with people, stand fast for what is right, but take care not to confuse yourself with God. It is a sin even to suggest that a priest does that, but we are all tempted, and no one more than a priest, I am afraid. Some priests more than others, though; it is well to be blunt. Maybe I am the worst of us all—sitting here and making my comments about 'them' and about myself. Beware of the preacher, especially one as old and ingrained in his habits as I am."

A nervous smile is followed by a serious, reflective look, then a broader, more relaxed smile. Hands hold on to a chair; one of them quickly moves toward the right thigh, to brush aside some dust on the pants, caught by a sunbeam. Soon the hands are folded around the belly, which possesses a certain prominence: a perfect resting place for the forearms as well as the fingers. A few remarks about one parishioner, then another, and, as always, blessings on both of them: "May God offer them His grace; they are among the oldest who come here on Sundays, and I always seek them out after I talk to the people: make my announcements, deliver my sermon, offer my congratulations and give my warnings—a dangerous moment for a priest, I am convinced. For a long time I never gave a second thought to what my words meant to people; I was too busy preparing the speech and in my mind giving it. By the time I *did* give it, I had already decided whether it was one of the better ones, or one of the less useful ones. But I have been given enough time to look back and take stock—a mixed blessing, I assure you. Some of my former sermons, like ghosts, have come to haunt me. I preached charity with a complete lack of it; and mind you, I am no stranger here, but a man who ought to understand his own people."

With that, silence; a hard silence to interrupt with a clever bit of nonsense or a face-saving compliment which would only make matters worse by suggesting that self-criticism requires reassurance or is a subtle, self-assertive maneuver aimed at obtaining praise. The head bows, but not for any embarrassing length of time. A glance at the crucifix on the opposite wall, then a direct stare at the visitor, followed by an inquiry: shall some tea be brought in? Yes; so he is up and out of the room for a second. Soon an elderly lady brings in a tray. On it, besides the tea, are an assortment of cookies and some cake, too. He looks at them, casts a quick look at his belly, then smiles at himself indulgently and reaches for the tray—to serve, but also to eat heartily. Just as the lady is leaving he refers to her, and she leaves hearing—not for the first time, one is sure—his comment: "I am a spoiled child, an old, old, one, but that is all the worse. And she is the one who does it!"

When the door is firmly closed he continues, perhaps hoping she can hear, anyway: "The two of us should stay away from such sweet things. I do not weigh myself because it is rather prideful to do so; but I know deep within my heart that I am playing a wicked game: my pride urges me to avoid facing the scale, and I call upon 'the sin of pride' as an excuse. It may be a devious move on my part, but I doubt the good Lord fails to see through my purposes. And all the time my lady friend, so anxious to care for me, urges me on to greater excesses: not only cookies, but her tasty cake! She knows only too well how weak I am; and I can't blame her, tempted though I am to do so. She offers, but I need not accept. Anyway, I have joined her in a conspiracy: I make sure she finishes what I don't. As you can see, neither of us is lean and hungry. I fear there will be a lot of fat to burn in Hell all too soon—for we are both about to go there in the near future, I would think."

Another pause, this time followed by a sigh not in the least stifled; then he shifts to a more philosophical vein: "There's no point worrying about the future. That is one of the virtues of our Spanish heritage: we are not lazy; we work hard; but we trust in God, not our own dreams of glory. Anglos believe in themselves. I should not say it, but I will: even Anglos who are Catholic do not think as we do. I would go further and add Anglo *priests* to the list. Irish priests come here and the people submit to them—yes, they do—but they do not really follow them spiritually. It is difficult for me to talk like this; I find it hard to explain what I mean in English—or in Spanish either. Some might say I am getting old—over seventy, and so given to sentiment, exaggeration, melodrama. I will stand up for my beliefs, though. For almost a half century I have been a priest here in New Mexico, always with my own Spanish-speaking people, always in the small towns, where the culture and traditions and customs are most pure and least influenced by the Anglo Americans. (They call us all those names; well, I have always liked to call *them* Anglo Americans, and I think of myself as a Spanish American.) Now in all these years I have learned more than I have taught. I have come to know the people; after all, I hear their confessions and they come to me every day for advice. But I must never forget how much they have helped me to understand my own life—what my parents brought me up to believe, why I think the way I do about so many issues.

"I suppose I would be considered by some Anglo priests strict, by others far too lenient. I have no use for many of the changes now taking place in the American Church. I am grateful for being up here, far removed from those changes. I am grateful for being old; I will soon go—well before the Catholic Church I love so much becomes before our very eyes conquered by the American evangelists: practical-minded businessmen; university agnostics; experts in technology; and, I have to say it, the psychiatrists and Unitarians and—what do they call it? 'ethical culture' people, with their talk of 'community.' You see, the hippies have come near here, with their communes. I have talked with them. They give me things to read, while all the time denouncing books. So I keep up with the world! The children of hippies, I fear, are lost: they know too much, have seen too much. They have no knowledge how to control themselves, only give way to their own demands. How sad, to see seven- or eight-year-old children so sure of themselves, so cynical, so demanding and bossy with strangers. But I do not want to sound shrill and narrow about hippies. The truth is, I feel sorry for them. I pray every day for them. I know they don't want my pity and my prayers. I know the danger of smugness. Still, I must pray.

"I read magazines; I have tried to keep my mind open—without success, no doubt many would say. I love the Latin mass. So do our people here. They do not want English or Spanish; they want their Latin mass—it truly is *theirs*. And they go to church to pray to God, not to man, not to the society. I did not become a priest in order to celebrate man; nor do my parishioners come here to stare in the mirror and exult at their 'capacities.'

"I respect each generation's right to see things in a new way. But the Catholic Church is devoted to one Man, who turned out to be God Himself. If we fail to center our attention on Him and His teachings; or if we go against His teachings for the sake of keeping up with 'modern times,' then it is best we close all our churches and say there is no longer a Catholic Church, just a collection of buildings to which egoists and materialists take themselves on Sundays out of some nostalgia, or because they get bored, or because they have a 'religious need,' and are trying to give it 'expression.'

"Oh, I have to tell you that I have no patience with all that. A few years ago, before I became hopelessly old-fashioned—and even bitter, I would have to admit—I would go to retreats, or to conferences; I would listen to lectures about the 'new' Church, and I would try hard to go along. But I know a Protestant when I see one—even up here they have made their inroads! And I know a truly agnostic or atheistic person. I don't want to win such a person over. I respect them—that may well be one way I differ (in the more 'free-thinking' direction) from some other priests. I simply want to stand up for my own beliefs, and I do not want to fool myself or fool the families who come here by giving the name Catholic to a porridge of secular notions, any of which may be valuable and important, but none of which are meant to be worshipped in Christ's name, in the name of our Lord and Savior."

He stops, and seems to be going into a moment of intense self-absorption. He looks up at a picture of the Bleeding Heart of Jesus; it was given to him by one of the better-off families. The man and his wife had gone to Mexico and South America, and while there had remembered him. They made sure he hung the picture where he would be able to look and look—and be somehow affected. He had once before told the story: how they were so proud to have the gift for him, how they chose a place for it, having been given carte blanche with his walls, how the señora personally hung the picture, having had it framed in Santa Fe. Now, as he stared, the Bleeding Heart seemed a refuge for him: let others make their "adjustments" to the twentieth century; let others be embarrassed by the ancient imagery and ritual of Catholicism; let others feel more comfortable with toned-down iconography or updated theology or scripture interpreted defensively in the face of convictions asserted by theoretical physicists, paleontologists, observers of African chimpanzees, Marxist historians, ever so knowing and self-conscious psychoanalysts, the last with their nervy interest in a dozen other "fields," including his own. He would not wince at that representation of the Bleeding Heart, not run in shame from it, nor "reinterpret" it, nor fit it into someone's "archetypal pattern." He would simply look and meditate and gain strength. "The Lord's agony has meant peace and wisdom for millions over the years," he had said several months earlier, after a similar moment spent with that picture; now a moment was becoming a minute, which can be a long time indeed when two people are alone and talking.

Then abruptly, words begin to come—and forcefully: "I will surprise you. I acknowledge superstition within the Church. There was a time when I wanted to study philosophy and theology—not be a parish priest. And I did, by myself. There was a time, even decades ago, before the recent changes in the Church, when I had little use for those flaming fires, those blood-drenched Hearts. My father was well-to-do—a prosperous landowner, and a self-educated man. He never left the Church, but he did business with the Anglos—too much business. He made too much money, and their Protestant ideas went to his head. My mother prayed for him. Only in his last year did he really become part of the Church again. He taught me to distrust the excesses: the festivals and cards and pictures and what he called 'the smell of ignorance and fear' that hovered over the church and the parish house all week.

"My mother said, 'Why not?' She said, 'Is it better to crave the newest automobile, or a machine that washes clothes?' She loved her scrubboard. She had no use for servants. She loved her rosary beads. She hated gasoline fumes and would stop by the side of the road and pick up trash left there. That was a long time before we ever heard of the word 'ecology.' She worried that the people of this town would soon be hanging pictures of cars on their walls, rather than the Bleeding Heart of Jesus. She worried that the president would come before Christ, the skyline of Albuquerque before the Church's mission. She was educated by nuns, and no doubt they were hard on her. But she knew how hard used-car salemen can be on their customers, and politicians can be on the voters, and the commercials on radio can be on a poor worker, trying to keep his self-respect and trying to live a decent, honorable life. Thank God she never lived to see television. I watch it and ask, Who is superstitious, who is ignorant, who is backward: an old lady coming to me holding on to her rosary or doing a Novena or handing cards with Christ's face or His heart to her children and grand-children, or those people who write the commercials and speak them and act in them, or worse, listen to them, then jump to pay attention?

"But I am ready to go back on my own ideas; to a degree I am. I know that I am old, and I have never done much, only take care of the souls God has entrusted to me. This world is full of injustice, and I haven't done much to change things. I preach. I ask the members of my flock to be kinder to one another. I ask them to look with care at *me:* am I mistaken in my ideas? They become uncomfortable when I talk like that. After the sermon they say, 'Father, you cannot mean what you say! Father, you must know you cannot be wrong!' I reply, 'So, you think I am dishonest when I ask you to question me!' That makes them stop and think! There is so far I have gone, though. I haven't marched to the cities with words of protest. I haven't tried to become a Chicano, a fighter in the world of politics and social activism. Christ fought the moneylenders. I know that. Christ was turned upon by the 'powers and principalities.'

"I do not deny the Church's responsibility: to be on the side of the poor, the hungry, the downtrodden. Here, of course, most people are barely able to get by, day after day. There are few rich people, and not many like my parents were—the middle class, they could be said to come from. No matter: our people are stubborn about their lives; what they have inherited they will keep, and what others want for them, they will look at with great suspicion. Am I the one to shout at them, call them fools, backward fools? Am I the one to demand that they stop being so grateful for so little, and instead, rise up, start marching, tear aside the curtains of self-doubt and hopelessness, begin forcing themselves and their reasonable and just demands upon today's pharisees and moneylenders, upon today's Pontius Pilates and the emperors who employ them?

"Any curate worth his salt tries to arouse his people; but he is also bound to feel their presence and respond to their view of life—as opposed to his own wishes for them. I will tell you: in the 1930s, when it was much more desperate a time than now, I stormed about, I was ready to lead an army down from this hill. Don't ask me where we would have gone. It never came to that. And it wasn't rich people or a sheriff who turned anyone back. There was no one to turn back. Maybe some today would say I should have raised my voice even louder, or if that failed to arouse people, march by myself. Maybe some would say I should have left here—told them all how ignorant and unimaginative they are, how little vision and little ambition they possess. I might have found willing supporters in Santa Fe, among the comfortable artists and writers, and those who hang onto them, look up to them as *their* priests. In more recent times I might have gone to Albuquerque, a noisier, less settled city, not so self-assured and full of itself, not so interesting to Easterners—and a place where a justifiably angry priest, anxious to link arms with his people's forward-looking organizers and spokesmen, might be quite welcome. I am glad, very glad, there are priests who have done so—become leaders of the very broadest kind. If I get sullen and meanspirited, if I try to protect myself, justify myself, by saying uncharitable, snide things against such priests, I can only pray that I learn better in another life. But today a man like me has little voice; his bad remarks, his rudeness toward others, matter little (except before God), because there is no one to hear. Everyone listens to the men of outrage and alarm. Few pay much attention to the millions of Catholics all over the world who are not unlike my own parishioners—or to priests like me, who are so quickly dismissed as out-of-date.

"I may sound as if I am asking for pity or attention—or both! At my age, though, a man loses a bit of the vanity we are all heir to. It is dangerous, I know, for one like me to make such a judgment, but I will take the risk. I am simply asking that 'the people' be heard—a cry worthy of a reformer, even an agitator! I do not mean that we limit our vision to their vision. Those of us in a position to lead should try to lead; it is sad to see leaders justifying their own prejudices and inertia by pointing out the presence of both in 'the people.' But it is also sad to see leaders lose touch with their followers, or those supposed to be their followers. And some leaders are self-appointed, and speak for audiences or groups other than the ones they claim to be from, or working for.

"I have nothing more to say. I have been held back by the climate here—so cold in winter, so hot in summer—I occasionally say to myself in justification for my lethargy. At other times I feel that I have done my best. And then there are those moments when I have to confess to myself: I have been a coward, even as so many of my superiors in the Church have betrayed Christ. But I love being here, and have been privileged to earn a certain place here, a certain measure of affection and respect from people I have grown to care for and love, for all their failures and blindness. I am old, and I suppose it is the old Church I represent. I am Spanish, and so I have a streak of the mystical in me, and a streak of indifference—I should admit it—to all that is new and yeasty. I tend to fold my hands and say that this too will pass, and afterwards there will be the same problems: those with power and those with much less; those who live better than others; those who die young and the old, grouchy ones like myself who hold on to life longer than seems fair, considering all the children who are doomed by fate. So it was in Christ's time; and the Spanish Church has never been inclined to think it will be much different any time this side of Armageddon.

"But I am American, so if I am of the Spanish Church, I am also of the American Church: I may dislike a lot of changes I see these days (the television set my parishioners bought me!) but I am also glad that there is a lot of ferment in this country; and there are even times when I wish I could lose all this weight and shed my wrinkles and gain back the energy I had, in order to go picket somewhere! Maybe more important to gain back than the energy would be anger: good, clean anger at the rich and powerful, the self-contented and the hypocritical. Americans are always looking for solutions, answers; they are—we are—so restless, and so taken up with oursleves. It is a bad trait—the danger of pride; it is a good trait—the courage to change, the strength to oppose what is wicked but entrenched. Don't ask me to give percentages of how much bad, how much good. When one is old one tends to rest with the oars; when one is young, one has one's eye on new goals. Perhaps the Spanish Church is old, the American young. As for me, I am half and half. What I know without question is that I have given up searching for consistency. My mother influenced me a lot, but one thing she taught me I no longer believe: consistency is *not* a virtue. Or, I should say this: it is not a virtue I will ever possess."

His eyes now look to his visitor, then through the window to some cattle moving down the road, followed by a young man on horseback. The cattle are wandering all over, and the man is trying to hold them together. Behind him are cars: one, two, three—a line of them. The man seems not to notice them, let alone show any signs of hurrying his herd. Finally, one driver loses his patience and honks his horn which gives the other drivers courage to do likewise. Now the man angrily stops his horse: he will leave the cattle to their own devices; he will stay there all day if necessary; he will make his point. The priest is amused. It is not the first time he has witnessed such a confrontation, nor is it likely to be the last. Yet, each time he wonders what to think. Who is in the right? The man on horse is stubborn, maybe a bit spiteful. Still, he was there first, and the cattle have to be moved to another pasture, and they, too, belong to the town. The drivers probably don't; they are coming through to look, enjoy, feel a tinge of awe or envy—but soon enough they will leave, glad to be on their way to some city, some other part of the country, where they can talk about "the beauty of New Mexico," but live their more urbane, sophisticated, progressive lives.

A shrug of the priest's shoulders, another sigh; the protagonists have moved up the road and out of sight. He must prepare for tomorrow. He has confessions to hear. He has homes to visit. He is heavy and gets short of breath, but he is a walker: the families within two or so miles are reached on foot. As for the rest, he asks for help from young people who have cars. He enjoys driving with them; they are so full of joy and enthusiasm: the noise of the motor, the speed, the quick stop that defies the worst expectations of older people. Sometimes he wishes he had learned to drive. Sometimes he has pictured himself at the wheel, going along at a fast rate, waving at his many friends. Younger priests do so many things he has not done, and it is good they do them, he knows. Nevertheless, when he comes back from a drive he is not only refreshed but pleased to take a walk, or simply sit and doze, or read—or else do something else: "Occasionally I sneak into the church, when I know no one is there. I sit at the very back; and to be honest, my mind doesn't do much. I'm not praying. I'm not thinking very hard. I just say a word or two to our Savior: 'It is up to You to make sense of all this; all we can do is try to be as upright as possible until we are summoned—and told how well we have done, or how badly.' Then I am ready to go outside and pick up again: the next obligation."